P9-CJQ-503
BISON
BOOKS

Indians of the Southeast

Theda Perdue

CHEROKEE WOMEN

Gender and Culture Change, 1700-1835

University of Nebraska Press, Lincoln & London

∞

Second cloth printing: 1999
First Bison Books printing: 1999

Library of Congress Cataloging-
in-Publication Data
Perdue, Theda, 1949–
Cherokee women : gender and
culture change, 1700–1835 /
Theda Perdue. p. cm. –
(Indians of the Southeast)
Includes bibliographical
references and index.
ISBN 0-8032-3716-2 (cl:
alk. paper) ISBN 0-8032-8760-7 (pa:
alk. paper) 1. Cherokee women
– History. 2. Cherokee women –
Social conditions. 3. Cherokee
Indians – Social life and customs.
4. Sex role – United States.
5. Sexual division of labor –
United States. I. Title. II. Series.
E99.C5P3934 1998
305.48′89755 – dc21
97-30486 CIP

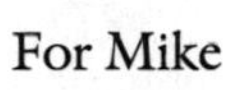
For Mike

CONTENTS

Acknowledgments

An author always incurs many debts in the process of research, writing, and revising. Because this project began over twenty years ago when I was a graduate student, I perhaps have run up a greater tally of debts than most scholars. Some of those people are not here to see the finished product. Charles Crowe, who always had faith in me, guided me toward a dissertation on slavery among the Cherokees and away from a study of Cherokee women. Women's history was in the dark ages, and I would have written a very different, far less satisfying book if I had persisted in the latter. Charlie, I think, knew that I did not know what questions to ask, but he encouraged me to begin taking notes for both books because he also believed that someday I would be able to formulate the questions as well as offer some answers. William McLoughlin, the dean of Cherokee history, helped me arrive at that point through years of correspondence and conversations. His own example of political activism challenged me to make a personal as well as a professional commitment to Native people. I think that Bill made me a better historian; I know that he made me a better person. The American colonialist Alice Mathews and the Byzantinist Constance Head, my friends and colleagues at Western Carolina University, were the first women historians I ever knew. (I guess it was the dark ages in lots of respects.) Alice was a wonderful mentor, and she gave me enormous emotional and intellectual support. Constance was a role model, and I greatly admired her commitment to scholarship and the unconventional. They died in their forties—Alice of breast cancer, which claims the lives of far too many women, and Constance of colon cancer, a disease her doctors did not think a young woman should have. Charlie, Bill, Alice, and Constance were never far from my mind as I finished this book.

Fortunately, some people who have known me a long time lived to see this book completed. Two deserve special note. Charles Hudson's influence is apparent in my work, even when I take it in directions that he thinks are fruitless. Mary Young has been a mentor in many ways. I first encountered her in a convention book display reading a new work on Cherokee slavery that had come out just as I was mailing my manuscript on the same subject off to a press. She sat there poring over every word as I stood first on one foot, then on the other. Finally, she looked up, smiled, and said something like, "I have your manuscript, and I don't think you have anything to worry about. Let me send you some notes that I took on slavery from the American Board papers." She was right—and she did. I have taken advantage of her wisdom and generosity ever since, and I have tried to follow her example.

Over the years, a number of people have commented on papers and articles drawn from this research and have engaged me in productive conversations about my ideas. For their questions and their interest, I would like to thank Bill Anderson, Jim Axtell, Kathryn Braund, Bill Chunestudie, Catherine Clinton, Jane Dysart, Dave Edmunds, John Finger, Don Fixico, Ray Fogelson, Elizabeth Fox-Genovese, Jean Friedman, Pat Galloway, Lynn Harlan, Tom Hatley, Sarah Hill, Leanne Howe, Nancy Joyner, Carol Karlsen, Clara Sue Kidwell, Jim Merrell, Devon Mihesuah, June Namias, Mary Beth Norton, Katherine Osburn, Linda Oxendine, Laura Hill Pinnix, Margaret Scarry, Russ Thornton, Dan Usner, Richard White, and Peter Wood. I also thank Mary Young, Nancy Shoemaker, Rayna Green, Carolyn Johnston, Daniel Blake Smith, Chris Taylor, and Karen Raley for taking time from their own work to read the entire manuscript and offer comments and suggestions. This book is much better for the time they invested.

I have thoroughly enjoyed working with the staff of the University of Nebraska Press on this project and on the series Indians of the Southeast. My thanks go to Paul Wilderson and Bill Regier, who were there at the beginning. I also appreciate the editing skills of Sally Antrobus.

In these days of computers, hardly anyone gets to thank secretaries for typing (or to blame them for errors). Although I typed this manuscript myself, I still depended on the office staff at the University of Kentucky to take care of minutiae that ranged from collating copies to ordering pizza for lunch. Thanks, Lynn Hiler, Darlene Calvert, and Dottie Leathers.

Several research grants gave me time to work on this project. I presented the first part of this book in a seminar while I was a fellow of the Newberry Library's D'Arcy McNickle Center for the History of the American Indian. The National Endowment for the Humanities provided a summer stipend, and the University of Kentucky awarded me a research professorship for 1991–92. The staffs of the Newberry Library, Houghton Library of Harvard University, the Georgia Department of Natural Resources, Western History Collection at the University of Oklahoma, the Alabama State Archives, the Gilcrease, and the National Archives Branch in East Point, Georgia, were very helpful. I also appreciate the use of the libraries of the University of Kentucky, the University of North Carolina, Dartmouth College, and Western Carolina University. I am especially grateful to librarians Mary Ann Hawkins, John Aubrey, and Brad Carrington.

I also want to thank the students who have helped me sharpen my arguments on a wide range of topics, in particular George Frizzell, Susan Hult, Brian McKown, George Ellenberg, Craig Friend, Adriane Strenk, Rowena McClinton, Jamey Carson, Lorri Glover, Matt Schoenbachler, Tim Garrison, Andrea Ramage, Greg O'Brien, Izumi Ishii, David Nichols, Kristen Forrester, and Randolph Hollingsworth.

My mother Ouida Perdue and her friend Telia Rountree, who recently died, introduced me to the concept that people who share a culture can have very different responses to change. I love them both, but one lived in the old South and the other lives in the new. Along with Audrey George, Lavine Williamson, Neva Atwood, Avis Bell, Lisa Bell, Vivian Ross, Carolyn MacArthur, Josephine Parsons, Wynette Fletcher, Mary Frances Hall, Dot Cate, Esther Thomas, Mary Nell Pharr, and Ruth Wooten, they taught me a great deal about a community of women.

Finally, I want to thank my husband Michael D. Green. Long before we married, Mike and I attended the same conferences, read each other's work, and edited a book series. At middle age, we discovered that our serious interests included each other. Since then, the personal as well as professional collaboration has exceeded all expectations. Mike balances me and makes my world complete.

Prologue

In August 1993, I attended a Cherokee stomp dance in northeastern Oklahoma. Located just off a well-traveled dirt road in a grove of trees, the stomp ground looked like a small, if somewhat temporary, community. Campers, tents, cook sheds, and public sanitary facilities surrounded the central dance ground. Cherokee people came to the stomp ground to spend the weekend, but visitors like me were welcome to drop in for shorter stays. I arrived in late afternoon. Children played while their elders, seated in aluminum lawn chairs, looked on. Two young men drove up in a pickup truck and asked if anyone wanted to play ball. Several other young men and women appeared, and they began to play on a ball ground adjacent to the dance ground. Women and men played against each other; the men had ballsticks and the women used their hands. It was a good-natured game in which people followed the rules appropriate to their sex and immensely enjoyed contact with one another. As they struggled to hit a wooden fish atop the pole in the center of the ball ground, young men and women careened into one another laughing and screaming. Soon the ball game ended. People began to gather at the sheds where women served dinner. Some visitors contributed food—I brought a watermelon—or offered cash to help defray the expenses, but the women provided food to anyone who wanted to eat without asking for recompense.

About dark, the stomp dance began with the man who served as chief of the stomp ground addressing those present in Cherokee. In English, he reminded participants that stomp ground regulations prohibited alcohol and drugs. In the center of the smooth, level stomp ground burned the sacred fire, earthly representative of the life-giving sun. Seven open-sided, roofed arbors, one for each Cherokee clan, surrounded the dance ground. In each arbor, the spiritual leader of the clan sat with clan members who came and went throughout the evening. One of my companions, an ethnomusicologist whose father is Cherokee, explained that he had no real place in the arbors because clans are matrilineal and his mother is not Cherokee, but that when he had questions, he asked the leader of his father's clan, who always tried to help him even though he was not technically a clan member. A lead singer followed by several of his relatives began circling the fire, calling people to dance. Women alternated with men in the moving circle that radiated out from the fire. Only men sang, in call-and-response style, but the women set the rhythm. Several women wore turtle-shell rattles that had been sewn to the split tops of old cowboy boots. As they moved their legs up and down, the pebbles in the turtle shells made a sound that equaled the volume of the men's singing. As midnight neared and dancers tired, a young singer and some of his youthful relatives began to circle the fire calling for people to dance. No women joined the circle. For several minutes, probably an eon to the stranded singer, he continued to call for women to join him. Ultimately, a woman dancer, perhaps a relative, stepped in behind him, set the rhythm, and permitted him to sing. Without a woman, the dance could not have taken place.

The men and women who circled the fire that night live in a modern world. They included lawyers, teachers, farmers, mechanics, secretaries, and housewives. They had arrived in late-model cars and trucks, and they wore clothing that would not have attracted attention on any main street in America. When they danced, however, they expressed a cultural tradition that has ancient roots, far older than the dance itself. The stomp dance taps a deep reservoir of feelings about sacred fire, the earth and the people who inhabit it, the Cherokees and the world beyond the stomp ground. Most significantly, it embodies a Cherokee construction of gender. The sound of the rattles summons a world in which women and men balance each other as surely as rhythm and words combine to make the stomp dance. That world is the subject of this book.

Introduction

Native American women exist in the historical shadows. We know little about their lives, how historical events affected them, and the cultural changes that reshaped their world. Feminist archaeology is beginning to reveal a material culture that draws an outline of women's lives beyond historical documentation.[1] Oral traditions offer insights into women's place in belief systems and ceremonies, oral histories reveal women's perceptions of the changes they have seen, and autobiographies provide a glimpse of individual women's lives.[2] Most historical sources, however, obscure women's experiences. The problem lies with the sources and with historians themselves. Until the mid–nineteenth century, non-Natives generated the bulk of the written record about Native people. Explorers, naturalists, soldiers, traders, agents, and missionaries recorded astonishing details about the appearance, behavior, and beliefs of the Native people they encountered. They did not always understand what they saw, and their misinterpretations make the scholarly use of their observations risky. Recognition of the biases and preconceptions inherent in this particular body of documentary evidence has given rise to the methodology of ethnohistory.[3] By relying on anthropological models of kinship, political organization, economic systems, and worldview, ethnohistorians can distinguish valuable information from the original, flawed interpretations and analyze that information in a new, presumably less flawed, interpretative context. Ethnohistorians, however, have their work cut out for them when they begin to try to write about Native women, because most people who recorded the Native past were men, and men of European origin at that.

The gender of observers poses substantial problems for writing the ethnohistory of Native women because Native men and women lived remarkably separate lives. A sexual division of labor underlay much of this separation, and tasks largely defined gender. Although Native men sometimes helped women with their chores—and women helped men—men knew relatively little about women's work, nor were they privy to women's conversations, rituals, and various gender-specific behaviors and beliefs. Although they usually occupied the same dwellings, women and men sometimes lived apart: Wahpeton Dakota women and men, for example, spent three months of the year in separate camps as men hunted muskrats and women made sugar.[4] Even when they lived in the same camps, men and women in some societies seem to have had different domestic space. At the Creek town of Tuckabatchee, archaeological excavation reveals that tools associated with women's work cluster in certain sections of houses while men's tools appear in others, a pattern suggesting that households had areas for women's tasks distinct from those for men.[5] When they were together in the same room, men and women often kept social distance. In some cultures, they did not sit together but kept to opposite sides of the room, and they could not speak to each other unless they had specific kin relationships.[6] Men and women sometimes spoke variants of the same language, using gender-specific words for the same thing.[7] Many Native peoples employed gendered rites in matters of production and reproduction. Men, for example, probably did not know the corn songs that Hidatsa women sang.[8] More exclusive rituals revolved around menstruation and childbirth, events associated with spiritual power.[9] Menstruating women, in particular, had great power, and men regarded them as dangerous; consequently, they kept their distance and knew nothing about the rites women performed to control and channel that power.[10]

Like the Native men who provided most of their information, male European observers had virtually no access to the private lives of women or to women's culture. Even those who married Native women usually had only scant insight into the most basic matters. James Adair, arguably the most astute observer of eighteenth-century Native life in the Southeast, garnered considerable information about menstrual seclusion, perhaps because it struck him as exotic and because it tended to bolster his argument that Native Americans were the lost tribes of Israel, but he completely missed the fact that southeastern Indians were matrilineal—although he had a Chickasaw wife and children.[11] Since women's status in the Southeast rested in part on their place in the kinship system, many of Adair's conclusions about women are suspect. Far less observant men either ignored women altogether or fell into a pattern of depicting them as slaves or harlots. Bernard Romans succinctly presented this view: "Their strength is great, and they labour hard, carrying very heavy burdens a great distance; they are lascivious, and have no idea of chastity in a girl."[12] European men could fit slavery and promiscuity into their understanding of the eighteenth-century world: gender parity and sexual autonomy were concepts that they simply could not fathom.

Ethnographers of the nineteenth and early twentieth centuries often seem to be as culture bound as the European observers of an earlier era. Anthropology grew out of the Enlightenment interest in culture and the extension of Darwinian theory to social evolution. Its emergence as an academic discipline in the late nineteenth century coincided with historian Frederick Jackson Turner's announcement of the closing of the frontier.[13] In Turner's view, which many Americans shared, "civilization" had conquered the wilderness. The Darwinian implications for Native peoples were obvious: the triumph of "civilization" doomed them to extinction. Consequently, ethnographers, people trained to document culture through participant observation, rushed to record all they could about these "vanishing" Indians. They couched their observations in comparative terms: they analyzed "primitive" customs, that is, Native behavior, against the backdrop of "civilized" practices, their own. By focusing on the differences between cultures, ethnographers often missed or gave too little weight to differences, including gender, within the specific cultures they were studying. They simply defined cultures in terms of what men did and moved on to recounting their deficiencies. Not only did they fail to use gender as a category of analysis, they often overlooked women altogether.[14]

Academic paradigms such as the Turnerian frontier and Darwinian evolution, however, were not alone in shaping the sensibilities of early ethnographers. Victorian propriety led them to talk primarily with men or to exclude menstruation, childbirth, and sexuality from their conversations with women. Furthermore, ethnographers tended to equate Indians to impoverished people in their own societies. Alice Kehoe has described the consequences of this approach for women: "The traditional [ethnographic] picture of the Plains Indian woman is really that of an Irish housemaid of the late Victorian era clothed in a buckskin dress."[15] Ethnographers also believed that what men did was intrinsically more important than what women did. Archaeology reinforced this view by identifying virtually all the artifacts collected with men and male activities, a classification that made men the dominant and most productive members of the community.[16] The result was an anthropology of gender that presented men as active and women as passive, a view that endured in some quarters into the 1980s.[17]

Not surprisingly, early Indian-centered history had little to say about women. In *The Road to Disappearance,* for example, Angie Debo described the domestic role of Creek women early in the book and interjected references to women throughout, but the story she told was one scripted, directed, and acted out by men.[18] Men generated most documents, the evidence on which historians relied, and they wrote about the matters that concerned them, not women. The discipline of history discounted that which was not written—indeed, people of literate cultures tend to assume that anything not written down is insignificant. Consequently, male activities and concerns dominated professional renditions of the past. Even when women took center stage, as they did in Carolyn Thomas Foreman's *Indian Women Chiefs,*[19] it was in roles usually ascribed to men, because the assumption was that only male roles were important.

James Axtell has demonstrated in his counterfactual account of colonial America without Indians that Native people, who did not amass records, had an enormous impact on the events that unfolded. If the Americas had been uninhabited, many colonists would have perished from lack of food and medicine, a cooperative ethic would have given way to unbridled materialism, evangelicalism would not have had as pronounced a role in shaping American culture, disparate colonies would not have joined together for common defense, and British identity would have endured far longer because no one would have challenged it or offered attractive alternatives.[20] A Native American past without women is equally unimaginable. Therefore, we must take an intellectual leap. Interaction between Native peoples and European invaders produced colonial America; similarly, interaction between Native women and men shaped the societies in which they lived and the changes they experienced. At the same time, the demands that the dominant society made on Native people rested on conceptions of gender and often became a discourse on gender. As Joan Wallach Scott has written, "Gender is a primary way of signifying relationships of power," and by decoding its meanings, we can come "to understand the complex connections among various forms of human interaction."[21] If we do not pay attention to women as well as men and to the language that culturally defined them, we risk writing history as counterfactual as the one Axtell presents.

In order to include women as well as men in our recounting of the

Native American past, we must accept the notion that gender itself is a cultural construction: physical features may determine who is male and who is female, but culture shapes how men and women dress, speak, think, and behave. Culture—learned rather than innate behavior—also largely determines how men and women act toward each other. Early attempts to explore systematically the relationships between men and women in various cultures focused on the universal subordination of women.[22] Flawed by the implication that cultures are static, these studies did not take into account change over time. Other scholars began to pay attention to the transformation of women's roles and the changes in their status, particularly the experiences of Native American women following European colonization.[23] The result was a "declension model" which juxtaposed high precontact female status with the subordinate women found in postcontact societies and held colonization responsible for the decline. More recently, Nancy Shoemaker has suggested that the declension model does not appropriately describe the history of Native women, at least Iroquois women, and a number of essays in her anthology suggest that her observation has broad applicability.[24] At the same time, a recent collection of anthropological essays demonstrates that the notion of universal subordination is far too simplistic and that North American ethnographic data point instead toward gender parity and complementarity of roles.[25] Like all ethnohistory, the study of Native women must walk a fine theoretical line between history and anthropology. Too great an emphasis on change led us to the declension model, whereas obsession with cultural continuity obscures the dynamic nature of cultures. We must recognize the complexity of both culture and change and try to integrate the two.

One of the important contributions of ethnohistory is a recognition that each Native people has a distinct history and culture. Any attempt to generalize about gender in Native America runs the risk of serious distortion when applied to specific peoples. Native cultures differ from one another in significant ways, and, consequently, so do the relationships between women and men. As Richard Sattler has pointed out, even neighboring Creeks and Cherokees, who shared an agricultural economy, matrilineal kinship system, and many religious beliefs, regarded women in profoundly different ways.[26] Similarly, the events that prove decisive in one tribe's past may have no parallel in the history of others. As a result, my conclusions about Cherokees may have some applicability to other tribes, but they may not. I do hope, however, that my approach and the questions I ask will prove useful to ethnohistorians examining gender issues among other Native peoples.

In order to analyze change over time, we need a cultural baseline, a starting point from which to plot change. Establishing such a baseline is difficult because cultures are dynamic. In one sense, the baseline for this study is the early eighteenth century, before the Cherokees had extensive contact with Europeans, but elements of that culture endure to the present. Persistence, in fact, is one of the themes of this book. Although some individuals abandoned particular cultural forms over time, others preserved them. Later eras, therefore, provide evidence for what I call "traditional" Cherokee culture. The best example of this is the work of James Mooney, a late-nineteenth-century anthropologist who collected a great deal of evidence on Cherokee myths and sacred formulas. I use Mooney's material, as well as the research of other scholars, to describe practices in a period earlier than that in which they were assembled because they seem to have very deep roots in Cherokee culture. I also occasionally use nineteenth-century observations to augment discussions of eighteenth-century culture. This well-established practice, which ethnohistorians call "upstreaming," involves following cultural patterns from the known present to the less well understood past.[27] This is a technique borrowed from anthropology, and more hidebound historians may be troubled by sources that seem anachronistic. Unfortunately, the demarcations in cultural history are not as clear as they are for wars or presidential administrations.

I write about a traditional Cherokee culture and a society and people whom I characterize as traditional with an understanding that the Cherokees experienced considerable change before my eighteenth-century baseline. From a sixteenth-century perspective, the world I explore in this book is a profoundly new world. In that earlier era, the Southeast was a very different place, and the peoples and cultures that appear in eighteenth-century accounts are not necessarily the ones that dominated the Southeast region two centuries earlier. Beginning about A.D. 800, the Mississippian cultural tradition shaped life in the Southeast until Hernando de Soto arrived in 1539. Centralized chiefdoms, hierarchical social structures, agricultural economies, and large earthen temple mounds characterized Mississippian societies, which exhibited far more coercive power and military might than did eighteenth-century tribes. The Cherokees did not organize themselves into chiefdoms until about 1100, and they may well have remained more economically diversified and socially egalitarian than their neighbors. In any event, they seem to have survived the decline of Mississippian culture in a relatively stronger position.[28]

Soto's *entrada* almost certainly destabilized Mississippian societies. His military victories, such as the one at Mabila in present-day Alabama, destroyed the balance of power in the Southeast, and the diseases that his expedition as well as others brought caused massive depopulation.[29] As a result, the great chiefdoms in the Southeast collapsed. The impact of these cataclysms on women is difficult to ascertain. Some chiefs in these Mississippian chiefdoms may well have been women. Hernando de Soto's encounter with the "Lady of Cofitachequi," who had several attendants and great wealth in the form of food stores and freshwater pearls, suggests that there were powerful women in the protohistoric Southeast. Later observers, including John Lawson, also describe Native "cacicas" or "queens."[30] Class and hereditary rights determined the status of these women, but with the disintegration of social hierarchy, gender was more likely to shape the lives of Native people. Towns, clans, and matrilineages became the basis for social organization, and a relatively egalitarian government by council replaced elite rule. In this new world, at least among the Cherokees, women had considerable power and prestige.

The history of the Cherokees has been written many times, most eloquently by William McLoughlin, whose work I admire. In this study, however, I depart from McLoughlin's interpretation of Cherokee history in terms of anomie and renascence. Certainly many Cherokees, particularly young men, lost their cultural moorings in the late eighteenth century, as McLoughlin has argued, and in the nineteenth century some Cherokees embraced a new vision for the Cherokee Nation. Cherokee history, however, is far more complex than these constructions permit. By focusing on gender in the process of cultural change, I have suggested that in the eighteenth century women may have become more secure in some roles—as farmers and as socializers of children, for example—and in the nineteenth century, Cherokees incorporated aspects of Anglo-American culture into their lives without fundamentally altering values or totally restructuring gender.

The story of most Cherokee women is not cultural transformation, as McLoughlin describes it, but remarkable cultural persistence. At the same time, some Cherokee women did experience profound change. They attended mission schools, converted to Christianity, and became paragons of domesticity. These women were primarily members of a Cherokee elite that emerged in the late eighteenth century and shaped the Cherokee history that McLoughlin wrote. Elite women may have lost power in relation to men, but this minority did not epitomize Cherokee womanhood. I do not mean to underestimate the power and influence of the Cherokee elite, particularly the role of men in dealing with the United States government, but their experiences are only a small part of the Cherokee past. Using gender as a category of analysis provides a glimpse into that other Cherokee world, one that perhaps was not so new.

The "decline" of Native people is embedded in contact history, largely because scholars have focused on military defeat and land loss. There are, however, other indices to culture change, including production, reproduction, religion, and perceptions of self, as well as political and economic institutions. Women, like Native people more generally, may well have had less "power" or "status" if we define those words in political and economic terms. The deerskin trade *did* make Cherokee women less central to the new commercial economy and centralized political authority *did* exclude women from publicly participating in decisions of national importance. Hunting and foreign affairs, however, had always been the domain of men, and even though European contact accentuated the activities of men, trade and warfare did not significantly alter the world of women. Women had their own arena of power over which they retained firm control. The growing involvement of men in the world beyond may, in fact, have enhanced the power of women within Cherokee society. Even the "civilization" program, the most direct assault on Cherokee conceptions of gender, failed to transform the relations between men and women in most Cherokee households. Other cultural measures, therefore, produce results that make a declension model more problematic.

At the same time, Native men as well as women became marginalized in the American society that emerged following the Revolution. A broader world, in which a different conception of gender prevailed, impinged increasingly on Cherokee men and women in the nineteenth century. Missionaries and government agents who sought to "civilize" the Cherokees made some inroads, but their limited success had far less effect than their failure. In part because many Cherokee women and men did not conform to the gender norms of the United States, their critics branded them as "uncivilized" and sought their removal west of the Mississippi. Proponents of removal encoded a host of attitudes about Indians in gendered language, a discourse perfectly intelligible to a United States citizenry largely isolated from contact with Native peoples.

Native women emerge from the historical shadows only if we approach their study on two levels. We must pay attention to how women and men related to each other within their own societies, and we must look at ways in which those relations became part of the larger debate over Indians and Indian policy. Thus viewed, Native women become major players in the great historical drama that is the American past.

Part I

A Woman's World

The Cherokees lived in the fertile valleys of the southern Appalachians. Archaeologists think that their ancestors had built villages along the region's rapidly flowing creeks and rivers for thousands of years and that since about A.D. 1000, they had grown corn in the rich alluvial soil.[1] The Cherokees believed that they always had lived there and that their ancestral mother, Selu, had given them the corn on which they depended for subsistence.[2] They conceived of their world as a system of categories that opposed and balanced one another. In this belief system, women balanced men just as summer balanced winter, plants balanced animals, and farming balanced hunting. Peace and prosperity depended on the maintenance of boundaries between these opposing categories, and blurring the lines between them threatened disaster.[3] Such rigidity may well offend modern sensibilities conditioned to expect equal opportunity and to seek the destruction of gender barriers. The balance that Cherokees sought to achieve between their categories and, in particular, between men and women may not have permitted equality in a modern sense, but their concern with balance made hierarchy, which often serves to oppress women, untenable. Men did not dominate women, and women were not subservient to men. Men knew little about the world of women; they had no power over women and no control over women's activities. Women had their own arena of power, and any threat to its integrity jeopardized cosmic order. So it had been since the beginning of time.

Among the first inhabitants of the world, according to a Cherokee myth recorded by the nineteenth-century anthropologist James Mooney, were a hunter named Kana'ti and his wife, Selu.[4] They had one son whom they often heard playing with a mysterious child who came from the river. The parents conspired with their son to capture his playmate and bring him home to live with them. Although Kana'ti and Selu tamed the child from ɪe river, he was often unruly and mischievous, and so they called him "Wild Boy."[5]

In this family, Kana'ti provided the meat and Selu contributed corn and beans, but no one else knew the source of the food. One day the boys followed Kana'ti into the forest and discovered that he kept the game in a hole. They secretly watched their father release a buck from the hole, shoot it with an arrow, and take it home for dinner. The next day the boys tried to imitate Kana'ti, but they became excited and confused, and they accidentally allowed all the animals to escape. As a result, according to the myth, Kana'ti and all men who followed him on earth have had to hunt throughout the forest for game to feed their families.

The boys returned home hungry, and so Selu went to the storehouse to get corn and beans for their dinner. At Wild Boy's instigation, they spied on her and discovered that by rubbing her stomach and armpits she filled a basket with corn and beans. They decided that she was a witch who must be killed. Selu knew their thoughts and, reconciled to her fate, told them: "When you have killed me, clear a large piece of ground in front of the house and drag my body seven times around the circle. Then drag me seven times over the ground inside the circle, and stay up all night and watch, and in the morning you will have plenty of corn."

The boys killed Selu and began following her instructions. They grew tired, and instead of clearing all the ground in front of the house, they prepared only seven spots, which explains why corn grows only in a few places in the world. They began to drag Selu's body over the circle, and from her blood sprang corn. Failing once again to follow their mother's instructions, the boys dragged her body only twice over the circle, and so the Indians still cultivate their corn but twice a year. The boys did watch the corn all night and in the morning it was ripe. Strangers came to get some of the grain, which was unknown to all other peoples, and the boys told them to plant the kernels and stay awake each night of their return trip. For six nights, they followed these instructions, and each morning they had ripened corn. On the last night of their journey, however, the strangers went to sleep and the corn did not sprout. Consequently, Indians must tend their crops carefully through half the year instead of for just one night.

When Kana'ti returned home and discovered what the boys had done, he vowed to leave home and go to the Wolf people. Wild Boy changed himself into a tuft of down that fell onto Kana'ti's shoulder so that he could eavesdrop when Kana'ti arrived at the council house of the Wolf people. The Wolves admitted Kana'ti to their council and agreed to his request that they "play ball" against his "two bad boys"—that is, kill the miscreants. Because Wild Boy knew the plan, the boys were able to outsmart the Wolf people and defeat them.

They waited for their father, but he did not return home. After a while, they went in search of him. They finally caught up with Kana'ti and joined him on his journey where they had adventures with a panther and with cannibals, but ultimately the boys lost sight of him. Then they came to the end of the world. They waited until dawn when the sky rose up to let the sun out, and they slipped through to the other side: "There they found Kana'ti and Selu sitting together." In the upper world, beyond the solid vault of the sky, man and woman sat side by side. In the realm of past time, predictability, and perfection, harmony and balance were restored.

Just how long Kana'ti and Selu had been living in the upper world when Europeans arrived is unknown. Cherokees in the eighteenth century, however, constructed gender and created community based on the principles embodied in their account of Kana'ti and Selu. The concept of balance was central to their perceptions of self and society, and the responsibility for maintaining balance fell to men and women. We can discover how they fulfilled this responsibility by paying attention to what the men and women described in historical documents did. By taking Kana'ti and Selu as our reference point in reading these documents, we can learn a great deal about the world of Cherokee women, the lives that they lived, and the ways in which they bonded with others.

ONE

Constructing Gender

The myth of Kana'ti and Selu provided the Cherokees with an explanation for why men and women in their society lived the way they did, occupying separate categories that opposed and balanced each other. Cherokee men and women performed different tasks, followed different rules of behavior, and engaged in different rituals. They knew little about each other's lives because any intrusion, any crossing of boundaries, involved a certain amount of danger. Yet men and women lived together in villages, they joked with each other, they made love, they shared houses and children, and they joined together in celebrating the harvest. On occasion, men could be found in fields, the realm of women, and sometimes women went on the winter hunt or even to war, normal pursuits of men. But Cherokees always understood their society in more absolute terms and tried to conform to those expectations.

Like their progenitors, the Cherokees divided labor according to gender. Men hunted because the first man had been responsible for providing his family with meat. Women farmed because Selu first gave birth to corn in the storehouse and then became the source of corn, which the Cherokees called *selu,* for all Indians. Men helped clear fields and plant crops, but the primary responsibility for agriculture rested with women. When women accompanied men on the winter hunt, they confined their activities to gathering nuts and firewood, cooking for the hunters, and perhaps preparing skins. By modern standards, such a division of labor was not very efficient. Men spent many summer hours gambling, smoking, or talking while women worked in the fields. And in winter, most women stayed in warm winter houses while men traveled great distances in bitter cold to search for game. But the Cherokees were not particularly concerned with the optimum utilization of their labor supply because for them, tasks involved far more than the production of commodities. A person's job was an aspect of his or her sexuality, a source of economic and political power, and an affirmation of cosmic order and balance.

Theoretically, the sexual division of labor was very rigid, but in reality, men and women often willingly helped one another. Men assisted in several agricultural chores including the arduous task of clearing fields and harvesting the crops. The men chopped down saplings with stone hatchets and burned the underbrush. From large trees they stripped away bark, which they used in constructing houses. When the trees died as a result of this girdling, the Cherokees either burned them or waited for them to fall so that they could use the wood for fires.[1]

Although they did not hoe and weed, Cherokee men helped women plant the large fields that lay on the outskirts of their towns. Nineteenth-century missionary Daniel Butrick, who was unusually interested in traditional Cherokee practices, wrote: "Anciently it was common for a whole town to inclose a large field, in which each family had its particular share, separated by some known marks. In this all the town, men and women, worked together, first in one part and then in another, according to the direction of one whom they had selected to manage the business, and whom, in this respect, they called their leader."[2] The trader James Adair identified this leader as "an old beloved man," or priest, who appointed a day for planting after the wild fruit and berries had ripened sufficiently to entice the birds away from the corn. No one was exempt from labor in the fields at planting, and Adair noted that he had seen "many war-chieftains working in common with the people." According to Adair, the laborers actually enjoyed this annual event: "About an hour after sunrise, they enter the field agreed on by lot, and fall to work with great cheerfulness; sometimes one of their orators cheers them with jests and humorous old tales, and sings several of their most agreeable wild tunes, beating also with a stick in his right hand, on top of an earthen pot covered with a wet and well-stretched deer-skin: thus they proceed from field to field, till their seed is sown."[3]

The Cherokees grew two types of corn in their large fields—a flinty multicolored "hominy corn" and a white-grain "flour corn." They planted these varieties in hills about a yard apart by dropping seven kernels into a small hole. They usually planted beans close to the corn so that the stalks could support the vines. Between the hills, they grew squash, gourds, pumpkins, sunflowers, watermelons, potatoes, and peas.[4] After the first cultivation of crops, either a priest or the head of the household stood at the edge of the field at the cardinal points and wept loudly, perhaps for the death of Selu. At the final cultivation, the owner of the field, either accompanied by a spiritual leader or alone, built an enclosure in the center of the field and sang songs to the spirit of the corn. In late summer or fall, men and women once again joined together in the fields to harvest their produce.[5]

Except for ashes from burning underbrush, the Cherokees did not fertilize their fields. Consequently even the rich alluvial soil they farmed eventually became unproductive. As late as the nineteenth century, missionaries of the American Board of Commissioners for Foreign Missions observed: "When they have exhausted a field by planting it with corn, they know nothing of recruiting it, by sowing other grains and laying it down to grass, and for lack of this knowledge, they are either working their old fields to very little profit, or forsaking them to open new ones." Even so, the soil's natural fertility apparently sustained crops far longer than was acknowledged by the American Board missionaries, who usually had to buy corn from the Indians. The Moravians reported: "Our field which has been used for 30 years still grows an excellent crop of corn."[6] Complementary plantings of corn, which removes nitrogen from the soil, and beans, which replace nitrogen, helped preserve fertility.[7]

Between planting and harvest, the men retired from agriculture and the women assumed total responsibility. Women not only tended the crops in the large fields but also planted smaller gardens near their homes. These they fenced, at least in historic times, with hickory or oak saplings tied to stakes. In their "kitchen gardens" the women cultivated a third kind of corn, which was smaller than field corn and ripened in only two months, and they grew beans, peas, and other vegetables.[8]

Most non-Native observers minimized the effort required to cultivate fields and gardens. According to Lieutenant Henry Timberlake, Cherokee territory was a veritable Eden, "the soil requiring only a little stirring with a hoe to produce whatever is required of it."[9] Adair attributed the brief time women seemed to invest in cultivation to their work habits: "They often let the weeds out-grow the corn, before they begin in earnest with their work."[10] Louis-Philippe, who toured the Cherokee country in 1796 when he was a refugee from the French Revolution, wrote that they dug only the weeds close enough to choke the plant, "but seeing the fields that result, one would not believe that they had been cultivated at all."[11] Women hoed with a sharpened stick or stone mattock, implements that encouraged them to be relatively tolerant of weeds.

Although they probably spent far more time farming than European men credited them with, women did have other means for supplying their families with the earth's bounty. In particular, Cherokee women were prodigious gatherers. In the fall, they burned the underbrush in the woods and collected vast quantities of nuts, which they used in bread or for oil. In summer, they picked berries and fruit. Throughout the year, they relied on wild plants for seeds, leaves (which were never eaten raw), roots, and stems to add variety to their diet and to tide them over in case provisions ran out before the harvest or the corn crop failed. The women searched for bee trees and collected honey, and they made sugar from maple sap. Benjamin Hawkins, the United States Indian agent, observed Cherokee women using "small wood troughs, and earthen pans to ketch the sap, and large pots for boilers in making sugar."[12]

The responsibility for ensuring a bountiful harvest fell to women. If the Cherokees experienced a drought, the women summoned a priest who tried to produce rain.[13] In addition to ensuring favorable growing conditions, women were also responsible for protecting the crops from predators, one of the most dangerous and demanding chores associated with farming. In the outlying fields, the Cherokees built large scaffolds from which they could watch for crows and raccoons. The task of sitting alone on the scaffolds all summer, the season for war, fell to elderly women, whose vigilance Adair described: "This usually is the duty of the old women, who fret at the very shadow of a crow, when he chances to pass in his wide survey of the fields; but if pinching hunger should excite him to descend, they soon frighten him away with their screeches." Introduction of livestock by Europeans made the work of these sentinels more difficult. The Cherokees thought that fencing fields—"childishly confining their improvements, as if the crop would eat itself"—was ridiculous and a waste of time. When they acquired livestock in the eighteenth century, they permitted the animals to forage for food. As a result, the women had to tether any cows or horses that were near the large fields and pen all hogs.[14] Animals that persisted in escaping and damaging the crops incurred the wrath of the women. In the late eighteenth century, a Moravian missionary reported with some horror: "No cattle are kept except by the traders; for if a Beast comes into the Fields they are used to shoot it."[15]

Because of their association with and involvement in agriculture, it is not surprising that women were also the cooks in Cherokee society. They prepared food in the morning, and since Cherokees had no formal meals but ate when hungry, they simply set it out for whoever wanted to eat. European opinion of Cherokee cuisine varied. John Howard Payne, who visited them in the nineteenth century, thought the Cherokees to be "among the best cooks in the world," whereas James Adair complained that they overcooked meat and boiled eggs until they resembled bullets.[16]

Europeans did agree, however, that corn was the staple in the Indian diet and that the variety of corn dishes was amazing. Although the Cherokees ate some fresh, or green, vegetables in summer, they allowed most of their corn and beans to dry in the fields. They could then store vegetables in cribs and use them throughout the winter. They soaked dried beans in water and then boiled them. To render dried corn palatable, the women soaked it in lye made from wood ashes, which removed the husks. Then they used a mortar and pestle instead of a mill to grind their meal. The mortar was constructed of a large log in which a bowl was formed by chopping and burning one end. The upper end of the pestle was much larger than the pounding end in order to give it weight. They considered meal made from this corn "not only a luxury, but a great support to nature," and they used it for a variety of breads.[17]

To bake bread, the women placed dough on a clay or stone hearth and then heaped coals over the loaf, which was sometimes covered with a pot, basket, or leaves. Cherokee women also boiled small loaves of bread wrapped in corn leaves. Usually bread contained ingredients other than corn, in particular chestnuts, beans, and pumpkin. The most common method of eating bread was to dip it in bear grease or oil made from hickory nuts, acorns, or black walnuts.[18] The women prepared a beverage from fine cornmeal and water, which they let sour and then drank cold. Sometimes they added other ingredients to this broth and served it as a soup. A favorite combination was parched cornmeal and grapes, but they also added beans, hickory nuts, or black walnuts.[19]

A Moravian missionary described a meal consisting of two kinds of soup and bread: "The women had prepared a supper for us. In a large earthen vessel, made by themselves, a cold soup of honey-locust pods and in another sour corn-broth were served. The whole company used a large wood spoon, which was passed down the row. The procedure was very informal. One ate awhile and then, perhaps, warmed himself in between. The locust broth had a sweet, but wild, taste. The bread made of corn and beans, and which consisted by more than half of whole black beans, was pleasant to the taste."[20]

The Cherokees roasted some vegetables, particularly sliced pumpkins, and most meat over open fires. They also parboiled green corn and then roasted the ears. Often corn prepared in this manner was subsequently boiled with venison or other meat. Generally, however, the Cherokees barbecued rather than boiled meat and fish. They particularly enjoyed bear fat cut into small pieces, stuck on sassafras skewers, which imparted a sweet taste, and then cooked over a slow fire. They also dried venison over embers or in the sun and then dipped the pieces in oil before eating them.[21]

Cherokee women made a variety of other things not directly related to food but necessary to the well-being of their households or for their own pleasure. They made their cooking utensils and other pottery from native clay.[22] Vessels included pitchers, bowls, dishes, basins, and platters. Adair said that "their method of glazing them, is, they place them over a large fire of smoky pitch pine, which makes them smooth, black and firm."[23] The black color of Cherokee pottery led a Moravian to remark that it "looks like the iron Ware from the Foundaries."[24] Cherokee women constructed baskets, which served as containers and sieves, out of river or swamp cane, which they cut into strips.[25] Adair found their double-weave baskets particularly attractive: "They make the handsomest clothes baskets, I ever saw, considering their materials. They divide large swamp canes, into long, thin, narrow splinters, which they dye of several colours, and manage the workmanship so well, that both the inside and outside are covered with a beautiful variety of pleasing figures; and, though for the space of two inches below the upper edges of each basket, it is worked into one, through the other parts they are worked asunder, as if they were joined a-top by strong cement." Dyes for baskets included bloodroot, walnut bark, and butternut. Rectangular baskets, according to Adair, usually measured about three feet long, a foot and a half wide, and a foot deep.[26]

Adair observed: "The women are the chief, if not the only manufacturers; the men judge that if they performed that office, it would exceedingly depreciate them."[27] In addition to baskets and pots, gourds and skins served as containers. Women hollowed out large bottle gourds for carrying water. For storing oil and honey, they turned whole deerskins into flasks by cutting off the head and feet and sewing up all openings except the neck which served as "the nose of the bottle."[28] Women made their clothing from a number of materials, including buffalo hair they collected after the animals had shed, which they wove into garments and pouches. Deerskins as well as fabrics made of hemp and mulberry bark were sewn into clothing with bone needles and thread of sinew. For their houses, women wove cane mats and hemp carpets, which they painted bright colors. They also probably carved the soapstone (steatite) pipes they smoked incessantly.[29] Women provided wood and water for their households. William Bartram noted that women "undergo a good deal of labor . . . cutting and bringing home the winter's wood."[30] Women also always carried the water, and "it was considered disgraceful for men and boys to be seen carrying water," probably because carrying water, associated with fertility, was a gender-specific task.[31]

As the farmers, cooks, and "chief manufacturers," Cherokee women had relatively little free time. Even in the winter they had to keep the fire going, prepare food, and make any items they could indoors. In addition, some women followed the men on long hunts lasting three or four months in order to perform their customary chores—carrying water, gathering wood, and cooking. Consequently, it is not surprising that Europeans generally believed Cherokee women to be victims of male exploitation. Bernard Romans, who traveled through the Southeast in the eighteenth century, reported: "A savage has the most determined resolution against labouring or tilling the ground, the slave his wife must do that."[32] Louis-Philippe, who visited the Cherokees in 1797 long before he became king of France, also was appalled at what he supposed to be the degraded condition of the women: "The Indians have all the work done by the women. They are assigned not only household tasks, even the corn, peas, and beans, and potatoes are planted, tended, and preserved by the women. The man smokes peacefully while the woman grinds corn in the mortar."[33] It was certainly true that beyond their help at planting and harvesting, Cherokee men had no role in cultivating gardens or fields, a circumstance Europeans attributed to the men's laziness. Native people in the Southeast tried to excuse themselves to a disapproving James Adair for this "long-contracted habit and practice" by explaining that between planting and harvest "the men improve this time, either in killing plenty of wild game, or coursing against the common enemy."[34]

John Norton, a Mohawk who came to the Cherokee Nation in 1810 to visit relatives, was more understanding. Norton readily admitted that Cherokee men were "not so remarkable for steady industry" as were women, but their obligations to the community differed from those of women. Norton explained the contribution of men in his journal: "The Chace was the field of industry for man; and the only necessary preparation was to have his quiver filled with arrows, or, latterly, to provide himself with a gun and ammunition and to arrive at his hunting ground in season. . . . Should the voice of glory, or the defence of the Nation, call them to the field, the talents which hunting has improved, are there exerted in a higher degree." Norton assured his readers that during the hunting season or in times of war, "there are no symptoms of laziness, or an indolent disposition."[35]

While Norton defended the behavior of men, the missionary Butrick made a remarkable observation on Cherokee women's attitude toward the apparently inequitable division of labor: "Though custom attached the heaviest part of the labour to the women, yet they were cheerful and voluntary in performing it. What others may have discovered among the Indians I cannot tell, but though I have been about nineteen years among the Cherokees, I have perceived nothing of that slavish, servile fear, on the part of women, so often spoke of."[36] Perhaps women willingly performed most of the work in Cherokee society because they also controlled the fruits of their labor, the crops; the means of production, the land; and ultimately, the result of production, the children.

The primary landholding unit in Cherokee society was the household, and the produce from the household's fields went into its own crib. A household consisted of an extended family linked by women, typically an elderly woman, her daughters and their children, the women's husbands, and any unmarried sons. Married sons did not live in the household. They resided with their own wives because the Cherokees were matrilocal; that is, husbands and children lived in the households of their wives and mothers. A husband and wife, therefore, occupied buildings belonging to the wife, or rather to the wife's family, and marriage did not alter a woman's right to her property. An anonymous writer commented: "The property of husband and wife . . . is as distinct as that of any other individuals, they have scarcely anything in common."[37] According to Bartram, "Marriage gives no right to the husband over the property of his wife."[38] Such an arrangement gave women control over the crops they produced and a proprietary interest in their houses and fields.

Women also tilled the soil because it was their responsibility, a task they performed as part of their sexual as well as social identity. Although biology plays a major role in defining gender in modern society, Cherokees traditionally took a much broader view of gender identity. A common early-nineteenth-century marriage ceremony symbolized the centrality of task to the construction of gender. In 1819 the missionary Cephas Washburn described a Cherokee wedding: "The groom and bride now commence stepping towards each other, and they meet in the middle of the council house, the groom presents his venison, and the bride her corn, and the blankets are united. This ceremony put into words is a promise on the part of the man that he will provide meat for his family, and on the woman's part that she will furnish bread, and on the part of both that they will occupy the same bed."[39] Similarly, the Cherokee inquired about the sex of an infant by asking, "Is it a bow or a (meal) sifter?" or "Is it ballsticks or bread?"[40]

The connection between women and corn gave women considerable status and economic power because the Cherokees depended heavily on that crop for subsistence. John Norton believed that the relative proportion of meat in the Cherokee diet was so low that game "killed for this purpose did not perhaps equal the natural increase in the temperate climates." James Edward Oglethorpe, the founder of Georgia, reported that the Cherokees were "more accustom'd to labour and live upon corn, then to procure their sustenance by hunting." Certainly corn was the preferred food, particularly by those who faced competition or danger. Warriors carried only parched corn, and the Cherokee excluded from the ball game any who had recently consumed meat because they could not "endure hardships and bear up under fatigue." Menstruating women took only a little hominy, while pregnant women generally avoided meat. Apparently, therefore, the Cherokees considered meat to be more debilitating than corn and its consumption problematic for those who faced various kinds of trials.[41] In the seventeenth century before the advent of the deerskin trade, hunting conceivably had become so insignificant to the Cherokee economy that it was largely ritualistic. Traditional Cherokee ceremonial life may, in fact, reflect the relative importance of agriculture and hunting: most public ceremonies, and in particular the Green Corn Ceremony, were associated with farming; none related directly to the chase.[42]

The association of women with corn found expression in the Cherokees' most important community ritual, the Green Corn Ceremony, which placed women squarely in the center of Cherokee religion. Originally, the Cherokees observed festivals at various stages of corn development, but in the historic era, they held their major celebration in July or August when the corn was first edible. They did not eat any of the new crop until they had performed the appropriate rites. The Green Corn Ceremony also became the occasion for the forgiveness of debts, grudges, adultery, and all crimes except murder. According to oral tradition, in an earlier era, disputes and crimes that could not be settled by the families involved, with the exception of murder, found resolution at the "annual feast of propitiation and cementation." All wrongs were forgiven; retribution was arranged; unhappy spouses were released from their marital bonds. This ceremony forced restoration of internal order whether or not the parties desired reconciliation.[43] This separate feast became subsumed in the Green Corn Ceremony, and corn became emblematic of community harmony.

The Cherokees began the ceremony with a feast and a rigorous cleaning of the town's public structures and square ground, or plaza. The men swept the council house, made new seating mats, built brush arbors, painted and whitewashed public buildings, carried out the ashes from the council house's central hearth, and covered the square ground with new dirt. The women cleaned their own houses, disposed of ashes, washed their cooking vessels and utensils, and discarded any food left from the preceding year, an act Adair believed "helped greatly to promote a spirit of hospitality" throughout the year.[44] From the previous year's crop, they saved only seven ears of corn that had been put aside "in order to attract the corn until the new crop was ripened."[45]

When everything was in order, the warriors and "beloved women" retired to the square ground where they fasted for two nights and one day. Sentinels prevented other women, children, and "worthless fellows who have not hazarded their lives" from entering the square. Those beyond the bounds only fasted until the sun reached its zenith. During the fast, the beloved women brewed and served warriors sacred medicine that acted as an emetic, purging their bodies of spiritual as well as physical pollution. At the end of the fast, the women brought samples of the new crop to the square ground and washed common utensils. On a freshly swept hearth, the community's spiritual leader kindled a new fire and placed in the fire corn given him by a beloved woman. All those seeking forgiveness could now come forward without fear of retaliation or reprisal. The medicine man called all the women to the fire, spoke to them about their obligations, and gave them new fire to take to their homes. When the women returned to the square ground, everyone joined together in dancing and singing. They feasted on the new crop, which could be eaten safely for the first time, but they were careful not to blow on it to cool it "for fear of causing a wind storm to beat down the standing crop in the field." Finally, they painted themselves with a white clay symbolizing peace and prosperity and ritually bathed in the river.[46]

The Green Corn Ceremony marked the social and spiritual regeneration of the community, and the role of women in the ceremony symbolized that which they played in Cherokee society. Selu was not only the first woman; she also was the spirit of the corn. By honoring the corn, Cherokees paid homage to women. The social renewal that accompanied the Green Corn

Ceremony connected the corn to the community and women to rebirth and reconciliation. Most women observed the occasion separately from men—as indeed they lived most of their lives apart from men—and we know little about their separate ceremonies. Beloved women, however, entered the square ground and joined the men in fasting and purification. They also performed the central act of the ceremony, the presentation of the new crop, corn that, like Selu, linked the present to the past and bound Cherokees to one another.

A communitarian ethic pervaded Cherokee life. The effort to reconcile aggrieved people at the Green Corn Ceremony was one manifestation; another was the redistributive aspects of the Cherokee economy. In a redistributive economy, the people contribute a portion of their goods and produce for the welfare of the community, a kind of voluntary taxation. The naturalist William Bartram described the harvest: "Each gathers the produce of his own proper lot, brings it to town, and deposits it in his own crib, allotting a certain portion for the Public Granary."[47] Cherokee redistribution was not as highly structured or as formalized as that found among other Native people in the Southeast, who depended on their chief to redistribute a portion of the hunt or harvest.[48] Among the Cherokees, women seem to have handled redistribution. Each household set aside part of the harvest to feed visitors, to provide for feasts, and to aid those whose crops failed. By the end of the eighteenth century, women also held special dances "twice a year or oftener" in which participants made contributions for "Use of the Poor who suffer Want."[49]

Community well-being depended on the maintenance of spiritual purity, which often manifested itself in temporal benefits. The Cherokees did not separate spiritual and physical realms but regarded them as one, and they practiced their religion in a host of private daily observances as well as in public ceremonies. Purification rituals cured and prevented disease and prepared people for war, hunting, fishing, planting, housecleaning, childbirth, and other worldly undertakings. The focus of ceremonies, however, was a spiritual cleansing, and the "medicine" Cherokees consumed during these rituals addressed spiritual as well as physical ills. Lieutenant Henry Timberlake, a member of a British garrison at Fort Loudoun in what is today east Tennessee, witnessed a "physic-dance" in which women played a central role:

A vessel of their own make, that might contain twenty gallons (there being a great many to take the medicine) was set on the fire, round which stood several goards

> filled with river-water, which was poured into the pot; this done, there arose one of the beloved women, who opening a deer skin filled with various roots and herbs, took out a small handful of something like fine salt; part of which she threw on the headman's seat, and part into the fire close to the pot; she then took out the wing of a swan, and after flourishing it over the pot, stood fixed for near a minute, muttering something to herself; then taking a shrub-like laurel (which I suppose was the physic) she threw it into the pot, and returned to her former seat.

A lull in activity followed the mixing of the medicine, and so Timberlake took a walk. When he returned some time later, he discovered that a great throng had assembled. They danced around the pot of "physic" for about an hour before they began to dip a gourd into the pot and drink the medicine. At the insistence of one of the headmen, Timberlake took a drink, although he confessed, "I would have willingly declined." He conceded that the concoction was "much more palatable than I expected, having a strong taste of sassafras." The headman told Timberlake that "it was taken to wash away their sins; so that this is a spiritual medicine, and might be ranked among their religious ceremonies."[50]

The Christian concept of sin does not have a direct corollary in the Cherokee belief system: for Cherokees, sin involved violating basic categories, blurring the boundaries, and upsetting the equilibrium. Purity resulted from the preservation of categories while pollution came from violating boundaries. On one level all Cherokees, both male and female, sought to maintain a state of purity and to avoid sources of pollution, but on another level, Cherokees sought out the very things that seemed to defy their system of categorization. Power in large part rested at the edges of the Cherokees' categories, in the interstices between categories, and with the anomalies that defied categorization. Laurel, for example, was a powerful medicine because it did not drop its leaves in winter like most other plants. Rather than ignore this attribute or identify laurel as something other than a plant, the Cherokees simply imbued it with special power. They also believed in fantastic anomalous creatures that had extraordinary power. The Uktena, for example, had the body of a snake, the wings of a bird, and the antlers of a deer, attributes of three separate categories as well as animals representative of the three levels of the universe—the underworld, the upper world, and this world. Although the mere sight of the Uktena paralyzed humans and its breath killed, people who managed to obtain the sparkling crystal from the creature's forehead acquired extraordinary abilities that included foreseeing the future. Anomalies, therefore, were the source of both great peril and amazing power. As anthropologist Mary Douglas has pointed out, many peoples respond to emissions or body fluids in the same way as they do other anomalies because these belong inside the body but escape through orifices.[51] Breath and saliva, both belonging inside the body rather than outside, had enormous power and figured prominently in the Cherokees' sacred formulas.[52] The most powerful of these substances, however, was blood, and women by virtue of their periodic contact with blood were both powerful and dangerous.[53]

Cherokee beliefs about purity and pollution help explain their attitudes toward women's life cycle, in particular menstruation, childbirth, and menopause. Because it involved bleeding, the Cherokees regarded menstruation as polluting, that is, the blood flowed outside its appropriate place within the body. During their periods, Cherokee women retired to specially constructed menstrual houses. Adair described these structures as "small huts, at as considerable a distance from their dwelling houses, as they imagine may be out of the enemies reach."[54] Nonmenstruating women left food, which consisted of a little hominy, outside the hut and quickly departed. If a woman's period coincided with an important ritual such as the Green Corn Ceremony, the headmen had ceremonial food taken to her; under no circumstances did a menstruating woman participate. Nor did a woman perform her normal tasks of farming, cooking, and caring for her children. Other women in the household or even men, if necessary, assumed her chores. The Cherokees were most particular that a menstruating woman stay away from the ill. As late as the nineteenth century, James Mooney found that the Eastern Cherokees prevented strangers from entering the house of someone who was sick in order to prevent his contact with either a menstruating woman or someone who might have come from the house of a menstruating woman. The presence of such a person in the sickroom was "considered to neutralize all the effects of the doctor's treatment."[55] Any breach of the rules regarding menstruation was an extremely serious offense. According to Adair, "Should they be known to violate that ancient law, they must answer for every misfortune that befalls any of the people."[56]

Regulations regarding menstruation extended beyond the individual women involved. Men whose wives were menstruating marched and danced behind the others on ceremonial occasions. In order to minimize the danger, the Cherokees prohibited sexual intercourse with a menstrual woman, and violation required her partner to undergo purification rituals: "He was obliged to take an emetic and then dipped himself in a river and then continue in his uncleanness till night. Unless he did this he was pronounced unfit to hunt and engage in war." Minor infractions of the prohibition against contact with menstrual women had less drastic remedies. Mooney reported that a decoction of skullcap (*Scutellaria lateriflora*) was "drunk and used as a wash to counteract the ill effects of eating food prepared by a woman in the menstrual condition, or when a woman by chance comes into a sick room or a house under the tabu." At the end of their menstrual periods, Cherokee women underwent ritual cleansing by plunging seven times in running water and changing their clothes before returning home.[57]

Many Europeans interpreted Cherokee behavior toward menstruating women as reflective of the belief that "females during their monthly courses were unclean."[58] A more accurate explanation for strict rules of avoidance is that the Cherokees believed that menstruating women possessed great power, which made them dangerous. Female physiology, according to the Cherokees, was not the consequence of original sin or divine displeasure. Adair reported that "they ascribe these monthly periods, to the female structure, not to the anger of Ishtohoolo Aba."[59] The seclusion and avoidance of women, which often has been cited as evidence for their subjugation and oppression, actually signified their power.[60] Women secluded themselves; men did not force restrictions and rituals on them. Men, in fact, often observed similar restrictions before and after warfare, and they, like women, regarded seclusion as a practical precaution and a demonstration of the elevated plane they had achieved.

The power the Cherokees attributed to menstruating women is illustrated by the myth "The Stone Man." The Stone Man was a cannibal with skin of solid rock and an appetite for Indian hunters. When a hunter spotted the Stone Man heading for a village, he hurried to the medicine man, who stationed seven menstruating women in the cannibal's path. The Stone Man grew progressively weaker as he passed the women and collapsed when he came to the last one. The medicine man drove seven sourwood stakes through the Stone Man's heart, and the people built a large fire on top of him. While he was burning, the Stone Man taught the people songs for hunting and medicine for various illnesses. When the fire died down, the people found red paint, which they believed brought success, and a divining crystal. Through the power of menstruating women, therefore, great tragedy was averted and good fortune brought to the people.[61]

Pregnancy did not bring the rigorous seclusion of menstruation, but an expectant mother curtailed many of her activities. She did not attend ceremonies and ball games or visit the sick. The Cherokees did not eat food prepared by a pregnant woman or walk on a path she had traveled. If she waded in a river upstream from fish traps, she spoiled the catch, and if she looked on a person suffering from snakebite, the victim died.[62] Many similar restrictions applied to the father-to-be. Husbands of pregnant women did not play ball and danced apart from other men in ceremonies. They did not dig graves, loiter in doorways, or wear neckerchiefs or hats with folds (which caused creases in the baby's head). Furthermore, some evidence suggests that men did not hunt, fish, or fight during their wives' pregnancies.[63]

Many of the restrictions on the activities of pregnant women protected the unborn child and aided delivery. The Cherokees believed that certain foods affected the fetus: raccoon would make the baby sick, for example, and pheasant would cause death. A child risked a birthmark if the mother ate speckled trout, ridiculously large eyes if she ate rabbit, and a big nose if she consumed black walnuts. Because squirrels climb trees, the Cherokees believed that the consumption of squirrel meat by an expectant mother caused the baby to go up instead of down during labor. Eating crayfish, which run backward, also impeded delivery. Any meat an expectant mother ate had to be trapped rather than killed by arrow or bullet—perhaps to avoid spilling its blood—and many pregnant women refrained from eating meat altogether. A woman who combed her hair backward might have a child whose hair bristled, and if she saw a mask, her baby would have its exaggerated and grotesque features. Wearing a neckerchief supposedly produced umbilical strangulation, and lingering in a doorway slowed delivery. The Cherokees also prohibited a pregnant woman from visiting a menstruating woman or viewing a corpse.[64]

In the late nineteenth century, anthropologist Frans Olbrechts studied Cherokee practices regarding childbirth, and he found that mother and father participated together in rituals guaranteeing safe delivery of their child. Occasionally, a relative of the mother replaced the father, a participation that may hark back to an earlier era for which evidence is unavailable. Each morning, they washed their hands and feet, and every new moon, they employed a medicine man to perform certain rites. The ritual took place at the river, but before leaving home, the woman drank a decoction of slippery elm bark (*Ulmus fulva*), which ensured an easy labor; touch-me-not stems (*Impatiens biflora*), which frightened the child into a quick appearance; and speedwell roots (*Veronica officinalis*) and pine cones (*Pinus pungens*), which, as evergreens, gave the child a long and healthy life. The parents took a white skin or cloth and two red or white beads, symbolizing good fortune, to the river. The priest and the woman entered the river while the husband waited on the bank. Holding the beads brought by the couple in one hand and black beads in the other, the priest sought answers to questions about delivery, the child's sex, its disposition, and its future. Following this divination, the husband folded the beads in the fabric and presented the items to the medicine man as payment.[65]

Some sources maintain that Cherokee women traditionally gave birth unassisted in the forest or in a special building. Olbrechts found that four women including a midwife attended the mother in her cabin, which all other residents left. Early-nineteenth-century sources suggest that "the presence of men is disgusting on such occasions," but Olbrechts reported that sometimes the husband or medicine man was present, although these men carefully stood behind the mother and, therefore, they did not actually witness the birth.[66] When labor started, the woman drank an infusion of wild cherry bark (*Prunus serotina*). Various formulas existed to speed delivery. According to Mooney, a female relative of the mother recited these while anointing the patient with decoctions. One formula Mooney recorded was intended to frighten the child out of its mother's womb: "Listen! You little man, get up now at once. There comes an old woman. The horrible [old thing] is coming, only a little way off. Listen! Quick! Get your bed and let us run away. Yu!" The person reciting then repeated the formula substituting "little woman" and "your grandfather." Another formula sought to entice the child to make an appearance: "Little boy, little boy, hurry, hurry, come out, come out! Little boy, hurry; a bow, a bow; let's see who'll get it, let's see who'll get it." The next verse appealed to a little girl to come out and claim a sifter.[67]

During delivery, a woman stood, knelt, or sat, but she never gave birth lying down. Usually no one bothered to catch the baby, who simply fell on leaves placed beneath the mother. The Cherokees considered it a bad omen "if the child, at birth, happened to fall on its breast." In this event, they wrapped the baby in a cloth and threw him in a creek. The child was rescued when the wrapper sank and carried away the "ill-fortune." If a child fell on its back, the Cherokees viewed this as a good omen.[68] After delivery, the mother ceremonially plunged the infant into the river, an act she repeated daily for two years. Sometimes the Cherokees also waved a newborn over the fire, the sun's earthly representative, and asked for spiritual guardianship.[69] The father buried the placenta. The number of ridges he crossed between the site of the birth and the interment of the placenta determined the number of years before another child would be born. The Cherokees believed that if he merely threw away the placenta, another child could be born at any time, whereas if he buried the placenta too deep and covered it with stones, there would be no more children.[70]

The mother and other relatives took immediate steps to form the child's personality and character. In the late nineteenth century, James Mooney observed Cherokee women giving their infants a drink made of pulverized cockleburs and water "taken from a fall or cataract, where the stream makes a constant noise" in order to make their children "quick to learn and retain in memory anything once heard." Mothers also rubbed beans on their children's lips to make them "look smiling and good tempered" or a lizard on their throat and head to make them sleep quietly. Scratching the hands slightly with a crayfish claw produced a strong grip and bathing the eyes with water in which a blue-jay feather had been soaked made them early risers. A child destined for the priesthood received special sustenance prepared and administered by a medicine man, whereas other children were nursed by their mothers or, in the event of maternal illness, by a relative.[71]

Many Europeans credited the treatment of newborns for the absence of deformity among Indians. John Gerar William de Brahm, the Crown's surveyor-general, claimed that he "never met with an Indian who was born a cripple," and Adair found it "remarkable that there are no deformed Indians."[72] Timberlake believed that bathing babies daily in cold water made "the children acquire such strength, that no ricketty or deformed are found among them."[73] Although such rituals may have been responsible for universal good health, another possible explanation is that Cherokee mothers simply abandoned weak newborns in the forest. Infanticide may have been practiced by the Cherokees as the only acceptable means by which people could control population growth.[74] Apparently, the mother alone had the right to abandon a child; for anyone else to kill a newborn constituted murder. Olbrechts found abortion unknown and the use of spotted cowbane (*Cicuta maculata*), purported to be a contraceptive, frowned upon.[75]

The mother's physical recovery from childbirth was rapid, according to European reports. Cherokee women "were not subject to any of the complaints attending modern childbirth, when delivered. They were often able to be in the field hoeing the next day."[76] Timberlake observed: "Though three days is the longest time of their illness, a great number of them are not so many hours; nay, I have known a woman delivered at the side of a river, wash her child, and come home with it in one hand, and a goard full of water in the other."[77] These accounts almost certainly exaggerate postpartum activity, because Cherokee women normally curtailed their activities for a period of time following delivery. A woman remained apart from her family for seven days following delivery; then she bathed, put on clean clothes, and returned home. A Cherokee woman, therefore, observed postpartum restrictions and underwent ritual cleansing that paralleled those of menstruating women. If she continued to bleed, a priest "took a bird, plucked off the feathers, and took out the innards and then offered it as a sacrifice for her." The treatment for problems resulting from delivery were spiritual because, unlike Europeans, the Cherokees integrated spiritual and physical worlds.[78]

In Cherokee cosmology, fertility, change, and future time were all within the province of the underworld, whereas purity, order, and past time rested with the upper world.[79] Good as well as evil could come from the underworld, but venturing into this realm was dangerous because the possibility of disaster existed. Even fertility was not an unmixed blessing since the Cherokees believed that there could be too many people. In one of the origin myths recorded by James Mooney, "At first there were only a brother and sister until he struck her with a fish and told her to multiply, and so it was." The Cherokees associated fish with the underworld and fertility because they swam in rivers, which led to the underworld. The pair's experience with fertility soon threatened disaster because the sister produced a child every seven days "until there was danger that the world could not keep them. Then it was made that a woman should have only one child in a year, and it has been so ever since." As the myth illustrates, fertility could be both a blessing and a curse. Furthermore, any contact with the elements of the underworld demanded extreme caution.[80]

The similarity of attitudes regarding menstruation, pregnancy, and parturition is not surprising because the Cherokees associated menstrual blood with childbirth: menstrual blood was, they believed, a child who had not been born. Menstrual blood, therefore, was invested with the power to bring about change, and while the Cherokees did not actually fear new things, they recognized that innovations could be for better or worse. Consequently, they regarded any potential change with some apprehension and attempted through rituals to control its direction. Because they were the embodiment of fertility, women occupied a particularly precarious position in Cherokee society. They were dangerous because they were powerful: that is, they were capable of bringing about change in the family and in the community through the addition of a new, unknown member. Chaos could accompany that shift since both chaos and change existed within the domain of the underworld. The restrictions and rituals surrounding procreation formalized the community's apprehensions, as well as any personal anxiety women might have about childbirth, and allayed fear. Through sexual abstinence, avoidance of the sick and menstrual women, and other practices, women attempted to control the danger and to minimize its negative effects.

Men underwent similar periods of seclusion before going to war and after their return from battle. For several days after the organization of a war party, the members remained in the council house, where they fasted and purged themselves with specially prepared emetics. Through these actions they hoped to attain a state of ritual purity that would ensure their own safety and bring them success in battle. Upon their return from war, the men retired to the council house, which had been carefully cleaned in their absence, and remained secluded until they presented no danger to the community or to themselves. Men or women captured by the enemy and freed also underwent a period of confinement and ritual purification.[81]

A warrior's avoidance of women stemmed largely from beliefs about sexual intercourse. The Cherokees believed that if a warrior slept with a woman after the prebattle purification rites, "the medicine lost all its virtue, and he was easily killed in battle."[82] Men observed a similar period of celibacy after battle. James Adair found this practice to be universal among southern Indians, even the Choctaws, whom he thought particularly susceptible to pleasures of the flesh: "Although the Chocktah are libidinous, and lose their customs apace, yet I have known them to take several female prisoners without offering the least violence to their virtue, till the time of purgation was expired;—then some of them forced their captives, notwithstanding their pressing entreaties and tears."[83] Young Cherokee men training to be hunters also abstained from intercourse, perhaps to prepare them for the hunting season in fall and winter, and while hunters were away from the village for months at a time in search of game, they refrained from engaging in sex even though a few women accompanied them on the hunt.[84] Pregnant and menstruating women adhered to the same sexual taboo as hunters and warriors.

War, hunting, childbirth, and menstruation required strict rules of behavior because they all involved blood. James Adair maintained that the Indians' aversion to blood stemmed from their belief that "it contains the life, the spirit of the beast."[85] Unleashed, the spiritual power that blood contained was dangerous. In myth, children sometimes sprang from blood; these children exhibited wild natures and upset the normal order.

Wild Boy, for example, came from the blood of game that Selu had washed in the river. He forced radical change: instead of an effortless subsistence, men subsequently had to hunt for game and women had to farm.[86] Good as well as evil, however, resulted from Wild Boy's actions: all men—not just Kana'ti—gained access to wild animals and all Native people received kernels of corn to plant. Nevertheless, human beings had to be wary of blood and its power. Consequently, hunters performed special rites when they killed animals: to appease the spirit of the deer, for example, and to prevent the rheumatism that spirit could cause, hunters asked forgiveness and cast bloodstained leaves into the river and a piece of meat into the fire.[87]

Human blood, of course, posed even greater dangers, and the distinct ways in which Cherokees encountered human blood helped define them as women and men. Menstruation and childbirth, hunting and warfare deeply embedded a person in a category: these were the times when women were most female and men were most male.[88] The categories of woman and man were so opposite at this point that they could not risk contact. Cherokees recognized these categorical extremes in other contexts: for example, they extinguished fire with soil rather than water because fire represented the upper world and water the underworld, opposites so powerful that they needed the soil of this world to mediate.[89]

Although women could not avoid the physical and spiritual dangers brought on by menstruation, pregnancy, and childbirth, they could gain a spiritual power through these trials.[90] Perhaps in recognition of that power, the Cherokees held postmenopausal women in high regard, and they became responsible for tasks requiring a high degree of purity. Adair reported that the war ark that accompanied military expeditions contained "consecrated vessels, made by beloved superannuated women." The trader also observed that six "old beloved women" sang and danced with the priests and warriors. During the Green Corn Ceremony, an "old beloved woman" carried medicine to the women, children, and "worthless fellows" waiting outside the square ground.[91] Timberlake reported that old women brewed the ceremonial medicine, and Norton noted that "their principal superstition is pretending to foretell events, by casting some kind of die which is performed by men and old women." Elderly women nursed wounded warriors, and an old woman cared for Norton after he sprained his shoulder. Furthermore, the Cherokees had traditionally held a special ceremony every seven years to purify the high priest, a ritual undertaken by "a very aged and honorable woman" who washed the priest with warm water.[92]

Despite the Cherokees' rigid construction of gender, they could not maintain impermeable boundaries. Some men and women, by circumstance or choice, crossed the line between them. Cherokee beliefs about menstruation and the female role in child rearing prevented women from becoming full-time hunters and warriors, but men sometimes did opt for a life of farming rather than one of hunting and warfare. Native reaction to such behavior is difficult to ascertain. European observers, of course, brought to the subject their own culture's expectations of men. Adair, for example, derided men who farmed as "worthless fellows" or "He-hen-pickers" and recounted how a beloved woman gave them only a child's portion of sacred tobacco "because she thinks such spiritless pictures of men cannot sin with married women."[93] Some evidence suggests that a kind of sexual reclassification occurred for men who preferred to farm and that these men functioned sexually as well as socially as women. Reflecting European homophobia, Romans mentioned transvestites in Choctaw society: "Sodomy is also practiced but not to the same excess as among the Creeks and Chickasaws, the *Cinaedi* among the Choctaws are obliged to dress themselves in woman's attire, and are highly despised especially by women."[94] Cultural similarities with the tribes mentioned by Romans make it quite likely that such individuals existed in Cherokee society. In the nineteenth century, a Cherokee recalled in far less pejorative terms that "there were among them formerly, men who assumed the dress and performed all the duties of women."[95]

The Cherokees' response to men who became women is unclear. They may have ostracized such people for upsetting the cosmic order. The trader James Adair reported an incident in which a young man whom the Cherokees considered too effeminate and suspected of homosexuality was scratched and ridiculed.[96] Within the Cherokees' carefully categorized universe, anything that did not exactly fit, such as men acting like women, elicited one of two reactions. Some anomalies, such as the mythical dragonlike *Uktena,* inspired fear and respect while others prompted joking. Bears, for example, appeared to defy categorization by exhibiting many characteristics, such as grasping and walking upright, that seemed more appropriate to humans than animals. As a result of their appearance and behavior, these humanlike animals became the object of jokes and represented inept and humorous characters in many myths.[97] The Cherokees probably regarded effeminate men or men who preferred farming to hunting in a similar way. Joking did not necessarily imply scorn. Instead, Cherokees used joking to recognize deviant behavior and incorporate it into the repertoire of acknowledged behaviors. By drawing attention to men who did not conform to their notions of manhood, Cherokees confirmed what they considered to be normal behavior for men.

When women crossed the gender boundary, however, the Cherokees responded in precisely the opposite way. War parties sometimes included women whose primary responsibility was to carry water and prepare food. In 1751, for example, the colony of South Carolina commissioned 12 Cherokee women along with 128 men to go to war against enemy tribes. Occasionally women actually became warriors. In the American Revolution, one of the casualties of the Cherokee defeat by General Griffith Rutherford at Waya Gap was a woman "painted and stripped like a warrior and armed with bows and arrows." The Moravian missionary John Gambold had an opportunity to converse with one of these women warriors, whose age he estimated to be one hundred: "The aged women, named Chicouhla, claimed that she had gone to war against hostile Indians and suffered several severe wounds. Vann's wives verified this and said that she was very highly respected and loved by browns and whites alike." One of James Mooney's informants in the late nineteenth century had known an old woman whose Cherokee name meant "Sharp Warrior." The Wahnenauhi manuscript, which Mooney obtained from a Cherokee medicine man, contained an account of a Cherokee women who rallied the warriors when her husband died defending their town against enemy attack. This woman, Cuhtahlutah (Gatun'lati or "Wild Hemp"), saw her husband fall, grabbed his tomahawk, shouted, "Kill! Kill!" and led the Cherokees to victory.[98]

Women who distinguished themselves in battle occupied an exalted place in Cherokee political and ceremonial life. William Bartram translated the title accorded female warriors as "War Woman," and he noted that a stream in north Georgia bore the name War Woman's Creek. A trader told him "that it arose from a decisive battle which the Cherokees formerly gained over their enemies on the banks of this creek, through the battle and strategem of an Indian woman who was present. She was afterwards raised to the dignity and honor of a Queen or Chief of the nation, as a reward for her superior virtues and abilities, and presided in the State during her life."[99] Mooney heard about a woman who had killed her husband's slayer in battle during the American Revolution: "For this deed she was treated with so much consideration that she was permitted to join the warriors in the war dance, carrying her gun and tomahawk." War Women also participated in the Eagle Dance, which commemorated previous victories. Athletic young men actually performed the dance, but in one part, old warriors and War Women related their exploits. These women sat apart from other women and children on ceremonial occasions and partook of food and drink not normally given to women. War Women also decided the fate of war captives. Some sources use the terms *War Woman* and *beloved woman* interchangeably, and they may have applied to the same women. But Cherokees distinguished between pre- and postmenopausal women, and evidence suggests that beloved women were elderly while War Women were of indeterminate age. War Women probably became "beloved" when they passed menopause.[100]

Why did the Cherokees joke about men and honor women who crossed gender lines? Both were anomalies, but only women acquired considerable prestige by crossing the line. Perhaps women who excelled in battle presented a greater challenge to the Cherokee categorization of humanity. Women were not supposed to engage directly in warfare; only men who had carefully prepared themselves for war through fasting and purification could expect to meet with success. How then could they explain a woman who killed enemy warriors and led Cherokee warriors to victory? Such a woman was obviously an anomaly: she was no longer merely a woman nor, of course, was she a warrior. As an anomaly, she possessed extraordinary power: through war and menstruation she had male and female contact with blood. Each experience singly was a source of power and danger; when the two came together, the power was phenomenal and permitted these women to move between the worlds of men and women. Men who farmed had neither opportunity—war or menstruation—to obtain power, and therefore the Cherokees had no reason to fear them.

Two anomalies of myth, the Uktena and the bear, provide parallels. The Uktena drew victims to it with the crystal on its forehead and then choked them to death, but according to Mooney, whoever managed to obtain the crystal was "sure of success in hunting, love, rainmaking, and every other business" and able to see the future. The Uktena, therefore, was the source of both good and evil because it possessed great power. The bear, on the other hand, was unable to kill humans even to avenge the loss of its own kind. Consequently, "the hunter does not even ask the Bear's pardon when he kills one." The bear had a place in the world, but it had little power.[101]

The Cherokees understood what it meant to be a woman or a man even when individuals confounded that understanding, but because gender did not shape their organization of the world, they were able to incorporate individuals who defied gender into their social organization. Language provides clues to that organization. In the Cherokee language *asgaya,* "man," and *agehya,* "woman," are distinct words that apply to different human beings. Cherokee is not a gendered language, like French or Spanish, nor is it a language that has gender-specific pronouns, like English. Linguistically, gender implies hierarchy, and languages that do not use gender as a "universally applicable classification" have "no implicit assumption of hierarchy or ranking of the categories just because they are different." According to linguist Durbin Feeling, "forms like ga²wo³ni²ha can be translated either 'he's speaking' or 'she's speaking,' depending on the context."[102] Indeed, the context revealed all one needed to know. Cherokee women farmed and men hunted; women spilled blood in menstruation and childbirth and men in hunting and war. Female and male, feminine and masculine, women and men had no real meaning apart from the context in which they lived.[103]

The Cherokees' conceptualization of the cosmos helped them understand their place in the world. The anthropologist Peggy Sanday has suggested that the existence of an important female deity indicates the acceptance of female rights, privileges, and even power. Although the Cherokees did not have "deities" in the sense of physical representations of spiritual beings they worshipped, they did personify many things in the natural world and assign them religious significance. A female spirit sometimes appeared as corn, while the Cherokees regarded thunder and rivers as male spirits. The most important "deities" were the sun and moon: the sun was female and the moon was male. In some ways, this depiction of the sun and moon epitomize Cherokee gender roles. The day belongs to the sun, the night to the moon. Rarely can both be seen in the sky at the same time. Similarly, men and women had separate and distinct responsibilities. But the Cherokees viewed the tasks both women and men performed and the contributions they made as essential to their society and, like the sun and moon, to the integrity of the universe.[104]

TWO

Defining Community

The descendants of Kana'ti and Selu defined themselves as a distinct people in ways that did not always make sense to European observers. Cherokees called themselves Ani-Yun Wiya, the Real People, which distinguished them from others with whom they had contact, but the bonds that held them together were obscure. Living in scattered villages separated by rugged terrain, Cherokees spoke several dialects of a common language, but no clear boundaries demarcated their territory and no political authority delineated citizenship. Only kinship seems to have bound Cherokees together in the early eighteenth century. Unlike the civic duties of European citizenries, the prerogatives and responsibilities of kinship extended to women as well as men. Furthermore, the Cherokees traced kinship solely through women. This circumstance gave women considerable prestige, and the all-encompassing nature of the kinship system secured for them a position of power.

Unfortunately, few early European observers managed to grasp the principle of matrilineal descent. In his otherwise perceptive account of Cherokee culture, J. P. Evans admitted that he simply could not comprehend "their mode of calculating clan kin" because "it appeared so incongruous."[1] Some Europeans such as John Lawson were cognizant of the essentials, but they tried to impose a European logic on what appeared to them to be an illogical way of reckoning kin. Lawson explained how a Congaree became headman of a matrilineal Saponi village: "He got this Government by Marriage with the Queen; the Female Issue carrying the Heritage, for fear of Impostors; the Savages well knowing, how much Frailty possesses the *Indian* women, betwixt the Garters and the Girdle."[2] Only the combination of primary source material and modern anthropological theory have enabled us to understand matrilineality and the complexity of Native American kinship. In aboriginal Cherokee society, matters of kinship affected social interaction, demography, internal order, and foreign policy, and the status of women derived in part from their place in the kinship system.

The basic unit of kinship in Cherokee society was the clan. All members of a clan supposedly descended from the same individual, and although the exact connection had long been forgotten, according to Evans, "this relationship seems to be as binding as the ties of consanguinity."[3] Although there may have been other clans in earlier times, the Cherokees of the historic era had seven clans: *Aniwahiya* or Wolf; *Anikawi* or Deer; *Anidjiskwa* or Bird; *Aniwodi* or Paint; *Anisahoni,* perhaps meaning Blue; *Anigotigewi,* perhaps Wild Potato; and *Anigilohi,* perhaps Twister.[4] According to the principle of matrilineal descent, people belonged to the clan of their mother: their only relatives were those who could be traced through her. Blood relatives included siblings, the maternal grandmother (mother's mother), maternal uncles (mother's brothers), and maternal aunts (mother's sisters). The children of mother's sisters were kin, but those of mother's brothers were not. Children were not blood relatives of their father or grandfather; a father was not related to his children by blood.

An entire clan did not live together, of course, but the stationary members of a household belonged to the same clan. A matrilineage, or subdivision of the clan descending from a particular known individual, formed the core of a typical Cherokee household. When households became unwieldy, members of the matrilineage separated and new households came into being. Similarly, households could be too small, a situation often intolerable for the women who did the heavy labor. For this reason, a Delaware woman, whom a Cherokee had married while he was in captivity, brought her sister with her when she and her husband moved to the Cherokee Nation in the late eighteenth century.[5] A fellow Mohawk with whom John Norton spoke told him that her elder sister "had married a Cherokee, who had visited the Mohawk river. A few years later, she, also, having married another of the same Nation, followed her sister." These women lived together (and their husbands with them) and provided each other kinship ties and enough woman-power to operate a household.[6]

Generally, Cherokee households were quite large. Norton described a multigenerational household he visited as "a little village."[7] The Moravians gave the following description of an elderly white man with whom they became acquainted: "For the last thirty years he has lived with the Cherokees and by his Cherokee wife; they and their children and their children's children live together."[8] Daniel Butrick observed that "family connexions generally settle together so that it frequently occurs that a whole settlement is made up of near relatives."[9] A number of buildings including summer houses, winter houses, menstrual huts, corn cribs, and various storage buildings accommodated these people. Summer houses, where the family slept in the appropriate season, were large rectangular structures with gable roofs and clapboard sides. The size of the round winter houses, or hot houses, depended on the size of the family, with some as large as thirty feet in diameter and fifteen feet high. Constructed of wattle and daub, hot houses had no windows, no chimney, and only a small deerskin-draped opening for a door. Berths lined the walls, and a fire, which the women maintained, smoldered throughout the day to keep warm all those who had no reason to be out of doors.[10]

The only permanent members of a household were the women. Husbands were outsiders; that is, they were not kinsmen. When a man married, he moved from the household of his mother to that of his wife. A man's move to his bride's residence did not mean that he became a part of her clan and lineage; in Alexander Longe's words, "Their wives is nothing akin to them."[11] Several myths collected by James Mooney depict matrilocal households. In "The Man Who Married Thunder's Sister," for example, a warrior fell in love with Thunder's sister at a dance. When she obtained her brother's permission to marry, the warrior accompanied his bride to her home in the underworld. The bridegroom had behaved appropriately, but in "The Slant-Eyed Giant," the newlyweds refused to follow established practice. In this myth, a young woman married a giant despite her mother's objections, and the giant took her to live in his house. The woman's brother, who lived with his wife, tried in vain to convince his sister to return to their mother's house. She persisted in her abnormal behavior, and in the end, she never saw her family again.[12]

The Cherokees regarded marriage as a family affair. Both parties had to obtain the consent of relatives and while kinsmen sometimes strongly encouraged young people to marry, kin did not normally force mates on them against their will. The relative freedom Cherokees exercised in matrimonial matters stemmed from the basic relationship between parents and children, which Payne described: "Parents generally, are excessively fond of their children to a degree which often proves their ruin, especially at the present day. Children and young people, however, used to manifest great respect for their parents and the aged generally."[13] This respect sometimes prompted children to accept matches other than those they would have preferred. The Moravian missionaries recounted the experience of one reluctant bride: "We were told, that she was by no means pleased by his visits and attempted to avoid him . . . [but] the marriage had been approved by Anna Johanna's parents and relatives. We could do nothing about it because her parents demanded it and we would have offended them had we objected." Anna Johanna acquiesced to her parents' wishes and married the unwelcome suitor.[14]

Kin relationships played an important role in selection of marriage partners. Cherokees did not consider clan members to be appropriate mates. Longe reported that Cherokee men would "in no wise marry with a woman of their own family counting them their proper sisters."[15] A person generally married into the clan of his or her grandfather, and such a marriage reflected a certain relationship between two clans. Love formulas, which rank second only to medicinal formulas in number, had phrases such as "I belong to the ——— clan, that one alone which was allotted into for you."[16] In the marriage ceremony, according to Payne, the bride's male relatives undressed the groom and clothed him in new garments, confirming their relationship to him. When a spouse died, the survivor usually took as a new mate a close relative of the deceased.[17]

Sometimes, a man did not wait for his wife to die in order to marry one of her female relatives.[18] No evidence for multiple husbands exists (although some women changed husbands frequently), but the marriage of a man to more than one woman was relatively common. Practicality encouraged men to marry women of the same lineage, often sisters. That way, he only had to reside in one household rather than divide his time between the lineages of unrelated wives. Although early European observers decried polygamy and suggested that the practice "renders the women contemptible in the men's eyes and deprives them of all influence," some modern anthropologists have postulated that in societies where sororal polygamy is common, women enjoy a high degree of personal autonomy and suffer little from male domination or sexual competition.[19]

In the event of divorce, the husband left his wife's house and returned to the household of his mother or sister. Although he may have been unwilling to leave his children and a household in which he had grown comfortable, an estranged husband had little recourse if his wife wanted him to go. In two myths recorded by Mooney, "The Owl Gets Married" and "The Huhu Gets Married," women drove their husbands from their homes.[20] Among humans, similar things happened. Dismayed Moravians wrote in 1813 that George Harlan's "evil wife had driven him from their house and he had found refuge with his relatives the Crutchfields."[21] Children always remained with their mothers and kinsmen rather than going with fathers to whom they were not related. John Lawson observed the consequences of marital separation among the matrilineal tribes of coastal North Carolina: "The Children always fall to the Women's Lot; for it often happens, that two *Indians* that have liv'd together, as Man and Wife, in which Time they have had several Children; if they part and another Man possess her, all the Children go along with the Mother and none with the Father."[22]

The men who had a permanent connection to the household were the male members of the lineage, the brothers and sons of the female members. Whether the women of a household or their brothers were dominant on the domestic scene is uncertain. Most likely, few contests for hegemony arose. Brothers normally lived not with their sisters but with their own wives, and so opportunities for conflict were rare. The Moravians did record one disagreement between niece and uncle: "Our Str. Anna Tussusellcky came very early this morning because her Uncle had threatened her life. She had refused to permit him to perform incantations in her house. She had hidden from him for two nights and came to us from the woods completely exhausted and starved."[23] This event occurred after pacification, the collapse of a hunting economy, and the abandonment of most local council houses; therefore, Tussusellcky's uncle may have spent more time at "her house" than he would have several decades earlier. As a general rule even unmarried brothers and uncles spent little time in the household. They were either in the hunting grounds, at war, or in the council house.

Although brothers may occasionally have challenged the domestic authority of their sisters or uncles their nieces, men apparently never tried to dominate their wives. The eighteenth-century trader Alexander Longe wrote: "I have this to say that the women rules the roost and wears the breeches and sometimes will beat their husbands within an inch of their lives." According to Longe, who was given to hyperbole, husbands did not defend themselves against their wives' wrath: "The man will not resist their power if the woman was to beat his brains out; for when she has beat one side like a stalk fish, he will turn the other side to her and beat until she is weary. Sometimes they beat their husbands to that height that they kill them outright."[24] A social dance that John Norton witnessed may have symbolized the domestic situation. The women began the dance alone and then seized partners from the audience. The result of this conscription was occasionally humorous: "Sometimes a grave, aged Chief, is seized upon, and snatched from among his Brother Counsellors, by those merry

Dances, to make a Partner in their frolicsome dance. In this the Ladies have absolute command."[25] Even as late as the 1880s, James Mooney found women of the Eastern Band of Cherokees to be the dominant partners in marriage.[26]

In Cherokee society, home and hearth were part of a woman's domain. Whatever time she could spare from the fields was spent at the homestead with other women. Men probably felt somewhat uncomfortable there. If they were married, the lineage with whom they lived belonged to a clan different from theirs. If they were unmarried and lived with their own lineage, they had to contend with the presence of their sisters' husbands, who were men of another clan. This sort of intimacy between male members of different clans was awkward and, in the case of conflict between clans, disruptive. Consequently, a male presence in a household was irregular. The Cherokees, in fact, referred to the moon as male because it "travels by night" like men who paid only nocturnal visits to their wives' houses.[27] While men did make appearances at the households of their wives and of their own lineages, they could be found most frequently at a communal site in the company of other men. Single men often preferred to sleep in the council house rather than in the houses of their mothers and sisters. But the control exercised by women over domestic matters did not stem merely from male abdication of authority. Matrilineality placed women in a unique position: they alone could convey the kinship ties essential to a Cherokee's existence.

Members of each of the seven matrilineal clans were dispersed throughout Cherokee territory, and every town usually had representatives of all clans. Although an individual might be personally unknown in a town, he or she always found a warm welcome from clan kin. Adair noted: "I have observed with much inward satisfaction the community of goods that prevailed among them, . . . especially with those of their own tribe [clan]. . . . When Indians are travelling in their own country, they enquire for a house of their own tribe; and if there be any, they go to it, and are kindly received, though they never saw the persons before—they eat, drink, and regale themselves, as at their own tables."[28] The Cherokees based distinctions within clans on generation and gender and applied the same familial names to all those of roughly the same age and sex; wherever Cherokees traveled, therefore, they encountered parents and grandparents, brothers and sisters.

Clan members also cared for children whose parents had died. Longe observed that "if the mother dies before the child has left off sucking, any of the woman's relations that gives milk will take the child and give it to suck and they will make no distinction betwixt that child and their own proper children." In the nineteenth century, a Cherokee child attending a mission school wrote to a benefactor that the relatives of orphans "give them victuals and clothes and often they do as well by them as they do by their own children." Clan members accepted children whose natural mothers had died because "mother" was a social rather than a strictly biological role. Children, in fact, had many "mothers," maternal aunts and other female clan members of their biological mother's generation. The same rules of behavior governed their interactions with all their "mothers."[29]

Kin relationships determined how all Cherokees behaved toward one another. The anthropologist William H. Gilbert Jr. described Cherokee social interaction as expressing respect, satirical familiarity, or sexual familiarity, and he identified the type of interaction considered appropriate for particular kin relationships. Parents and children treated each other with respect, as did aunts or uncles and nieces or nephews, because the latter stood in the same social relationship as parents and children. Siblings and cousins were on familiar terms and could joke with and tease one another. People of the grandparent-grandchild relationship could be on terms of physical familiarity ranging from affection to sexual intercourse. This, of course, does not mean that elderly Cherokees had sexual relations with their grandchildren, but that the preferred mate was a person from grandfather's clan. Kinship terms and the relationship they entailed extended beyond close relatives to all members of one's clan. Consequently, the kind of relationship a person had with another depended on what they called each other.[30] Evans reported: "An Indian can tell you without hesitating what degree of relationship exists between himself and any other individual of the same clan you may see proper to point out."[31] Similarly, the clans of other people determined a person's behavior toward them: father's clan had to be respected, whereas sexual familiarity was permissible with grandfather's clan.

So descriptive were kin terms that Cherokees used them to explain nonkin relationships. In expressing their appreciation to Thomas Griffiths, an Englishman who escorted a woman captured in war from Charleston to her village, the Cherokees told him that he "had behaved like a True Brother in taking care to conduct their squaw safely home."[32] They also imposed taxonomical order on the animal world by classifying creatures in terms of kin relationships. The water beetle, for example, was the beaver's grandchild.[33] In one of the sacred formulas recorded by the modern scholars Anna and Jack Kilpatrick in Oklahoma, the priest addressed the spirits in kin terms: "Grandfather, I want water! Grandmother, I want water! Uncle, I want water!"[34] Kinship terms described Cherokee relationships with other tribes and with European powers as well. An informant told Daniel Butrick in the early nineteenth century: "All Indians came from one father. The Delawares are the grandfathers of all other tribes, while the Cherokees are uncles to the Creeks, Choctaws, and Chickasaws, and some other tribes are brothers to the Cherokees."[35] The Cherokees applied the term "brother" to the English, perhaps because their relationship was often competitive, but when they sought assistance in war, the Cherokees called the English "eldest brother" because this person was responsible for the safety and well-being of his younger siblings. They usually referred to the king or governor as "father" in order to indicate respect.[36] The kinship terms with which Indians addressed each other and Europeans were far more than quaint figures of speech; they were instead descriptive of a particular relationship and prescriptive of behavior toward another party.

The absence of kinship ties was a distinct liability in Cherokee society. First of all, people were unsure of how to behave toward someone who had no place in the kinship system. Consequently, the Cherokees once concluded a peace treaty with the Senecas by Cherokee women choosing Senecas for uncles and brothers. The Cherokees could interact peacefully with their old enemies only if they incorporated the outsiders into their kinship system.[37] The rules governing conjury also penalized a person without kin. Rainmaking required a representative of each clan to wade into the water with a club and strike seven trees on the bank.[38] In the event of illness, only a blood relative could summon the doctor; husbands and wives, being of separate clans, could not treat each other nor could a spouse send for the medicine man. In the late nineteenth century, James Mooney reported: "In one instance within the writer's knowledge, a woman complained that her husband was very sick and needed a doctor's attention, but his relatives were taking no steps in the matter and it was not permissible for her to do so."[39] If a person died, the responsibility for burial rested with kinsmen. According to Adair, the Cherokees buried clan members together, and if a person died away from home, relatives collected the remains and properly interred them. Other clans played no role even in mourning the dead. Adair provided an example of the lack of concern with which they regarded a death in another clan (or "tribe"): "In this time of mourning for the dead, I have known some of the frolicksome young sparks to ask the name of the deceased person's tribe; and once, being told it was a racoon, (the genealogical name of the family) one of them scoffingly replied, 'then let us away to another town, and cheer ourselves with those who have no reason to weep; for why should we make our hearts weigh heavy for an ugly dead racoon?' "[40]

The Cherokees may have regarded an individual without kin ties as something less than a person.[41] Hostility to early traders probably stemmed from the Europeans' lack of relatives and place in the social structure.[42] That their lives were often in jeopardy is certain: trader Ludovic Grant maintained that Old Hop, an influential chief, was "the sole Preserver with the Great Warrior of every White Man's Life in the Nation."[43] This hostility was neither racially nor politically motivated, because the Cherokees distinguished themselves from others not by skin color or political allegiance but by their membership in a Cherokee clan. Any person, regardless of ancestry or nationality, who was born or adopted into one of the seven clans was a Cherokee; any person who did not belong to a Cherokee clan was not a member of the tribe and was liable to be killed almost at whim. Adair reported that "sometimes the Indians devote every one they meet in certain woods or paths, to be killed there, except their own people; this occasioned the cowardly Cherokee in the year 1753, to kill two white men on the Chikkasah warpath . . . for when they have not the fear of offending, they will shed innocent blood."[44] The Cherokees had "fear of offending" fellow Cherokees because their relatives offered protection from and exacted vengeance for acts of violence.

By far the most important role that the matrilineal clan played was as the arbiter of justice. Cherokee jurisprudence was simple, and enforcement was swift and certain. An anonymous observer explained: "Retaliation is the principle of their criminal code. When an individual is killed, a relative of the deceased kills the murderer." The principle applied to lesser crimes as well. John Pridgett told Payne that "if in fighting one bruised the other, the same kind of bruise was made in his flesh. If one scratched the other, he was scratched in a similar manner. If one gouged the other's eye, his eye was gouged; and one knocked out a tooth, one of his teeth was knocked out &c." According to Adair the Cherokees inculcated the principle of retaliation in the very young: "A little boy shooting birds in the high and thick cornfields, unfortunately chanced slightly to wound another with his childish arrow; the young vindictive fox, was excited by custom to watch his ways with utmost earnestness, till the wound was returned in as equal a manner as could be expected. Then, 'all was straight,' according to their phrase."[45]

If one Cherokee killed another, the clan kin of the slain person had the responsibility for avenging the death. Death upset the cosmic balance, and only the death of the person responsible or of a person from that same clan could restore order. When the clan of the victim had exacted vengeance, both clans involved considered the matter settled because harmony had been restored. Retaliation did not continue and consequently feuds between clans did not erupt. The clan of the offending party was, in fact, as disturbed by the disruption of order as was the clan of the victim. When a death was avenged, "all things were considered straight": order was restored.[46]

Normally, the brother or nearest male relative of the deceased sought vengeance, but sometimes women may have participated in retaliation. One of John Howard Payne's informants claimed that the death of Doublehead, which other evidence indicates resulted from unscrupulous land deals, was an act of vengeance:

> Doublehead had beaten his wife cruelly when she was with child; and the poor woman died in consequence. The revenge against murder now became in the Indian's conscience, imperative. The wife of Doublehead was the sister of the wife of [James] Vann. Vann's wife desired with her own hand to obtain atonement for her sister's death. Vann acquiesced; and he and a large party of friends set away with his wife upon this mission of blood.[47]

Vann became ill, and while his wife cared for him, some of the men in the party killed Doublehead. The Vann family provides another example of how the Cherokees interpreted the principle of blood vengeance. James Vann, an alcoholic who frequently was cruel and violent when intoxicated, killed another brother-in-law in 1806 and fled to the Creek Nation to escape the dead man's avenging relatives. Vann's flight placed all of his clan in jeopardy since the death of any one of them would have satisfied the need for vengeance. Vann's mother told neighboring Moravians that she worried particularly about her daughter, the wife of the slain man, because she, of course, belonged to the clan responsible for the murder. Finally, Vann returned. Three years later, according to one account, a relative of the victim shot Vann, who was drunk once again, through a crevice of a log house. As was customary, the family did not seek retaliation for Vann's death since it had been an act of vengeance.[48] While other more verifiable explanations exist for each death, as late as the nineteenth century, many Cherokees understood crime and punishment only in terms of kin and clan vengeance.

The law of blood extended to anyone considered responsible for the accidental death of another. One observer wrote: "It is no excuse of a homicide, that it is accidental. A husband by mischance killed his wife with a ball that glanced obliquely from a tree; a brother of the wife thought it his duty to shoot the husband in retaliation." Adair suggested the following scenario to illustrate Cherokee reaction to accidental death: "If an unruly horse belonging to a white man, should chance to be tied at a trading house and kill one of the Indians, either the owner of the house, or the person who tied the beast there, is responsible for it, by their lex talionis." Moravian missionaries recounted in their journal an episode in which the notorious James Vann helped another inebriated man to his horse but refused to accompany him to the village of Estanally "for fear that he might fall from the horse, be killed, and he, Vann, would be accused of having killed him."[49]

Some confusion exists over what happened when a person killed a fellow clan member. This was the most horrible of all crimes, almost unthinkable and consequently very rare. Adair suggested: "If indeed the murder be committed by a kinsman, the eldest can redeem: however, if the circumstances attending the fact be peculiar and shocking to nature, the murderer is condemned to die the death of a sinner [without anyone to mourn him]." Elias Boudinot, the nineteenth-century editor of the *Cherokee Phoenix,* disagreed and insisted that no man was entitled to kill a relative and so those responsible for killing kin suffered no penalty. The latter is probably accurate, but it is also likely that such murderers were ostracized or even exiled. Shoe Boots, for example, who became prominent in the nineteenth century, lived a number of years among northern Indians after he killed a kinsman.[50]

Clans that were not involved in a fatal incident had nothing to do with it. No relationship, however close, other than that of clan kinship entailed or even permitted retaliation. Matrilineality and clan vengeance, for example, prohibited a child's revenge on behalf of a father or a father for his child: "A son therefore is not allowed to revenge the murder of a father, though he is required to punish that of a mother, a sister, or a brother."[51] Fathers and children, of course, were not members of the same clan and so any retaliation would not be "blood" vengeance. The principle of clan vengeance also meant that no warriors, chiefs, priests, or any other recognized leaders of the community had anything to do with crime. The responsibilities that today we associate with police forces and courts rested with families. No one outside the family, however respected, had anything to do with providing protection or dispensing justice.

Furthermore, no united Cherokee congress declared war: only the duty to exact retribution sent relatives of slain Cherokees against other Native people. Lawson compared Native and European motivations for war: "The Indians ground their wars on enmity, not on Interest, as the Europeans generally do; for the Loss of the meanest Person in the Nation, they will go to War." The Cherokees believed that the spirits of those killed by the enemy could not go to the "Darkening Land" until their deaths had been avenged. In the meantime, the spirits haunted the houses of relatives with whom the ultimate responsibility for vengeance lay. Cherokees, therefore, went to war in order "to quench the crying blood of their relations, and give rest to their ghosts." According to Adair, "when that kindred duty of retaliation is justly executed, they immediately get ease and power to fly away."[52] The spirits of women as well as men demanded retribution, and so Cherokees did not base the need for vengeance on the sex of the victim. The death of an old woman on a scaffold protecting the corn or a young woman gathering wild greens in the forest required the same attention to duty as the loss of the most courageous warrior.

Since the Cherokees' neighbors held similar beliefs about "crying blood," peace was a virtual impossibility: one side or the other always had unavenged casualties. Unlike interclan killings, vengeance against another Native people redressed the balance only from the perspective of those who conducted the raid. Their victims viewed the act as upsetting the balance. Principal Chief Charles Hicks wrote to John Howard Payne that in the mid–eighteenth century, the chiefs had favored a "permanent peace with the northern tribes, but the imprudence of one party or the other, had defeated this desirable event, by their seeking retaliation for lives of their relatives." Because vengeance was more of a family matter than a foreign policy, Cherokees often did not wait for the town to proclaim a state of war. According to Longe: "There is no mercy showed to them that kills one of their own nation. Life for life. And sometimes when such things happens, there are more than 8 or 9 and sometimes two only goes to set about it if it is not looked into betimes by the king and the senators."[53]

If "the king and the senators"—that is, a council—decided on military action, the war chief, who attained this rank through many victories, beat his drum and retired to the council house. At this point, according to Adair, "a sufficient number of warriors and others, commonly of the family of the murdered person," armed themselves and joined the war chief for three days of purification. The war chiefs, remarked Lieutenant Henry Timberlake, "lead the warriors that choose to go, for there is no laws or compulsion on those that refuse to follow, or punishment to those that forsake their chief." Normally from twenty to forty Cherokees decided to follow the war chief although occasionally "two or three only will go to war, proceed as cautiously, and strike their prey as panthers."[54] However many Cherokee men chose to go to war, they almost certainly belonged to the clans of people killed by the enemy.

Although women sometimes accompanied warriors, most women had to await the return of the warriors in order to participate in quieting the blood of relatives. If the raid was a successful one, the women helped celebrate victory in the Scalp Dance. Accompanied by a drum, they circled the fire in a crouch and sang about the warriors' valor and deeds. Periodically they raised their arms and struck out at an imaginary enemy, ritually reenacting vengeance. Finally men joined the dance and took turns recounting the events of battle. During the Scalp Dance warriors surrendered the spoils of war—scalps, war clubs, and captives—to their nearest female relatives, and at the conclusion of the dance, men retired to the council house for purification.[55]

The women then turned to exacting vengeance from the enemy by torturing the captives the warriors had taken. Usually they thrashed the prisoners, tied them to stakes, "larded their Skins with bits of Lightwood," and seared them with flaming torches. If a victim collapsed from the pain, his tormentors threw water on him and gave him time to revive. Sometimes torture lasted for over twenty hours. Adair observed: "Not a soul, of whatever age or sex, manifests the least pity during the prisoner's tortures: the women sing with religious joy, all the while they are torturing the devoted victim, and peals of laughter resound through the crowded theatre—especially if he fears to die." Most victims and particularly warriors manifested no fear but bragged about martial deeds. When the women concluded that vengeance had been sufficiently exacted or the victim died, they took his scalp and dismembered the body. War Women often had a central role in this drama. Mooney recorded an oral tradition in which two women with snakes tattooed on their lips directed the other women to burn the feet of a captive Seneca war chief until they were blistered. Then they put corn kernels under the burned skin, chased him with clubs, and ultimately beat him to death.[56]

War Women, however, also had the power to save captives. Lieutenant Timberlake pointed out that while "War Woman" was the only title awarded women, "it abundantly recompenses them, by the power they acquire by it, which is so great, that they can, by the wave of a swan's wing, deliver a wretch condemned by the council, and already tied to the stake." The historical record includes episodes in which a War Woman did save the lives of captives. In 1776 Nancy Ward, the War Woman of Chota, reportedly rescued from the stake Mrs. William Bean, who lived in one of the illegal white settlements along the Holston River in what is today northeastern Tennessee. The War Woman took Mrs. Bean to her house and, according to an oral tradition, learned from her how to make butter. Ultimately, Mrs. Bean was restored to her family.[57] In 1781 Ward rescued prisoners clandestinely, perhaps because the captives were held in a village other than her own. The Cherokees at Scitigi (Sitico) imprisoned five traders and intended to execute two of them before embarking on a raid against frontier settlements. Instead of publicly demanding the freedom of the traders, Nancy Ward and several other women helped them escape and reach safety.[58]

The imperative to quench crying blood was so strong that the Cherokees had to have good reasons to grant reprieves to prisoners. The most common seems to have been the desire to adopt them in order to augment the size of clans decimated by famine, war, disease, or low birthrate. Most accounts of adoption, even those by people who did not understand matrilineal kinship, indicate that the Cherokees adopted captives to fill particular slots in the matrilineal structure. Adair said that the Indians adopted those captives who were not tortured "in the room of their relatives, who had either died a natural death, or had before been sufficiently revenged."[59] Antoine Bonnefoy, a Frenchman whom the Cherokees took prisoner, reported: "My companions were adopted by other savages, either as nephews or as cousins, and treated in the same manner by their liberators and all their families."[60] The Cherokees captured the physician David Menzies in the mid-eighteenth century specifically to replace "one of their head warriors" who had been killed by the English. The mother of the slain man, however, rejected Menzies, and the Cherokees subjected him to torture before ultimately releasing him.[61] Menzies' account hints at the enormous power women possessed in deciding the fate of captives. He understood that he "was destined to be presented to that chief's mother and family in his room," and he realized that the mother's refusal to accept him as her son spelled doom: "The mother fixed first her haggard bloodshot eyes upon me, then riveting them to the ground, gargled out my rejection and destruction."[62]

Admission to a Cherokee clan derived from birth or adoption, and both depended on women. For this reason, the Cherokees included women in many activities, such as the Scalp Dance, that in terms of the rigid construction of gender seem appropriate only for men. Motherhood was not a trite sentimentality to Cherokees. Cherokee women invoked motherhood as the source of their power and used their status as mothers to make public appeals. In 1768 Cherokee warriors negotiating with Iroquoian peoples at Johnson Hall in New York presented a wampum belt, used to symbolize and record agreements, sent by Cherokee women to Iroquois women. Oconostota, a Cherokee war chief who was urging peace, relayed the women's message: "We know that they will hear us for it is they who undergo the pains of Childbirth and produce Men. Surely therefore they must feel Mothers pains for those killed in War, and be desirous to prevent it."[63] Mothers also conveyed Cherokee identity; no one could be a Cherokee unless he or she had a Cherokee mother. When Attakullakulla, a distinguished Cherokee headman, appeared before the South Carolina Governor's Council, he demanded to know why no women were in attendance. After all, he pointed out to the governor, "White Men as well as the Red were born of Women."[64] Women sat in Cherokee council meetings, and their presence led Timberlake to conclude that "the story of the Amazons [was] not so great a fable as we imagined, many of the Indian women being as famous in war, as powerful in the council."[65]

The nature of Cherokee government made participation by women possible. According to one anonymous observer, "the Cherokees cannot be said to have any regular system of government, laws or even permanent customs which supplies the place of laws in some nations." For Europeans accustomed to hereditary authority, broad governmental powers, and written laws, the Cherokees seemed remarkably devoid of political organization. Timberlake tried to describe Cherokee political institutions in terms Europeans could understand: "Their government, if I may call it government, which has neither laws nor power to support it, is a mixed aristocracy and democracy, the chiefs being chose according to their merit in war or policy at home."[66] Even these chiefs, according to Adair, had little coercive authority: "The Indians, therefore, have no such titles or persons, as emperors, or kings; . . . they have no words to express despotic power, arbitrary kings, oppressed, or obedient servants; . . . The power of their chiefs, is an empty sound."[67] Cherokee chiefs may have enjoyed more power in an earlier era,[68] but in the colonial period, everyone attended council meetings, and according to Adair, "their voices, to a man, have due weight in every public affair, as it concerns their welfare alike." War Women and perhaps other women also spoke in council. The chiefs only recommended a course of action and then waited for a consensus to emerge from prolonged discussion.[69] As mothers, women often had considerable influence on the debate: on occasion, they discouraged warriors from pursuing an enemy who had taken children hostage, or they prodded reluctant warriors into taking action.[70]

Until late in the eighteenth century, the Cherokees had no national council: "Each town is independent of another. Their own friendly compact continues the union."[71] The "friendly compact," of course, was kinship, but the Cherokees also found unity in an overarching principle that governed their behavior in both domestic and foreign affairs. Cherokees believed that human beings had the responsibility for maintaining cosmic order by respecting categories and maintaining boundaries. The Cherokee obsession with order and balance, or "harmony," as one anthropologist has called the fundamental ethic governing their behavior, extended to individual conduct as well as to relationships within the nation and with other peoples.[72] A clan collectively avenged the deaths of members to restore balance, but Cherokees also expected each person to follow the rules and to govern his or her own behavior carefully. The result was considerable individual autonomy, particularly in terms of personal relationships.

Autonomy translated into sexual freedom for Cherokee women because no one controlled their sexuality. Unmarried women engaged in sex with whomever they wished as long as they did not violate incest taboos against intercourse with members of their own clans or the clans of their fathers. Married women also enjoyed considerable latitude. Their behavior provoked James Adair to conclude that "the Cherokee are an exception to all civilized or savage nations in having no laws against adultery; they have been a considerable while under a petticoat-government, and allow their women full liberty to plant their brows with horns as oft as they please, without fear of punishment."[73] If the husband of an unfaithful wife took any action at all, he usually resorted to conjury.

Formulas existed to fix the affections of a wife who had a wandering eye, and priests had several methods, including colored beads and divining crystals, to determine whether she had been unfaithful.[74] If the wife proved guilty and the husband desired revenge, the priest took some dead flies in his hand. If one came to life upon his opening the hand, it would burrow its way into the body of the wife and bring her a painful death on the seventh day. Payne, who recorded this practice, commented: "Whether the fly received any assistance from the husband or the priest is not reported."[75]

The most acceptable course of action for the husband of a wayward wife, however, was to ignore the infidelity and, if he chose, take another wife. Louis-Philippe observed: "If a Cherokee's woman sleeps with another man, all he does is send her away without a word to the man, considering it beneath his dignity to quarrel over a woman."[76] According to Norton, in the case of a wife's adultery, "the husband is even disgraced in the opinion of his friends if he seeks to take satisfaction in any other way, than that of getting another wife."[77] Adair, however, recounted one episode in which the male relatives of a cuckold husband followed the wife who "loved a great many men" into the woods, where they "stretched her on the ground, with her hands tied to a stake, and her feet also extended, where upwards of fifty of them lay with her, having a blanket for covering." Adair quickly pointed out that such revenge was an exception.[78]

Although female infidelity rarely perturbed men, husbands who strayed caused considerable disharmony in the community. Women whose husbands abandoned them for other women were "unreconcilable" according to Longe, who suggested that women had more of a proprietary interest in men than men had in women. He described a pattern of behavior that we are more accustomed to find in reverse in modern America: "Sometimes the young maids comes and steals away women's husbands. Then the wife, the first time she meets her, there is a bloody battle about it. Sometimes one gets the victory and sometimes the other. They that gets the upperhand carried the husband. If these two women were to live a thousand years in the same town, nay, next door, they never will have any communication together, nor so much as speak the one to the other."[79] Since such conflicts probably drew in family members as well, the results could be terribly disruptive. Such difficulties, however, never became the town's concern; they remained personal and familial.

Consequently, the Cherokees normally resolved sexual rivalries through divorce and remarriage. Louis-Philippe claimed that an Indian man who had several wives "takes them on and turns them away like servants, and similarly they leave him when it suits them to do so."[80] Although many Cherokee marriages endured a lifetime, some ended in less than a fortnight, and Timberlake maintained that a few Cherokees changed spouses three or four times a year.[81] Adair placed the blame for the instability of Cherokee marriages squarely on the women: "Their marriages are ill observed, and of short continuance; like the Amazons, they divorce their fighting bed-fellows at their pleasure, and fail not to execute their authority, when their fancy directs them to a more agreeable choice."[82] The

Cherokees attached no stigma to those who dissolved their marriages. When Alexander Longe inquired about the reason for the divorce of a Cherokee couple, a priest told him "that they had better be asunder than together if they do not love one another but live for strife and confusion."[83] In a similar vein, an Indian attempted to explain his people's philosophy of marriage to Adair: "My Indian friend said, as marriage should beget joy and happiness, instead of pain and misery, if a couple married blindfold, and could not love one another afterwards, it was a crime to continue together, and a virtue to part and make a happier choice."[84]

While the Cherokees largely relied on individuals to conduct themselves appropriately, they had to be concerned about flagrant violations of the rules. Adair claimed that the Cherokees blamed the smallpox epidemic of 1738, which decimated the tribe, on "the adulterous intercourses of the young married people, who the past year, had in a most notorious manner, violated their ancient laws of marriage in every thicket, and broke down and polluted many of their honest neighbors bean-plots, by their heinous crimes, which would cost a great deal of trouble to purify again."[85] The Cherokees regarded semen, like other bodily emissions, as polluting. Following intercourse, they normally bathed in the river and cleaned or destroyed any material semen had touched. The polluting nature of semen made intercourse a forbidden activity to anyone who faced danger in other ways, including touching a corpse, digging a grave, and even handling a bone—or, as we have seen, going to war, hunting, menstruating, or bearing a child.[86] Sex among the beans defiled the fields and made their subsequent use, as well as consumption of the current crop, problematic.

Such personal infractions became community concerns when they jeopardized the order and balance that all struggled to preserve. Payne described a kind of female judiciary in each town that enforced regulations. A man or woman who violated mourning customs incurred the "court's" wrath. A person whose spouse had died was supposed to observe a period of seclusion during which bathing, hair combing, and changing clothes, as well as remarriage, were forbidden. If a violation occurred, the women had the right to punish the culprit "with whipping and cropping." A similar fate awaited a man who neglected his wife and children or a person who disregarded the taboos associated with childbirth, menstruation, and sexual intercourse.[87]

The court's authority probably rested lightly on most Cherokees because each person had a profound sense of responsibility for the well-being of the community. Furthermore, clans helped them live upstanding lives through instruction, support, and protection. Clans enabled Cherokees to place themselves in the world and establish appropriate relationships with the rest of the cosmos. Cherokees grounded their sense of self in the clan, and individual identity melded into clan affiliation. Women and men had equal claim on clan privileges, but both understood that women were the source of clan membership. Only those who belonged to Cherokee clans—regardless of language, residence, or even race—were Cherokee; only those who had Cherokee mothers were the Ani-Yun Wiya, the Real People.

Part 2

Contact

In 1781 Nancy Ward, the War Woman of Chota, addressed United States treaty commissioners at the Long Island of the Holston in what is today northeastern Tennessee. She opened her speech with a surprising comment about women: "You know that women are always looked upon as nothing."[1] How could the War Woman make such a statement? Her own exalted position and her presence before such an august body seemed to belie her observation. Furthermore, the society in which she lived and the culture that formed her sense of self pointed to a very different conclusion. Almost certainly, the War Woman employed a truism held by her audience rather than a belief she shared. By hastening to add, "But we are your mothers; you are our sons," she sought to counter the prejudice of the commissioners. In acknowledging deeply held European attitudes about women, however, Ward reminds us that Cherokee women did not exist in a vacuum in the eighteenth century.

Eighteenth-century Cherokees lived in a world on which Europeans and their culture increasingly impinged. Even before the century dawned, traders began to make regular trips into the Cherokee country, and by the second decade, they had set up year-round posts. Representatives of the Crown and colonial governments also began to call on the Cherokees, and Cherokee delegations visited both colonial capitals and London. Political alliances became military alliances in the imperial rivalries of the eighteenth century, and the Cherokees became embroiled in a series of wars not of their making. All of these developments touched women as well as men, but trade and war threatened to elevate men above women. Men were the hunters who provided the deerskins that became the currency of the eighteenth-century Indian trade, and men were the warriors who forged alliances with Europeans and committed all Cherokees to war. Furthermore, Europeans brought their own construction of gender into relationships with the Cherokees, and their beliefs and behavior often ran counter to Cherokee norms.

Despite national differences, Euro-Americans shared a host of beliefs about the proper role of women in society. Instead of viewing men and women as balancing one another, Euro-Americans regarded gender, like the rest of creation, as hierarchical, with women subservient to men. Christianity, both Catholic and Protestant, charged Eve with bringing sin into the world and demanded women's subordination. In British America married women lost control of their property and, by implication, lost many other rights under the principle of coverture, which maintained that a woman's husband legally "covered" her so that she had no independent legal standing. Classical political theory proclaimed the virtues of a republican citizenry ready to defend its freedom (and contributed to revolution in the British colonies), but its emphasis on landownership and military service excluded women from the very definition of citizenship.[2] At the time Nancy Ward spoke, Anglo-American women were about to gain respect as republican mothers who gave their allegiance to the new nation and trained their children for service to the republic, but even these enlarged civic roles differed dramatically from those of Cherokee women.

In *The Dividing Paths,* Tom Hatley suggested that the Carolinians, who had the greatest contact with the Cherokees, became apprehensive over the freedom that Cherokee women enjoyed.[3] They viewed women as emotional creatures who had to be restrained by marriage and other social roles that reinforced their subservience to men. Cherokee women presented a troubling alternative to Carolinians, who acted on their own views of appropriate female behavior in their dealings with Cherokee women. Such encounters led Cherokee women to understand that Carolinians regarded their agricultural labor, sexual autonomy, control of children, and other behavior as deviant.

Although Cherokee women had some contact with colonial women, the non-Native people they encountered were mostly men who had come into their country to conduct diplomacy, war, and trade. These men encountered women in many different situations, but they always regarded the women who engaged in commerce with them, gave birth to their children, and became victims of their wars as merely incidental to their presence in the Cherokee Nation. European men came on men's business—trade and war—and they expected women to remain on the periphery. The economic and political relationships that Cherokees established with

Europeans, however, subtly threatened to undermine the status of women and to alter their lives.

In many ways the story of Cherokee women in the eighteenth century seems to conform to the declension model: Europeans arrived and the status of women plummeted. The deerskin trade and imperial wars that drew the Cherokees and other Native peoples into a non-Native world concerned men far more than women. As the significance of trade and warfare in Cherokee life grew, the people who engaged in those activities assumed greater importance. Men became more central to life and livelihood. At times, they even seemed to threaten long-established prerogatives of women, such as the disposition of war captives, and to impose their will on recalcitrant women. Women became dependent on men for items they wanted but did not have the means to acquire. Attention focused on individual prowess rather than communal productivity, and town councils increasingly debated war and peace rather than domestic issues. Some Cherokees began to regard political position and wealth as attributes of power. Invasions disrupted the settled, village life over which women presided and forced communities into the forests, the domain of men. None of these changes boded well for women. The interests of men threatened to take precedence over the interests of women rather than balance them.

On the other hand, women did not completely acquiesce to a new order shaped by a European presence in their country and European attitudes toward women. They found ways to retain traditional prerogatives, preserve corporate values, and maintain the fundamental structures of Cherokee society on which their status rested. The long absences of men who were hunting or fighting may have left women in more absolute control of households and villages. In the uncertainty of frontier America, Cherokee women infused their society with an element of stability. The Cherokees continued to eat the corn that women grew—and they suffered when it was destroyed. They organized their society matrilineally and recognized the rights that matrilineality conveyed to women over children, captives, and even war itself. Finally, despite a new respect accorded to individuals who acquired wealth and political position, most Cherokees still subscribed to an ideology that located power in relationships with the spirits controlling the natural world, subsistence, health, and the future. Women, as well as men, had access to this spiritual power. Consequently, while the events of the eighteenth century may have placed Cherokee women on the slippery downhill slope, their own adaptability and resilience coupled with cultural conservatism permitted them to retain a foothold.

Trade, war, and other dealings with Europeans, however, threatened all Cherokees with decline. A world economy over which they had no control and military alliances from which they could not easily extricate themselves severely compromised Cherokee independence. In one sense, men may have felt this loss of tribal autonomy more keenly than women, and circumstances may have forced them to alter their traditional ways of hunting and fighting more dramatically than women changed their activities. Women, after all, continued to farm and raise children much as they always had, but men developed the strategies to deal with external demands and the power relationships to implement those strategies. The impetus for any shift in gender relationships among the Cherokee, therefore, grew out of the need to meet the challenges of European contact, not out of a battle of the sexes. As a result, Cherokee economic and political life began to move toward concepts of individualism, hierarchy, and coercive power that had become firmly rooted in male culture. Women tried to channel these changes in ways that validated their traditional roles, but increasingly, women became the conservators of traditional values while men entered a brave new world.

THREE

Trade

At the beginning of the eighteenth century, women farmed, men hunted, and Cherokee economic well-being depended on both. Self-sufficiency characterized male and female contributions. Men made the bows and arrows, traps, blowguns, and fish weirs they used while women fashioned baskets, pots and other utensils for housekeeping, and digging sticks and hoes to cultivate fields. The Cherokees normally found abundant raw materials—including stone, wood, bone, clay, and various fibers—close at hand, and they did not use metal. Europeans brought a variety of new products—including textiles, firearms, and metal tools—that the Cherokees found desirable, and the Cherokees in turn provided commodities in exchange for these goods. Trade also introduced new ways for Cherokee men and women to relate to each other and for the Cherokees as a whole to engage their enlarged world.

The first traders to the Cherokee country probably arrived in the late seventeenth century, but no one seems to have settled permanently among them until the second decade of the eighteenth.[1] After midcentury the trading community became quite diverse, with factors from several British colonies, France, and perhaps even Spain, but in the early years the Carolinians out of Charleston dominated the trade. The colony attempted to regulate and then to monopolize the trade, but traders often flaunted regulations or exerted enough pressure on the colonial government to change the rules or thwart their enforcement. Ultimately, debate over conduct of trade contributed to the demise of proprietary government and its monopoly and a return to the regulatory system. In the first half of the century, either the Indians took their goods to Savannah Town, an entrepôt at the falls of the Savannah River, or Indians and traders exchanged wares at individually operated factories in Cherokee towns. Some Cherokees even appeared in Charleston to deal directly with merchants. Packhorses or Native bearers carried goods back and forth between Charleston and the traders' stores.

Native desire for and dependence on European goods—and European demands for very specific Native products—lay at the heart of economic change. Many European products were more efficient and more convenient than their Native counterparts; others were simply in vogue. Whatever the attraction, their use became widespread, and gradually the Cherokees became dependent on them. As early as 1725 the headman of Tennessee told Colonel George Chicken, South Carolina commissioner for the Indian trade, that "they must consider that they could not live without the English." He no doubt had in mind guns and ammunition, without which the Cherokees would have been vulnerable to their enemies, but his statement certainly encompassed domestic items as well. Although women probably continued to use tools of their own making alongside trade goods, they began to replace their stone hoes and knives with metal ones, cane baskets and clay pots with brass kettles, and stone adzes with iron hatchets and axes. European-style clothing and jewelry became popular. Among men, firearms supplanted bows and arrows, and whatever the relative advantage of other European goods over those of Native manufacture, guns and ammunition gave the people who possessed them a perceived advantage not only for hunting but also for warfare and defense. Although all Cherokees sought trade goods and derived benefits from them, men became more directly connected to European trade, for they were the hunters and warriors and they provided the commodities that European traders found most desirable—war captives and deerskins.[2]

War captives held no economic value in Cherokee society until traders began to buy them.[3] In European eyes, land in eastern North America was plentiful, particularly after the demise of coastal tribes, but labor was at a premium. Consequently, the torture of war captives by Native peoples seemed to be a terrible waste of able bodies. English colonists began enslaving captives after the 1622 Powhatan uprising in Virginia, but by the end of the seventeenth century South Carolina had taken the lead in the Indian slave trade. Until rice culture produced a local demand for labor in the 1720s, the Carolinians transported most Native captives to Virginia or the West Indies. Although the export continued throughout most of the eighteenth century, Indians constituted a significant proportion of the enslaved labor force in colonial Carolina. In 1708, for example, South Carolina's population of 9,580 included 2,900 African and 1,400 Indian slaves.[4]

Historian J. Leitch Wright contends, however, that the number of Indian slaves actually may have been much higher because of imprecision in recording the race of slaves.[5] The number of Native captives became large enough that the colony tried to regulate the Indian slave trade. Instructions warned traders against purchasing free Indians. Initially traders were supposed to brand slaves with the same brand they used for deerskins, but colonial officials amended the order to provide for marking slaves with powder. They also issued regulations for the care, transport, and sale of Native war captives. Fearful of warriors, colonial officials only reluctantly raised the minimum age for the lawful enslavement of male captives from fourteen to thirty.[6]

Cherokee warriors played an active role in the slave trade. Although Cherokee slave raiding may have gone back to the seventeenth century when they joined other tribes against the Guales, Cherokee warriors began selling slaves with some regularity in the early eighteenth century. In 1703 the South Carolina Assembly recorded that "the Cheree Kee Indjans, have takent some of our Southern Indjans, our friends, Slaves and have sold them to our Indjan Traders." By 1713, when war broke out with the Tuscaroras, the assembly was only too happy that the Cherokees had seen an advantage in slave raiding, and the colony enlisted them in campaigns against the Tuscaroras. Cherokee warriors helped capture or kill nearly one thousand of the enemy, and many of the captives arrived at the colonial auction block rather than the village stake. The subsequent Yamassee War, in which Cherokee warriors joined Carolinians against a confederation of Native peoples, also produced slaves.[7]

Although men seized slaves and sold them at a profit, women were more likely to be enslaved. A Cherokee headman reported to Colonel Chicken that a war party had encountered several canoes of Cahokia Indians and their French allies. They killed the men and "took all their women and children slaves with abondnce of goods that ye frinch was going to Trade with all among them."[8] Sometimes the Cherokees managed to redeem their own women who had been taken as captives. Thomas Griffiths, who visited the Cherokees in search of clay for the manufacture of Wedgewood china, recounted the story of "an Indian woman belonging to the Chiefs of the Cherokees, who had been long stole away by the Youghtandus, tho afterwards Ransomed by our Indian deputy of the Illinois, who sent her Round to Pensacola, and so conveyed her back to Charles Town."[9] Most captives, however, were not as fortunate as this woman was and ended their lives as slaves. In 1713 the officials who supervised the Carolina Indian trade notified a colonist that "the Cherike Indians have made Complaint to this Board that there are two Women of their Nation detained Slaves att your Hous." These two women had considerable company: in 1724 at least two thousand Indians were slaves in South Carolina and many more had been exported to the West Indies.[10]

Wright maintained that British colonists enslaved perhaps three to five times more Native women than men. Men usually were killed in eighteenth-century warfare, whereas women and children typically were sold as slaves. Since the preponderance of Africans imported into North American were men, unions between enslaved Native women and African men became common. Many aspects of African-American culture, including handicrafts, music, and folklore, may be Native American rather than African in origin. In fact, Wright suggests, the presence of so many women from southeastern tribes where matrilineal kinship was the norm helps explain the prominent role of women in slave culture.[11] As archaeologist Leland Ferguson also has demonstrated, the cultures of Africans and Natives intertwined in complex and surprising ways in early South Carolina, and material culture, like social organization, often reflected the blending of two traditions.[12]

The slave trade dramatically changed the nature of Cherokee warfare. Reward joined revenge as a major motivation. An English woman captured during the Yamassee War reported that her captor told her "that rewards were given to Indians for their prisoners, to encourage them to engage in such rapacious and murderous enterprises."[13] In 1717 Theophilus Hastings delivered twenty-one captives he had purchased at the Cherokee factory to the Board of Commissioners for the Indian Trade and reported that he had paid the warrior who had owned one of them with a horse.[14] Sometimes traders incited warriors to raid for slaves so that they could clear their debts at trading factories. In a particularly notorious episode in 1714, traders Alexander Longe and Eleazar Wiggen induced Cherokee warriors who were heavily in debt to stage an unprovoked attack on the Yucchi village of Chestowe and seize "a brave Parcel of Slaves." The marketability of war captives also meant that torture and perhaps even adoption became less acceptable means of disposing of them.[15]

After 1730, the Indian slave trade declined. Native populations had been so decimated by then that the small number of slaves no longer provided acceptable recompense for the upheaval caused by warfare. The seemingly endless supply of Africans, who had no nearby armed relatives, appeared to be a better solution to the planters' labor problems. Furthermore, an emerging racial ideology distinguished between Africans and Indians and made slavery seem increasingly inappropriate for the latter.[16] Warriors subsequently found substitutes for Native captives: they seized Europeans and ransomed them. In the American theater of the various eighteenth-century European wars, someone—either friend or foe—was usually willing to pay for prisoners of war. Warriors also captured African slaves on one part of the frontier and sold them on another. Whether the person being bartered was Indian, European, or African, the vendor almost always was male.[17]

Women occasionally sold a prisoner, but the cases are few and far between. In 1716 a Cherokee named Peggy arrived in Charleston with a Frenchman. Her brother had purchased the man from the warrior who had captured him for "a gun, a white duffield matchcoat, two broadcloth matchcoats, a cutlash and some powder and paint." He then had turned the prisoner over to his sister, who conducted him to Charleston and received strouds—blankets manufactured explicitly for the Indian trade—equivalent in value to the goods her brother had paid plus a "suit of Calicoe Cloathes for herself and a suit of stuff and a hat for her son."[18] Although Peggy benefitted from the exchange, she clearly was a courier for her brother, and the original exchange had been strictly a male transaction.

The warriors' sale of prisoners challenged the traditional role of women in warfare. Until captives became commodities, the women of clans and lineages had determined whom to adopt, War Women had decided whom to send to the stake, and the women had tortured the condemned to avenge the deaths of their relatives. Warriors' desire to satisfy the European demand for war captives severely curtailed these activities. Not all women placidly surrendered their power, and competition for captives developed. John Gerar William de Brahm, the colonial surveyor general, observed the tactics used by some War Women whose prerogatives the slave trade had limited:

> All prisoners must be delivered alive (without any Punishment) as her Slave, if she requires it, which is a Privilege no man can enjoy, not even their Emperor, Kings, or Warriors; there are but a few towns in which is a War Woman; and if she can come near enough to the Prisoner as to put her hand upon him, and say, this is my Slave, the Warriors (tho' with the greatest Reluctancy) must deliver him up to Her, which to prevent they in a great hurry drive a Hatchet in the Prisoner's Head,

> before the War-Woman can reach him; therefore the War Women use that Strategem to disguise themselves as Traders, and come in Company with them, as if out of Curiosity to see the Spectacle of the cruel War-dance.[19]

Apparently, in the struggle over the control of prisoners, some warriors preferred a dead captive to one who fell into the hands of the women. The competition between men and women, however, involved far more than a contest over spoils of war. Men who had become immersed in the trade regarded captives as commodities. Women, on the other hand, sought captives for social reasons: they wanted to add to their families or avenge the death of relatives.

Unlike with captives, the ownership of deerskins was indisputable, and hunters had few social impediments to profiting from their sale. Colonists also found deerskins a more satisfactory commodity than slaves. As lucrative as the trade in captives was, particularly before 1730, it carried certain risks, including a constant state of warfare on the frontier, that became less acceptable to traders and colonial officials as time went on. The deerskin trade presented none of these difficulties and promised even greater returns. Consequently, deerskins dominated the southern Indian trade. De Brahm summarized the operation of the trade at midcentury: "Traders . . . who always live within the Indian Nations, and are licensed by the Governor, that they may encourage the Indians, in employing themselves to hunting for the Sake of the Skins, which are a considerable Branch of the Carolina Trade; for these Skins the Traders exchange European Manufactures."[20] Deerskins ranked second only to rice in cash value of exports from the colony of South Carolina.[21] The supply of skins governed the profitability of the trade. In the winter of 1754–55, the hunt was so bad that Cherokee men planned a summer hunt, and the traders as well as their customers were in dire straits because the trade "chiefly and solely consists in the Indians making good Hunts." The next year, the hunt was so good that the traders began to run out of goods to exchange for skins.[22] The procurement of deerskins, like the capture of enemy Indians, was a significant element in Cherokee life well before the advent of the trade, but hunting assumed a new importance when the hunters found an external market.

Men were the hunters in Cherokee society, but a few women sometimes accompanied the winter hunt in order to perform gender-specific tasks such as carrying water and firewood and preparing food. Women also helped dress and tan skins, and as the demand for skins escalated, the number of women on hunting parties may have increased. During times of intense warfare, and that included most of the mid-eighteenth century, however, few Cherokee women accompanied hunting parties, but their protection was only one concern. Because of the spiritual danger women posed through intercourse and menstruation, their presence had the potential to jeopardize the entire party. Furthermore, the larger the party, the more likely was detection by the enemy. References to women in hunting parties come primarily from the last decade of the eighteenth century, when more settled conditions prevailed. In the 1790s, for example, Benjamin Hawkins called at a Cherokee house and discovered that the children were alone since both parents had gone hunting. Moravian missionaries reported that the Cherokees left on their annual hunt in late October "partly alone and partly with their women and children," and Francis Baily encountered a hunting party that included men and women. The Cherokees, however, considered women to be merely auxiliary not essential participants in the hunt. While the majority of men went on the hunt, the majority of women stayed home. In 1783–84, for example, Moravians found few men in Cherokee towns in midwinter and had to delay discussion of their proposal to establish a mission until the men returned from the hunt. Fifteen years later, their colleagues encountered precisely the same problem.[23]

Cherokee women never became the laboring class of the deerskin trade.[24] Instead, they continued to work primarily in the fields. The failure of women to become more involved in the hunting economy may rest with the Cherokees' division of labor, which was more rigidly gendered than that found among some Native peoples, including neighboring Creeks. Along with hunting, Creek men cultivated the town fields, and Creek women confined their agricultural labor to small kitchen gardens. Cherokee women, on the other hand, farmed both large fields and smaller gardens, and Cherokee men normally appeared in the fields only at planting and harvest.[25] Just as Creek agriculture employed men, Creek hunting parties usually included women and children. The burden of transporting carcasses, butchering and preserving meat, and tanning skins fell exclusively to Creek women, and their workload increased dramatically in the eighteenth century.[26] Among the Cherokees, hunting and its attendant chores rested primarily with men, while farming was women's work.

The Cherokees deviate further from patterns described by historians of other peoples in the Southeast. According to Kathryn E. Holland Braund, the Creeks divided hunting grounds along kin lines, and men hunted on their families' land. In the eighteenth century, they began to take their wives with them to their hunting grounds, an act that both strengthened the nuclear family and strained matrilineal ties. Hunting removed married women from villages and homesteads for months at a time, and by the late eighteenth century, Creek "towns were virtually deserted during the hunting season."[27] Among the Cherokees, however, hunting grounds were commonly owned, and villages were devoid of men only in the winter months. Furthermore, men's long absences may well have strengthened matrilineages, because the only people who lived in households regularly were related; that is, husbands, who were not of the lineage of the household, were not as frequently in residence.

The Cherokees also differ from the people along the lower Mississippi, about whom Daniel Usner has written, in that Cherokee women participated only marginally in the Indian trade and seem to have understood exchange in very different ways than did men.[28] Unlike the Choctaws and their neighbors, the Cherokees had no outlet like New Orleans, where multiethnic bartering thrived throughout most of the eighteenth century, and both circumstance and attitude restricted Cherokee women's entry into a frontier exchange economy. Women did not seem to internalize basic assumptions about commerce as completely as did men. In her memoir, a Carolina colonist recalled that a Cherokee woman warned backcountry settlers of an impending attack because she "disliked very much to think that the white women who had been so good to her in giving her clothes and bread and butter in trading parties would be killed."[29] This "giving" was almost certainly trade, as Carolinians defined trade, and not charity. The white woman who recorded the incident, however, had spent several of her teenage years as a captive, and her wording genuinely reflects the Cherokee woman's attitude about the exchange—it was gift giving, not trade.[30]

The relative attitudes of men and women regarding trade were perhaps best expressed by Nicholas Carteret, an early Carolina colonist, who reported in 1670 that Indian men met his party at Bull's Bay and traded deerskins for knives, beads, and tobacco: "By and by came theire women clad in their Mosse roabs, bringing their potts to boyle a kinde of thickening which they pound and make food of, and as they order it being dryed makes a pretty sorty of bread. They brought also plenty of Hickery nutts." Women shared what they produced; men sold their bounty. These attitudes and behaviors long endured among Cherokees.[31]

Cherokee women's chief economic activity was raising corn and other vegetables, but they did not regard these products as having commercial value. The Cherokees' hospitality ethic plus their custom of constantly having food available so that they could eat when hungry meant that no casual visitor had to purchase dinner. In describing the subsistence-level economy of southern Indians, Adair noted: "As they were neither able nor desirous to obtain anything more than a bare support of life, they could not credit their neighbours beyond a morsel of food, and that they liberally gave, whenever they called."[32] After midcentury, women did sell corn to troops garrisoning forts in their territory, and at the end of the century women, by then well schooled in commerce, sold corn to United States agent Benjamin Hawkins. Women, however, continued to welcome casual visitors with food and generally neglected opportunities to exploit local markets for produce.[33]

The Indian trade as well as the presence of other Europeans in the Cherokee country did not change women's attitude toward food, but it did expand the variety of foodstuffs available to them. Peach orchards became widespread in the Cherokee country, as did the cultivation of watermelons, an African import.[34] Hatley has pointed to the incorporation of sweet potatoes and hogs into the Cherokee ecosystem in the eighteenth century as particularly good examples of the adaptability of Cherokee agriculture. The fact that women chose to plant sweet potatoes and other introduced crops in their kitchen gardens rather than in the large fields that men helped plant and harvest indicates that women claimed these innovations for their own. They also kept hogs in pens close to their houses and fed them on weeds, the by-product of farming and gathering.[35] Their expanded food supply made surviving the uncertainties of the weather and hunt more likely, but these innovations did not substantially change their relationship to the market.

Most attempts by Europeans to open a trade in foodstuffs failed. In 1716 the South Carolina Board of Commissioners for the Indian Trade instructed the chief factor at Savannah Town to "purchase of the Charikees, out of the Cargo, what Corn they shall bring you, for the Use of the Trade and give us due Accounts thereof." Traders, however, quite likely tried to buy whatever corn they needed from the wrong parties. Complaints from traders at Quanesee and Terraqua that the residents would not supply provisions or help repair the trading houses may have stemmed from a misunderstanding on the part of traders that these tasks belonged to women and that men, their usual customers, could not be expected to perform them. By 1718, corn purchased to supply packhorsemen and even Native employees came from whites, not Indians. Furthermore, most traders ultimately married Native women, who cultivated fields for them and obviated any need to purchase corn at all.[36]

The construction of Fort Loudoun west of the Appalachians in 1756 provided women with a rare opportunity to market corn. Unlike the garrison at Fort Prince George in upcountry South Carolina, the men at Fort Loudoun did not raise their own food. The British had intended to purchase food when they first arrived, but they believed that they could soon become self-sufficient. Governor James Glen wrote to Attakullakulla, a pro-British Overhill chief, to inquire about "the Quantity of Corn you may have that we may know what we can certainly trust to for the supply of our Men for some Months for I hope they will be there Time enough to plant sufficiently for themselves." Once established, the habit of obtaining corn from the Indians was hard to break. Soon after completion of the fort, the women held a dance for Raymond Demere, the commanding officer: "The Ladies of the Towns . . . presented me with a great Number of Cakes of Bread of their own make and green Peas and Squashes, every Woman bringing something of this Kind in a Basket and laying it before me, notwithstanding that Provisions are now scarcer than ever was known."[37] The women's generosity could not support the garrison indefinitely, and it did not seem to be capable of supporting itself. Ultimately Demere employed a woman to buy corn.[38]

Cupid helped alleviate any remaining food problem, at least until war broke out. Many of the women in the vicinity married British soldiers, and they brought their husbands food when they visited them at the fort. Tensions over these conjugal visits developed in 1760, however, when the Cherokee War erupted and the warriors placed the fort under siege. Ignoring the siege, some Cherokee women continued to visit Fort Loudoun with both information and provisions. Either the war chief ultimately halted the visits or they had little effect on the material well-being of the fort, because by the time they surrendered, the soldiers had been reduced to eating their horses.[39] There is no evidence that men intentionally thwarted the entry of women into the market economy; indeed women continued to sell some food as well as fabric and even livestock into the nineteenth century. Whatever commercial opportunities the experience at Fort Loudoun promised women, however, ended with the fort's surrender and the invasions that followed.

The only commodity women produced that had any commercial value was their double-weave baskets. Adair described these containers as "the handsomest clothes baskets, I ever saw, considering their materials."[40] As Sarah Hill has demonstrated, basket making extended into a distant Cherokee past and tied Cherokee women inextricably to places where river cane, as well as the sources of vegetable dyes, grew. Traders living in Cherokee towns probably bought some baskets directly from women. In 1716 resident trader Theophilus Hastings asked permission "to purchase a few Baskets, and such other small Things to the Value of Twenty Pounds per Annum, to make Presents of to his Friends." The commission refused to relinquish its control over the trade, however, although baskets rarely appeared in the inventory of goods delivered to Charleston. In February 1717 "Skins and Baskets" arrived together on packhorses sent from Savano [Savannah] Town to Charleston, but normally, records of shipments to Charleston reveal no baskets.[41] Deerskins and captives remained the focus of the trade. Baskets enter the early records of the trade only incidentally. In 1717, two Cherokee men complained about the loss of baskets. One claimed to have been cheated by the commander of the Edisto garrison of "eleven Skins, seven Bever and three Baskets"; the other lost one basket. These two do not seem to have been involved in a deliberate trade. Instead, the commander had taken the three baskets after their owner insisted that "he would not spare them." The other accepted the promise of a shirt in trade for his basket, but the commander failed to pay.[42] These Cherokee men apparently did not consider baskets an appropriate commodity for trade. Since men controlled commerce, this view may help explain why a more successful trade in baskets never developed.

Despite some demand for Cherokee baskets in the colonies, Cherokee women apparently began to abandon their production. Adair reported that "formerly, those baskets which the Cheerake made, were so highly esteemed . . . for their domestic usefulness, beauty, and skilful variety, that a large nest of them cost upwards of a moidore [gold coin]." Unfortunately, he explained, "the Indians, by reason of our supplying them so cheap with every sort of goods, have forgotten the chief part of their ancient mechanical skill."[43] In other words, women were no longer making the one item they produced that traders found desirable.

The failure of a viable commerce in food or handicrafts threatened to reduce women to a secondary and subservient economic role. Women had become dependent on the trade: more durable brass kettles replaced not only baskets but also pottery; iron hoes had a decided advantage over flint ones; scissors and metal knife blades made many tasks easier. Because the Cherokees no longer wore deerskins but sold them, women also required clothing. According to the trader Adair, "The women, since the time we first traded with them, wrap a fathom of the half breadth of stroud cloth round their waist, and tie it with a leathern belt, which is commonly covered with brass runners or buckles."[44] Women, however, lacked the means to purchase these necessities, and so they had to rely on the people who were able to obtain European goods.

Those people almost exclusively were men, for the Cherokee trade centered on deerskins, which men procured. In an address delivered to the Creeks in 1754, a visiting Cherokee headman described his people's relationship with Governor Glen of South Carolina: "When he made them any present of Axes, Hoes, Knives, Guns, or Ammunition as he frequently did, he always desired them to hunt briskly to kill plenty of Deer, that with the Skins they might buy Cloaths for their Wives, and with the Flesh that they might feed their Children." Because men controlled the trade, Cherokee women became dependent on men not only for their clothing but also for the economic well-being of their households. In 1794 Doublehead appealed to the president of the United States to permit the Cherokees to retain their hunting grounds "where we and other nations hunt upon it, and get our living and our support there, as we are a people that do not make our own cloaths as our brothers do. We are a people that depend on our gun to support our families." This headman perceived, correctly no doubt, that support of the family depended on hunting.[45]

The division of labor between men and women remained unchanged by this new trading economy. Women continued to grow corn and other vegetables, but the demands of hunting made the labor of men at planting and harvest less reliable. Consequently, trade may have accentuated the role of women as farmers. Two economies characterized by very different economic values began to emerge—an agricultural economy of women and a commercial hunting economy of men. Women farmed together just as they always had, and they gathered their crops into household cribs and public granaries. Plentiful food produced a healthy people. Commerce, on the other hand, profited the individuals who traded deerskins. While hunters purchased items for household use, they also acquired personal items that enhanced individual status. In addition, men gave women kettles, metal tools, and fabrics. Women used these new goods in old, familiar ways, but their relationship to the goods had changed. Women now needed deerskins—and the men who provided them—to purchase the very hoes with which they cultivated their corn.

Virtually every aspect of the trade reinforced the economic dominance of deerskins and the men who provided them. Deerskins were the currency of the Carolina trade: colonial authorities established prices in terms of deerskins. In 1716 a man could purchase a gun at Savannah Town for thirty skins while the same item in the Cherokee Nation cost thirty-five skins. In Cherokee towns, he paid eight skins for a yard of stroud; three skins purchased a hatchet or a narrow hoe; five skins bought a broad hoe or a shirt; and one skin was the equivalent of thirty bullets, a knife, a pair of scissors, two strings of beads, or twelve flints. By 1718 the South Carolina commissioners of the Indian trade had developed a more complex pricing system that distinguished between "heavy" and "light" skins. At midcentury, the distinction was between buckskins and doeskins, and prices had dropped dramatically. Men exchanged three buckskins for two yards of stroud and seven skins for a gun. Nevertheless trade goods were still expensive, since a hunter's average annual kill was twenty to forty deer.[46]

As Richard White has pointed out, the demand for most European goods was inelastic: the durability of goods threatened to depress the market and slow the harvesting of deerskins. Only an insatiable demand for alcohol kept the Indians providing a constant supply of skins.[47] The Cherokees were never awash in a sea of alcohol in the way White describes the Choctaws, but many drank to excess. Although a high rate of alcohol consumption was common among colonists as well, the prevalence of the problem in both communities does not diminish its effect on Native peoples. The Cherokees had no previous experience with its use or abuse, and the soldiers, traders, and frontiersmen who normally provided liquor to Indians were not good role models for responsible drinking. Indians, according to Adair, were "excessively immoderate in drinking.—They often transform themselves by liquor into the likeness of mad foaming bears." Individual alcohol abuse disrupted Cherokee society as a whole. Self-inflicted injuries, fights, and murders frequently resulted. Violence increased; wrongs had to be avenged; further violence occurred. Yet even Adair, who clearly recognized the deleterious effects of alcohol, sold liquor to the Indians. Although colonial officials made halfhearted attempts from time to time to outlaw the sale of alcohol to Indians, little could be done to stem the flow. When traders watered the rum—not for the Indians' protection but to maximize profits—Native consumers complained.[48]

The limited role of women in the trading economy shielded most of them from addiction to alcohol. No evidence points to Cherokee women as the purveyors of spirits that women became in other Native societies.[49] Individual women almost certainly imbibed, but their supply of alcohol normally came from men. On one occasion, the commander of a British garrison in the Cherokee country explained that he was guest of honor at a women's dance in "Thanks for the small Refreshment I had been so good as to send them the Day before." The "small Refreshment" almost certainly was not tea. Women were more likely to have an unpleasant association with liquor, for often alcohol was the catalyst for sexual abuse. In 1756, for example, the South Carolina officials received a complaint that one of the packhorsemen brought to Keowee by a trader got a woman drunk and then "used her ill."[50]

As addiction to alcohol and demands for European goods increased, the proceeds of a winter's hunt sometimes did not carry the Cherokees through the year, and they demanded that goods be advanced on credit against the next year's hunt. Although credit was always a controversial issue in the Indian trade, the consensus among traders seems to have been that if granting Indians credit could not be avoided, it should be tied directly to the hunt. In the 1720s Major John Herbert, South Carolina's Indian commissioner, told the Long Warrior of Tennessee: "You must tell all your people that they must not expect the White men to trust any of them for their goods Except Powder & Bulletts."[51] In the 1750s Ludovic Grant echoed Herbert's decree when he urged that credit be extended to Indians for "necessaries for hunting" and not for hoes or blankets.[52] Consequently, not only were prices set in terms of the commodity men produced, but credit was limited to those goods deemed necessary for hunting. A woman whose kettle rusted or whose hoe broke could not replace it on credit.

The deerskin trade gave Cherokee men experience with a market economy largely denied women. Early in the trade, hunters complained about the prices of goods at Savannah Town and pressed the South Carolina colonial government to lower them. They achieved their objective when they sold their skins to Virginians "who supply them at much cheaper Rates." By the end of the century, tactics had become more sophisticated. Moravian missionaries who visited the official United States trading post at Tellico in 1799 reported that Indians sometimes "take their skins and pelts to Pensacola, in Florida, which is reckoned 500 miles from here, receiving cash in payment, and afterward do their buying here in the store, because goods are cheaper here while skins and pelts are more highly priced in Pensacola."[53] Traveling abroad certainly conformed to men's traditional role, but now that role enabled men to learn the lessons of the market and to employ those lessons in enhancing their own wealth.

Men not only provided the raw material for the trade but also were the chief employees of the trading system in the early days. As such, they introduced the concept of laboring for someone other than one's household for remuneration: labor became a commodity that men alone sold. Traders in the nation had to rely on Native burdeners to transport skins to Savannah Town and then on to Charleston. These men normally received payment in the form of blankets or other fabrics—"one Yard and a Half blew Duffields for Match-coats, and a quarter Yard Strouds, for Flaps." In 1717 Creeks attacked twenty-one Cherokee burdeners on their way to Charleston and robbed them of 770 skins. Despite the gift of "two Coats, two Shirts, and a striped Duffield Blanket" to a Keowee headman and his wife, who were with the party, and to the chief burdener, the Cherokees decided that a burdener's job was too dangerous and ended the system. British attempts to revive it failed, and the Cherokees largely confined their transport of skins to their own nation. The use of male burdeners, however, strengthened the perception of the deerskin trade as the exclusive province of men, and the packhorses that replaced Native burdeners did not alter that perception.[54]

While they continued to urge the use of Native transport, the commissioners replaced the burdeners with packhorses in 1718. Although they were still novelties, these were not the first horses in the Cherokee Nation. When James Needham and Gabriel Arthur visited the Cherokees in 1673, the Cherokees erected a scaffold on which the white men could stand and tethered their horse at the center of the gathering so that the people could view it. By 1718 a number of Cherokee men seem to have owned horses. Traders even occasionally bought or borrowed horses from Native owners. Yet ownership of horses probably was not widespread when resident traders acquired their herds of pack animals. These horses presented a new set of problems for Cherokees, particularly women farmers, because they proved to be very destructive. The Cherokees traditionally kept no livestock, and so they did not fence their fields. English colonists, on the other hand, secured their fields and permitted livestock to roam freely and forage in the woods. The traders, of course, brought with them the colonial method of animal husbandry. In 1725 the Indian Commissioner George Chicken reported:

> This morning came to me Sevl of the head men of the Town Complaining that the Sevl Traders horses are here Continually amongst their Corn and that they have already destroyed a great deal and desiring a Stop might be put to it they not being wiling to Shoot a White Mans horse. I told them that the English did not Suffer

any such thing and that if they would Shoot some of their horses they would take more care of them for the future, and that I should Speak to the white Men about it.

It is interesting that men, not women, complained about the destruction: men had replaced women as the protectors of the crops, at least where foreigners were concerned. Despite attempts to deal with the problem, white men's horses continued to cause trouble throughout the colonial period. In the 1750s, the commander of the garrison at Fort Loudoun had to assign one of his men the sole task of keeping the horses out of the Indians' cornfields.[55]

While women became dependent on men in some respects, men also relied increasingly on women to plant corn, perpetuate lineages, and maintain village life. The deerskin trade may well have served to enhance the relative position of women within their villages by removing men for much of the year. The power of women within the matrilineage, unchallenged by uncles or brothers, conceivably increased as they assumed more of the responsibility for raising children, appropriating resources, and regulating a host of day-to-day matters. As Carol I. Mason points out in an article on the Lower Creeks, Cherokee women may also have served as "the thread of cultural continuity from generation to generation and certainly were a powerful force for cultural conservatism."[56] Indeed, the persistence of women's traditional roles and the differentiation of tasks suggest that this was the case.

Cherokee women found ways to adapt the deerskin trade to traditional practices. Communitarian values at the heart of Cherokee culture found public expression in agricultural redistribution, a rite for which women had responsibility. The gifts of food to Demere and the Loudoun garrison, who obviously had need, can be understood in this light.[57] As economic well-being came to depend on the hunt rather than the harvest, men may have tried to wrest this responsibility from women. Lieutenant Henry Timberlake observed: "When anyone is in need, the warriors dance & sing about their exploits & contribute to the needy."[58] Women apparently found ways to extend their power over community wealth by incorporating the deerskin trade into redistribution. Later in the century, Moravian missionaries reported "a great Danceing of Women" at Chota. Extending over four evenings, the dances took place about twice a year in all Cherokee towns. "No one has Leave to come," the missionaries wrote, "except he bring at least a Skin with him. And thus they get every time a pretty Number of Skins together, who are made Use of for the Poor who suffer

Want."[59] Deerskins instead of corn had become the commodity required to sustain Cherokees, and so women managed to appropriate these emblems of a more individualistic worldview to traditional community use.

Cherokee myth linked hunting to corn and the corporate values corn represented. A hunter who had found no game heard beautiful singing while he slept in the forest. Finally, he realized that the song was real, and he discovered that it came from a single corn plant, the form Selu took on earth. The plant told him to cut off some of its roots, chew them before dawn, and bathe before the other villagers awoke; then he would be successful in the hunt. According to the myth, "The corn plant continued to talk, teaching him hunting secrets and telling him always to be generous with the game he took." At noon, the plant transformed into a woman and disappeared, but the hunter did as he had been told and "from that time was noted as the most successful of all the hunters in the settlement."[60]

Dances and mythology suggest that Cherokees continued to recognize women's access to spiritual power. Dances were religious observances rather than social affairs, and their chief purpose was to restore spiritual order and balance to the community. When women arranged dances and participated in them, brewed and served sacred medicine, and assumed responsibility for implementing a material egalitarianism that reflected spiritual harmony, they demonstrated their power. Mythology sanctioned their behavior and gave expression to fundamental beliefs about men and women that trade threatened to subvert: men might hunt, but women gave them the spiritual tools to do so successfully.

Despite the fact that men monopolized most aspects of the trade, women did occupy one position that had long-term implications for the Cherokees—they became the wives of traders. All the traders Moravian missionary Martin Schneider encountered in 1783–84 had Cherokee wives. The advantages of taking a Native wife were many. First of all, she performed her customary domestic duties, including farming and cooking, and she minded the store while the trader was away. If she spoke English, a wife served as a translator until her husband learned the language, and in any case, she often acted as a tutor in the difficult task of learning Cherokee. Cherokee wives also provided traders with an entrée into Native society. Although a trader would never have Cherokee kin unless a clan (other than his wife's) adopted him, the fact that his wife had Cherokee relatives made him less anomalous. Furthermore, if he married well—the sister of a prominent medicine man or warrior, for example—he had a degree of protection in a society in which he otherwise was very vulnerable.[61]

Perhaps for these reasons, traders were not the only whites to marry Native women. The garrison at Fort Loudoun provides many examples. John Stuart, British commissioner for Indian affairs south of the Ohio River, was the progenitor of a large family of Cherokees who came to be known as Bushyheads, named so after the commissioner's unruly locks. Deputy commissioners also took Cherokee brides. Consequently, the complexions of the Cherokees changed literally in the eighteenth century.

John Lawson maintained that one reason Europeans took Indian wives was "that it preserves their Friendship with the Heathens, they esteeming a white Man's Child much above one of their own getting."[62] Although the Cherokees became increasingly color conscious in the eighteenth century, Lawson probably was incorrect on this count. What mattered most to Cherokees was kinship, and a child whose mother was Cherokee was also Cherokee. Louis-Philippe described the principle of matrilineal descent and then commented that "in consequence, the children of white men and Indian women are Indians like the others. The Americans call them *half breeds.* They live precisely as the others do, neither read nor write, and ordinarily speak only the tribal tongue."[63] The Cherokees, however, had no concept of a "half breed" or mixed-blood person: a child of Cherokee and European ancestry was Cherokee or European depending on whether the mother was Cherokee or European. Paternity had no bearing on identity, and non-Native fathers usually had little control over their children. This practice caused consternation and anguish for many Europeans who took Indian wives and then found that they had no claim to their children. When a French trader transferred his business to the Alabamas in 1756, he tried to move his Cherokee wife and son out of the Nation, but the "Indian of Great Tellico," probably the woman's brother or uncle, would not let her go.[64] Indeed, many children had little contact with their white fathers and remained culturally Cherokee.

Others, however, grew up in their father's household, and their impact on Cherokee society in the nineteenth century was profound. Normally bilingual, many also were bicultural. From their mothers, these children learned the Cherokee language and received clan affiliations and lineages; from their fathers, they acquired European names and the English language. Most traders tried to train their children in European customs, and for daughters this meant a far more restricted life than their mothers had known. Margaret Vann, the widow of James Vann, recalled that her father, a trader named Walter Scott, "safeguarded me from heathen reval-ries. On one occasion he called me away from an Indian dance. Since then I shunned such occasions."[65] Sons often inherited farms, stores, and other property, and with the education their fathers provided, many managed to parlay bequests into sizable estates. These children introduced the first real economic inequality into Cherokee society. Furthermore, they established a new domestic norm in which a wife lived with her husband, children in part belonged to their father's family, and the organizing principle in the life of the second generation became the father's property instead of the mother's clan.

Intermarriage in the eighteenth century may well have contributed to more subtle changes in the society. Cherokee men traditionally linked status to personal accomplishments—a good hunt or bravery in battle—while a woman's status, with the exception of that of War Women, seems to have been more communally based. A woman's status and even identity was bound up with clan and perhaps even more so with lineage. A woman, not a man, perpetuated clan and lineage. As Cherokees became more materialistic, wealth gradually began to contribute to status, and although Cherokees complained constantly about the ethics of traders, they held the traders in high regard. Adair, who was not particularly impartial on this subject, wrote that "their good sense led them to esteem the traders among them as their second sun."[66] The same could be said of agents and soldiers who resided among the Cherokees. Trade or diplomacy could enhance the status of a woman only if she married a European; by doing so she possibly provided her lineage with an important patron, but the source of her own status and identity came to derive from her husband rather than her mother, brother, lineage, or clan.

Intermarriage was only one source of growing individualism in Cherokee culture. Although hunting involved some cooperation, particularly in traditional methods such as the fire surround, success largely depended on individual skill and good fortune. The Cherokees hunted in large parties, but normally one man killed one deer, and that deer was his alone. Farming, in which women engaged, was a much more cooperative effort. While fields belonged to lineages, women worked together, moving from field to field. The lineages owned the produce, and any single woman's individual contribution was impossible to determine. Consequently, she received little individual credit for success. As long as agriculture was the bedrock of the Cherokee economy, the cooperative ethic of farming dominated Cherokee life, but the shift to hunting made individualistic pursuits and triumphs not only acceptable but expected. The precipitous growth of individualism threatened the Cherokees' communitarian values. Women struggled to keep both the values and their public expression alive.

Other ethical and ideological bases of Cherokee culture came under assault during the eighteenth century. An earlier notion of a world of discrete categories in which summer balanced winter, farming balanced hunting, and women balanced men no longer fitted the economic realities of Cherokee life. In some years hunting could not be confined to the winter months. Traders, in fact, expected men to hunt year-round and complained to colonial authorities when war made it impossible for them to venture from their villages except in winter. The winter hunt of 1754–55 was so bad that despite the danger, the Cherokees had to hunt again in summer. The absence of men from the villages made women far more vulnerable to attack, particularly when they were working in the large cornfields. The food shortages of the 1750s may have been related to the reluctance of women to venture into distant fields far from the relative safety of towns.[67] Selu, who promised the Cherokees endless bounty, seemed held hostage by forces beyond the control of women.

Participation in a commercial system beyond their control challenged the Cherokees to modify their attitude toward the exploitation of game and the acquisition of material goods. Traditionally, the killing of deer involved a complex set of beliefs. Animals, the Cherokees believed, caused disease, which plants could cure. Ideally, however, one avoided disease by placating the spirit of the dead animal. According to a myth recorded by James Mooney in the late nineteenth century, the deer had given the Cherokees a prayer asking for pardon "when necessity forced them to kill one of the Deer tribe." Whenever a hunter shot a deer, the Little Deer who was chief of the deer tribe asked the spirit of the slain animal if the prayer had been said properly. If the answer was no, then the Little Deer inflicted rheumatism on the hunter, who became "at once a helpless cripple." Hunters who did not say the prayer tried to thwart the Little Deer by building a fire behind them on the trail.[68]

Central to this myth is concern over the unnecessary killing of animals, yet in the early nineteenth century, Major John Norton wrote:

> The intoxicating beverage introduced by Europeans and their merchandize which seemed adopted to make a more gaudy and convenient apparel, excited the exertions of the hunter. He no longer bounded his desires by killing enough to supply with meat and clothing, his family, his aged relatives or unfortunate friends; but

hunted to obtain skins for the merchant, the number of which was only decided by his ability in killing them. The animals were destroyed for their skins alone; and frequently the bodies were left to be devoured by the beasts and birds of prey.[69]

The commercial hunting economy of the eighteenth century undermined an earlier aversion to the exploitation of the natural world. The Cherokees began to see distinct advantages in killing as many deer as possible for their skins alone, and in a society heavily dependent on the trade, failure to do so condemned one's family to severe deprivation. A hierarchical worldview began to emerge that gave men dominion over the animals and placed them at the top of a human hierarchy as well. When this worldview extended to gender, women no longer balanced men. Some Cherokee men, particularly those who grew wealthy in the trade, accepted this worldview. Some Cherokee women, most likely the wives and daughters of traders, also embraced new notions about the place of human beings in the world and the appropriate relationship of men and women. The people who were gaining economic power in the Cherokee Nation developed a radically different view of gender than Cherokees had traditionally held.

At the same time, a competing value system endured. After all, the myths that provide insight into a Cherokee worldview date from the late nineteenth century, long after the deerskin trade had ended. In this view, animals kept people in check through disease; plants cured disease and balanced animals. The whole Cherokee cosmology rested on this system of opposites that balanced each other, and maintaining equilibrium gave individuals' lives purpose and meaning. Similarly, men and women balanced each other and both contributed to subsistence. Although in the eighteenth century some tasks women performed came to depend on the tools and other goods that men provided, men did not take over women's domain. Their greater significance to the broader world in which Cherokees now lived, however, gave them superior visibility in and control over Cherokee relations with that world. In some respects, men may have eclipsed women, but in the shadows, most Cherokee women continued to construct their lives in ways that secured their own realm of power.

FOUR

War

Political changes accompanied the economic reordering of Cherokee society in the eighteenth century, and like the emergence of a commercial hunting economy, the centralization and delegation of political power had important implications for women. The almost continual warfare of the period provoked many of these changes. Warfare was not a European introduction: Native Americans had gone to war long before the European invasion. Nevertheless, the intensity, scale, and duration of warfare increased dramatically, and Europeans added new participants, methods, and motivations. Incessant warfare brought men to center stage in Cherokee society because war was the occupation of men, and political decision making came to focus on military and diplomatic matters, the business of men. Cherokees increasingly equated political power with military might and associated individual and national welfare with warriors.

The Cherokees and other eastern Indians became embroiled in colonial rivalries that stemmed from European empire building. The Spanish in Florida and the French in Louisiana challenged English hegemony in the Southeast. Although the Spanish threat declined with the English destruction of the north Florida missions in 1704, the French subsequently extended their sphere of influence eastward with the construction of Fort Toulouse near present-day Montgomery, Alabama, in 1717. The French were successful, in a way the Spanish had not been, at forging alliances with Native nations and enlisting their warriors in the French imperial scheme. The English too recruited warriors for expeditions against European enemies, and so the North American theater of eighteenth-century imperial wars involved many Native players. In this rivalry, the Cherokees assumed a major role because as the trader Ludovic Grant wrote to Governor James Glen of South Carolina, "Carolina hath no greater Barrier against the French."[1]

Women usually became involved in actual fighting by chance. Nancy

Ward achieved the title of War Woman in the 1750s when she seized her slain husband's gun and joined a battle against the Creeks. John Norton's grandmother related to him the story of a Cherokee woman who had married a Natchez, and while in his village, she overheard a plot to massacre her town at a dance in the Natchez council house. She told the headmen of her village what she had learned, and they instructed the Cherokees to attend the dance armed and to refuse to enter the council house, where they could be trapped. The dance took place without incident and the Cherokees returned the invitation. When the unarmed Natchez entered the Cherokee town house for the dance, they became victims of their own plan.[2] Few Cherokee women, however, played so central a role in military actions or strategy.

Most women whom warfare touched directly became its victims. Many of the tasks women performed—collecting firewood, carrying water, gathering nuts and other wild foods—were relatively isolated ones and made women likely targets of enemy war parties. Perhaps one of the most vulnerable occupations for Cherokee women was protecting the crops from birds, raccoons, and livestock. The scaffolds on which elderly women sat while keeping watch over the crops were in the large fields that often lay some distance from dwellings. Furthermore, summer, when the scaffolds were occupied, was the season for war. Since the enemy sought the most accessible victims, these old women alone on scaffolds outside the villages often became casualties of raiding war parties.[3]

Even the proximity of family and neighbors did not necessarily offer protection: "Northward Indians" took the life of one woman in her own house. The commander of Fort Loudoun reported that "an old Cherokee Woman and a young Girl were lately killed and scalped by the Enemies within a Mile of Great Tellico." At Chota, "the enemy had killed a beloved Woman in a canoe by the Town." In another village, "the Nantaucs shot at our People as they were hoeing corn and killed a Woman." Traveling posed obvious dangers: enemy Indians dispatched a woman and her male companion while they were "refreshing themselves by a River" on their return from a neighboring village.[4] George Chicken, the South Carolina commissioner of the Indian trade, reported that "about Six Nights agoe a Man and a Woman going over the river to geather some herbs to make Salt, the Man left the Woman for some small time in Order to go and Shoot a Turkey, and at his return back he Espyed some Enemies who he found had taken away the Woman he left behind him." The Cherokees could not recover the woman, and they told Chicken that they wanted to make peace with tribes to the south so that they could "Venture to leave their Women and Children at home" in order to fight other Indians and to hunt.[5]

Killing of women may have resulted from more than simply opportunity. Women perpetuated clans and lineages. If the women of a lineage died, the lineage died regardless of the number of surviving males.[6] Therefore an attack on a woman was an attack on lineage, clan, and even tribe (since to be a Cherokee, one had to have a Cherokee mother). Mutilation of pregnant women drove home the point: "[Savannah Tom] executed his inhuman, cruel, and barbarous Will on her Body by stabbing her several Times with a Knife, scalping and opening her Belly, and taking out a poor infant Creature that she had in her Body."[7] Native mutilation involved symbolism, and the murder of a woman coupled with feticide symbolized the end of a people.

Women's interest in war surpassed their actual involvement. Cherokees traditionally went to war to avenge relatives killed by the enemy. The death of kin was a family matter, not a foreign policy issue, and as such it directly concerned women. Only vengeance stilled the spirits of the dead, and so women often pressured their male relatives to act. According to Adair, "The lying over their dead, and the wailing of the women in their various towns, and tribes [clans], for their deceased relations, at the dawn of day, and in the dusk of the evening, proved another strong provocative to them to retaliate blood for blood." Apparently, women could also prevent reprisals against the enemy. The Cherokees told John Norton that the Tennessee militia attacked Turkey Town in 1794, killed twenty Cherokees, and captured twelve women and children. The warriors intended to follow the retreating soldiers in order to exact vengeance, but "the women, whose children had been taken prisoners, entreated them with tears in their eyes, not to follow the enemy, lest they might cause their children to be put to death." The war party disbanded, and the militia "escaped a pursuit."[8]

Whether Native Americans had been as bellicose before the arrival of Europeans as they were afterward is difficult to establish, but the chiefdoms encountered by Soto could field armies of considerable size.[9] In the late seventeenth century, Samuel Wilson, secretary to the Lords Proprietors of Carolina, wrote: "The Indians have been always so engaged in Wars one Town or Village against another (their Government being of no greater extent) that they have not suffered any increase of People." Wilson cast some doubt on his own assertion that Native warfare was endemic when he added that there had been "several Nations in a manner quite extirpated by Wars amongst themselves since the English setled at Ashly River."[10] Certainly the European presence exacerbated enmities long established and probably created new ones. Cherokee headmen, for example, complained to Governor James Glen that "the white people imprisoning the Savannahs has caused them to join the French against us because we would not join the Savannahs against the English."[11] Few Native peoples found it possible to avoid being drawn into such conflicts.

In the 1750s the English became increasingly concerned about Cherokee loyalty and employed a variety of tactics to discredit the French and strengthen their normally good relationship with the Cherokees. They told the Cherokees that the French intended "to spoil their Hunting and so incapacitate them from providing for themselves, Cloathing and other Necessaries of Life." Furthermore, the English offered material inducements to join their cause: Governor Glen instructed Cherokee visitors to Charleston to ride horses so that they could return home laden with gifts. The French complained: "The Cherokees have allowed themselves to be gained by the presents of the English."[12]

European rivalries began to shape Native warfare, but colonial ambitions often were compatible with Native enmities. The Cherokees, for example, usually sided with the English because the Choctaws and Shawnees joined the French. In the 1720s Herbert promised the Cherokees "that if they would go to Warr against the lower Creeks that they should not want Am'unition." The Cherokees had long been engaged in intermittent warfare that usually originated in their joint hunting grounds with the Creeks, and so while Herbert's promise probably did not alter policy, it may have shaped military priorities. In the Tuscarora War of 1713–14, the Cherokees provided more than three hundred warriors for the British cause. However, the Cherokees also sometimes ignored military commitments they made. In 1715, during the Yamassee War, the members of a delegation to Charleston "agreed they would with their whole strength fall upon any Nation of Indians of our Indian Enemies that we should desire of them." Yet they failed to send a promised army for an attack on the Upper Creeks.[13]

When Cherokees did go to war at the behest of their English allies, they expanded the scale of warfare far beyond what had been customary. War parties traditionally had been rather small—sometimes only two or three warriors—and consisted primarily of the kinsmen of people killed by the enemy. War itself amounted to little more than a raid, after which the war party returned home. The objective was simply to satisfy the need for vengeance without suffering casualties whose deaths subsequently would need to be avenged. Adair described the Cherokees as being "exceedingly cautious and averse to bold attempts in war, and they are usually satisfied with two or three scalps and a prisoner." The three hundred warriors dispatched to the Tuscarora War marked a radical departure for the Cherokees. By the 1750s war parties of a hundred or more had become fairly common, and warriors no longer limited their killing and capture of the enemy. Tuscarora captives and casualties numbered nearly a thousand; victims in the Yamassee War may have exceeded that figure.[14] The violence of warfare far exceeded that required to avenge the deaths of clan kin, and the entreaties, pressure, and bribes of the English provoked much of this violence.

The escalation in warfare may have led to a decline in the ritual complex associated with warfare. The requirement of European allies that Native warriors fight on command diminished the social and spiritual imperatives for war and the ceremonies that made those imperatives manifest. European schedules could not accommodate weeks of deliberation and days of fasting before each battle. Europeans considered withdrawal from battle and return home, which Cherokees might regard as prudent behavior, to be cowardly and treasonous. Moreover, British success in the absence of ceremonial preparation and attention to omens called into question the efficacy of Cherokee ritual. A decline in rituals and beliefs associated with male shedding of blood upset a gender parity with menstrual rituals and dissolved a link between men and women with respect to blood.

The new motives for war excluded women from the social and spiritual benefits that traditional warfare had brought them. Women had avenged the deaths of their relatives personally through torture, but by the late eighteenth century torture had waned. Europeans, who considered the practice "shocking to humanity," exerted pressure on the Indians to abandon "their unmerciful method of tormenting their devoted prisoner." Although they were not always successful, traders made "pressing entreaties and very high offers" to prevent the torture of captives, and certainly the marketability of captives discouraged the practice. During the Seven Years' War, Lieutenant Henry Timberlake noted the decline in torture: "This savage custom had so much mitigated of late." The shift in emphasis on vengeance as a motivation for warfare contributed to the gradual abandonment of torture, and so women ceased to be active participants in the activity that came to dominate their lives.[15]

The English did not appreciate fully the role of vengeance. Adair maintained that the English failure to avenge the deaths of two white men in

1753 caused the Cherokees subsequently to "dipt themselves too deep in blood" because they believed that the English would not retaliate. Certainly, factors other than the Native obligation of vengeance determined colonial Indian policy, and the English often attempted to negotiate truces between ancient enemies. In the 1760s John Stuart, the commissioner of Indian affairs for the region south of the Ohio, urged his superiors to bring an end to warfare between the northern Iroquois and the Cherokees because excessive Cherokee casualties threatened to tip the balance of power in the South toward the "insolent" Creeks. The efforts to achieve a peace between the Cherokees and the Iroquois, traditional enemies, actually dated to the 1730s, when the Lords of Trade described it as "extraordinary . . . that these five [Iroquois] Nations who are protected by the British government should employ their force to destroy other nations under the same protection." It did not occur to the lords that these nations might well have differences that had nothing to do with the British, and so throughout the eighteenth century, they invested considerable energy and expense in Native truce making. Peace, like war, did not always follow the course the British desired, but the Cherokees generally felt compelled to give the appearance of doing the bidding of their European ally.[16]

Although women did not normally become involved in negotiations with foreigners, both the Cherokees and their neighbors availed themselves of the diplomatic services of women from time to time. In 1725 the Creeks trusted a Cherokee woman who had been taken prisoner to represent them in treaty negotiations. She had been present during Creek council deliberations that centered on the mistaken belief that the Cherokees, rather than the "French Indians," had killed a number of their people and on the rumor that a joint attack of the English and Cherokees was imminent. Fully apprised of the Creek view, Slave Woman accompanied a Creek man, perhaps as a translator, to a Cherokee town to sue for peace. The man fled in fear, but he left Slave Woman behind and "particularly gave her in charge to talk about a peace."[17] Cherokee women also sometimes represented their own people in negotiations with foreign powers. In the 1750s a Cherokee woman traveled to Fort Toulouse, in what is today Alabama, with French John, a captive whom the English suspected of espionage, to act as translator and discuss the building of a French fort among the Overhill towns, located west of the mountains. In addition, the wife of the Mankiller of Tellico, who had conspired with the French against the English, joined her husband in complaining to Raymond Demere about

English treatment of the Indians.[18] As late as the Hopewell Treaty Conference of 1785, the War Woman Nancy Ward addressed commissioners of the United States.

European, particularly English, participation in and even imposition of decisions for war and peace robbed women of their considerable influence on these issues. They had been accustomed to demanding retribution and determining satisfaction, but vengeance alone ceased to motivate Native warfare. Instead, Europeans placed their own interests foremost and frequently tried to compel the Cherokees to further those interests. As a result, the Cherokees often went to war against people with whom they had little complaint and made peace with traditional enemies, such as the Iroquois, in total disregard of crying blood. In compromising their independence in respect to foreign policy, the Cherokees lost the voice of women in policy making. Furthermore, the responsibilities and demands of kinship no longer exclusively governed warfare. The status and prestige of women had depended in part on their role in a matrilineal kinship system, but in the eighteenth century, the kinship system gradually lost one of its political functions. Because women generally participated in politics at the clan level and concerned themselves with war because of their position in clans, this shift denied most women a role in the escalating warfare with which the Cherokee political system increasingly was concerned. "Kin" automatically included them while "warriors" did not. As the significance of kin ties in military decisions waned, so too did the connection of women and war.

Because military concerns came to dominate relations with Native peoples, colonial officials wanted to negotiate exclusively with warriors. In 1725 Colonel George Chicken, the South Carolina Indian commissioner, made this clear to the Cherokees he met during a tour of their country: "I desired that when ever they sent any of their people abt business to the English that they might be head Warriour, that We might know how to Use them, and those were the people among them that We must take the most Notice of." The practice of sending warriors alone to conduct diplomacy contradicted Cherokee practice, and they ignored Chicken's instructions. When Chicken's successor, John Herbert, met at Nequisey (Nequassie) two years later with representatives of seven towns, only three towns sent exclusively warriors to represent them, one town sent two warriors and one beloved man (or priest), and three others each sent one warrior and one beloved man.

As late as the 1750s, the Cherokees seem to have been somewhat uncomfortable with the makeup of diplomatic delegations. Twelve Cherokees attended councils in Winchester, Virginia, and Philadelphia, Pennsylvania, in 1758 during the Seven Years' War. In an address at Philadelphia, their spokesman began apologetically: "I am not a Chief Man myself, I am deputed by the Chiefs of my Nation to travel this Way. . . . The Warriors now present received a Message from the King of Great Britain to come to War against the French, and on receiving this Message, they have come with minds Exasperated against the French, and wherever they see a Frenchman they will knock his Brains out. . . . Some of these now present are very good Warriors, they have already killed two of the Enemy, two Shawonese [Shawnee]." The warriors' enthusiasm may have been fueled by their desire to collect "promised Cloathing and all necessities," and indeed they received "what is proper for them as Warriors." With Britain's growing power and the Cherokees' increasing dependency on European trade goods, few alternatives to outward acceptance of the new political order seemed to exist.[19]

Warriors rose to prominence in diplomacy not only with the British but also with other Native peoples. A Cherokee delegation to the Iroquois in 1757 was made up of warriors. When the council opened with an Iroquois condolence ceremony, the Cherokees replied: "Perhaps you will expect a formal answer upon the ceremony of condolence to us. Brethren we are Warriors and do not understand these Matters and hope you will excuse us." They had come to recruit Iroquois warriors for an attack on the French in the Ohio valley, and they were impatient to get on with the business at hand. A little over a decade later, the war chief Oconostota conducted a Cherokee delegation to a council in New York. No Cherokee women were present, and so he presented a wampum belt they had sent to Iroquois women and he delivered their message urging peace.[20] The English practice of attributing power to warriors and bestowing honors and gifts upon them excluded not only beloved men but also women, who had to turn to warriors to represent them.

The new power invested in warriors was a departure from the Cherokee political system that had operated until at least 1730. Characterized by widespread participation in councils and decision making by consensus, the traditional system involved little in the way of delegated power or coercive authority. Certainly some people commanded more respect than others and their words carried more weight in council meetings. Warriors who took many scalps and experienced few casualties organized war parties more easily than did less successful warriors; conjurors whose predictions came about and whose remedies worked had more clients. These were the people, particularly the warriors, whom Europeans identified as "chiefs," but they exercised limited power; they were leaders only because people followed them. Councils made decisions, and the debate surrounding an important issue could last for several months.[21] Elements of this political system continued into the nineteenth century, but from the 1730s, the realities of dealing with Europeans undermined consensual politics, and warriors came to dominate Cherokee decision making.[22]

Formal relations with the English also brought about the first steps toward the centralization of Cherokee villages into a nation. Until the second half of the eighteenth century, the Cherokees had little notion of an overarching political mechanism or centralized government. Adair described the nature of Native political organization: "Every town is independent of another. Their own friendly compact continues the union. An obstinate war leader will sometimes commit acts of hostility, or make peace for his town, contrary to the good liking of the rest of the nation."[23] This was particularly important to women because within the village they enjoyed considerable power. On the other hand, councils and conferences that brought together a number of villages or took Cherokee representatives to colonial capitals and other Native nations often excluded women. Colonial officials saw women as an unnecessary expense and did not normally receive them officially. Other considerations also kept women at home. They could not travel as readily as men, particularly in the summer when fields needed tending. But even at other times of the year, households demanded attention, and the care of small children further exacerbated the difficulties women faced in attending intertown councils. Since relations between Cherokee villages or with non-Cherokees tended to fall into the category of "foreign relations," which men normally conducted, the inclusion of women did not seem to be essential. By the time national councils began to address a broad range of issues, the precedent for excluding women was well entrenched.

The makeup of early councils involving more than one Cherokee town also stemmed from the demands of the British. Indeed, the British early tried to exert influence on the Cherokees to centralize their nation and delegate political power. Accustomed to a monarchy, they believed the Cherokees would benefit from such a form of government, which also would simplify relations with colonial governments. This, of course, was an alien concept to the Indians, who, according to Adair, "have no such titles or persons as kings; . . . no words to express despotic power, arbitrary kings, oppressed, or obedient subjects." In the 1720s, however, Herbert implemented the form of Native political organization preferred by the British when he awarded a commission to the Warrior of Keowee and "told them that they must allways remember to Obey him as their Comander." Within five years Sir Alexander Cuming, a self-appointed emissary of the British Crown, had made the warrior Moytoy "emperor" of the Cherokees and instructed him to enforce British law in the nation. The English expected these warriors, and others who were appointed in a similar fashion, to be in control of Cherokee political affairs.[24]

At first, of course, it did not work. Even warriors commissioned to raise large armies rarely delivered. The "great body of the Charikess" promised by Caesar during the Yamassee War never materialized. Of the 1,000 Indians for whom Oglethorpe began ordering provisions in 1740 for an expedition against St. Augustine, only 112 began the march (103 Cherokees and 9 Creeks), but this number soon dropped to 35. Far more serious than the failure of head warriors to raise armies, however, was an inability to control the behavior of their warriors, since the decision to fight traditionally was an individual one. In 1725 the Coosas (Creeks) attempted to make peace with the Cherokees, but negotiations broke off when a Cherokee war party from Tellico attacked Coosa without the approval of the head warrior. The only explanation offered to Colonel Chicken was that "They were Young Men and would do what they pleased."[25]

As long as the "Young Men" confined their unauthorized attacks to the Creeks, Shawnees, Senecas, or other Native peoples, the worst that was likely to happen was a retaliatory raid by the enemy, but by the late 1750s, the English were the enemy. After the murder of Cherokees on the Virginia frontier in the late 1750s, the headmen of the Cherokee Nation counseled first mediation and then limited action "to bring in an equal number of their scalps, to those of their own murdered relations." Their advice and instructions went unheeded: "The hearts of their young warriors were so exceedingly enraged, as to render their ears quite deaf to any remonstrance of their seniors." The result was the English massacre at Fort Prince George of nearly thirty Cherokee headmen who were trying to negotiate a truce, and an invasion that left hundreds, perhaps thousands, dead from wounds or dying of starvation and exposure.[26]

The most traumatic military events experienced by the Cherokees in the eighteenth century were the British invasions during the Seven Years' War and the American Revolution. In the earlier conflict, the Cherokees initially allied with the British despite the presence of French traders in some of their towns and considerable sentiment in favor of the French. In part, the superior goods and trade networks of the British dictated the Cherokees' choice of allies, but Native politics also influenced their decision. Ancient enemies of the Cherokees, such as the Choctaws and Shawnees, favored the French, and ultimately the conflict involved most Native peoples east of the Mississippi, who cared more about the Native outcome than the European one.

The Cherokees agreed to embark on an expedition against the Shawnees, who lived in the Ohio River valley, on the condition that the British would build a fort among the Overhill towns that would offer protection to villages while warriors were away. In 1756 the British completed Fort Loudoun in the Tellico River basin as well Fort Prince George in upper South Carolina. The purpose of Fort Loudoun ostensibly had been to offer protection to civilians while warriors raided the enemy in the Ohio valley, but colonial officials also intended to use it to keep an eye on these remote Cherokee towns, which had always been a bit too tolerant of French traders and ambassadors for British tastes. When Virginia frontiersmen attacked a party of warriors returning from the Ohio valley, many Cherokees shifted their allegiance to the French, and warriors began raiding frontier settlements. A peace mission in 1759 failed: British troops took the Cherokee emissaries hostage at Fort Prince George and then, in a state of panic, slaughtered the hostages. The Cherokees promptly placed Fort Loudoun under siege, and in the summer of 1760, they defeated a company of twelve hundred British regulars, who already had destroyed the lower towns along the Savannah River while on their way to relieve the besieged fort. The garrison at Fort Loudoun had no alternative but to surrender. After the surrender, warriors attacked the prisoners, killed the commander and thirty-two soldiers, and took the survivors captive.[27]

In retaliation, the British mounted an invasion of Cherokee territory with twenty-six hundred men, including a number of Catawba, Chickasaw, and other Indian warriors. The soldiers and their Native allies did not have a clear policy for dealing with noncombatants. Major Alexander Monypenny maintained that "such as remain'd quiet in their Houses, [would] be protected," but Captain Christopher French claimed that he "had orders to put every soul [in the belligerent towns] to Death." Usually the soldiers found no occupants in the villages: they had fled to the forests. At Ayoree, about twelve people remained, but all except two of them escaped. The soldiers scalped one captive. They took the other, an old woman, to their camp, and when it became clear that she had no intelligence to share with them, they let her go: "We gave her some provisions, and convey'd her privately out of camp lest she should be scalp'd by our Indians who wanted much to do it, soon after another poor old Sqwa was brought into camp, & the savages having got hold of her soon kill'd & scalp'd her, they threw her Body into the River." Several days later, Captain French reported that they found the released woman in her house and that Catawba allies, "(the same who kill'd the old Sqwa at Noukassi) kill'd our Sqwa for the Sake of her Scalp."[28]

When Cherokees were on the offensive, few women died, but with invasion, women became particularly vulnerable because they were the farmers, and consequently they were less mobile than hunters and warriors. Women were more likely to remain "quiet in their Houses" than men, but this offered them little protection. Monypenny reported that Tistoe, a warrior of Keowee, left "an old woman and a Boy, to keep his House; The Chickesaws scalp'd the Woman and Wounded the Boy." When women tried to escape, they were less successful than men. At one town, Native allies spotted three Cherokee men and two women who attempted to escape by crossing a river: "They were closely pursued, notwithstanding which the Men escap'd, but the Sqwas were taken."[29]

The invasion was devastating. The soldiers, according to Captain French, "pull'd up all the Corn, cut down the fruit Trees, & burn'd the Houses." Lord Jeffery Amherst, the British commander in North America, reported that the army destroyed fourteen hundred acres of "Corne, pease, & Beans, & has driven near 5000 Men, Women, & Children, into the Woods, where, if they do not make a proper Submission, they cannot fail of starving in the Winter." Reduced to eating their horses, the Cherokees suffered terribly: many of them did starve, and an epidemic claimed further lives. A Cherokee chief told the governor of South Carolina in 1766: "When I got up this Morning I cou'd hear nothing but the Cries of Women and Children for the loss of their Relations; in the Evenings there are nothing to be seen but smoak and houses on fire, the dwellings of the deceased; I never remember to see any sickness like the present, except the small Pox."[30]

When war between Britain and her colonies broke out, the Cherokees sided with the British, who had made some effort after the Seven Years' War to stem the tide of white settlement. Cherokee warriors attacked illegal settlements in the Holston River valley and raided the southern frontier. When the colonists retaliated with invasion, the Cherokees could offer little resistance. Altogether, soldiers destroyed more than fifty towns; they scalped women as well as men and sold children into slavery.

The war ended with the Cherokee Nation devastated. Most Cherokees favored peace, but a small band called "Chickamaugans" refused to accept a truce and relocated in northern Alabama and Georgia. With the assistance of the Spanish in Louisiana, they continued to fight until 1794, when their towns were destroyed. Once again starvation and disease probably claimed more victims than the fighting. Archaeological evidence points to a marked increase in root and wild food consumption and a decline in grains in the historic era; the destruction of fields and granaries as well as of the communal labor pattern may help explain this.[31]

The casualties from the invasions of the eighteenth century are difficult to ascertain, as indeed is the total number of Cherokees. Louis-Philippe gave one reason for this difficulty: "People always count Indian populations by *warriors,* that is, by *men capable of bearing arms.*"[32] Adair reported that twenty-three hundred warriors survived the Seven Years' War; this represented "a great diminution for so short a space of time." By 1797, Louis-Philippe reported, "Some tell me that the Cherokees were so depleted by the last war that they would have trouble raising 500 warriors. Others claim that they have 2,000, still others 1,000, 1,200, 1,500, etc. I presume that the last two figures are closest." In other words, the already severely depleted population may have been reduced by half.[33]

The Cherokees developed strategies to deal with the population loss. One option was the adoption of captives, and as John Norton noted, so many captives were adopted into the Cherokee nation that the Cherokees lost any distinctive appearance they might earlier have possessed. Polygamy was another option, particularly in light of the preponderance of women in some communities. Few Cherokees seem to have resorted to this traditional practice, however, because the disruption of hunting by war, land cessions, and game depletion made the male contribution to more than one wife or household very difficult. Another solution was for Cherokee women to marry outside their own people, and many women did just that.

Warfare claimed many women victims, but men probably suffered more casualties. In his section on the Cherokees, Adair observed that "in every Indian country, there are a great many old women on the frontiers, perhaps ten times the number of the men of the same age and place."[34] While the absence of men had little impact on the continuation of lineages, particularly since the Cherokees practiced polygamy, the imbalance in the sex ratio had other ramifications. Fewer hunters meant a decline in the number of deerskins that could be traded for European goods. This shortage, particularly in guns and ammunition, increased the danger of enemy attack. A diminished contingent of warriors provided less protection for villages in these perilous times, and surviving men could not readily seek revenge for their relatives' deaths without jeopardizing the safety of women and children left in the villages. Had it not been for the persistence of the Cherokees' definition of gender and of their rather rigid sexual division of labor, women might have stepped into the breach. However, the scarcity of men (along with other factors discussed in the following chapter) seems instead to have enhanced the status of men at the expense of women. The Cherokees were quickly becoming a warrior-dominated society.

The increasing political power of warriors grew out of changing relations with the British rather than self-aggrandizement. Until the late eighteenth century, incompatible political organizations had been merely an inconvenience. Colonial officials expressed annoyance at dealing with councils or at the inability of "chiefs" to keep their commitments; Cherokees, no doubt, found British attempts to create "emperors" to be strange and perhaps even amusing. English colonial settlement, however, at last had come to abut Cherokee country, and frontier relations between these two peoples were less than cordial. English settlers held all Cherokees accountable for the actions of any Cherokee; Cherokees retaliated according to the old law of blood. But English and Cherokee retribution differed in scale and scope. The entire Cherokee nation was at risk: a raid by a small war party on a frontier settlement could provoke a massive retaliation that brought destruction and death to hundreds, even thousands, of innocent people. A national consensus and voice was a matter of critical concern to warriors, and so they met in councils that gradually came to be considered national councils, while head warriors such as Attakullakulla, Oconostota, and Little Turkey emerged as "Principal Chiefs." These warriors—the people who normally dealt with the English and provided war material to the "Young Men"—and their councils assumed a coercive role and delegated power in order to control the actions of unauthorized war parties.

These national councils did not enjoy much success in enforcing their will until the next century, long after warfare had ceased, but the emergence of a national council, even an ineffective one, signaled important changes. Head warriors had come to believe that they had an obligation to define the national good and to force others to accept their decisions. In this nascent political hierarchy, women also presumably became subject to the warriors' power, but like the young men, they resisted.

When warriors in the Overhill towns began to shift their allegiance away from the English, Cherokee women who had husbands among the soldiers garrisoned at Fort Loudoun provided valuable information to the English. The commander, Raymond Demere, wrote to Governor Lyttelton of South Carolina that "intelligence from women amongst the Indians are always best." In 1756 the Indian woman employed to procure food told Demere that the "Old War Woman" at Chota had confided to her about an Indian and French conspiracy against the English. When the warriors placed Fort Loudoun under siege, women continued to visit the garrison and supply the soldiers with food. According to Timberlake, the women laughed at the threats of the war chief, who tried to stop them, and told him "that if he killed them, their relations would make his death atone for theirs." Consequently, the warriors could do little to prevent what they probably believed to be treasonous activities.[35]

The head warrior was powerless to stop the women for several reasons. First of all, the women controlled the production of food, and they asserted their right to dispose of the product of their labor as they saw fit. By providing food to their English husbands, Cherokee women confirmed their marriages and behaved in a way that Cherokees expected wives to behave. They did not defy the warriors out of rebellion or subversion—they acted according to long-established standards of behavior for married women. They were unwilling to permit warriors, implementing a novel military tactic and asserting unprecedented power, to thwart them in fulfilling one of their important roles.

Second, the behavior of these women and the head warrior's inability to stop them reflected the Cherokees' respect for autonomy. A corporate ethic guided Cherokee actions, but individuals decided on the course that they thought best served community interests. Each person determined whether or not to engage in war, and corporate decisions did not bind individuals. Youthful war parties exercised this right when they raided the frontier in defiance of chiefly pronouncements against warfare. Exercising their own autonomy, Cherokee women warned colonists of impending attacks by Cherokee warriors.[36] In 1781 Nancy Ward, the War Woman of Chota, followed the dictates of her own conscience rather than national policy in providing intelligence to the invading Virginia militia that had burned several Cherokee villages and captured Chota.[37]

Finally, the women's defiance illustrates the viability of clan vengeance and the matrilineal kinship system. They did not laugh at the potential danger or at the head warrior; they laughed at the absurd notion that he might ignore the ancient law of blood. Their response to the crisis was conditioned by social expectations because they continued to understand politics in terms of social relationships. Women did not see themselves as citizens of an abstract Cherokee nation ruled by warriors. Instead, they were members of a clan and lineage, wives of men with whom they had reciprocal responsibilities, and mothers of warriors as well as cultivators of corn.

When Nancy Ward addressed United States treaty commissioners at Holston in 1781, she did not represent the views of a united Cherokee nation. Instead, she spoke for Cherokee women: "Let your women's sons be ours; our sons be yours. Let your women hear our words."[38] Peace could be sustained, she believed, only if the Cherokees and their enemies became one people bound by ties of kinship. She called for the women to respond because only women could accomplish this goal. In 1785 the Cherokees met treaty commissioners at Hopewell, South Carolina. The chief spokesman at the conference introduced Ward as a "beloved woman who has borne and raised up warriors," and the War Woman reiterated the theme of her earlier talk: "I look on you and the red people as my children. Your having determined on peace is most pleasing to me, for I have seen much trouble during the late war." Her maternal concern was not based on any biological connection but on a more encompassing conception of kinship. Nearly fifty at the time of this speech, Ward spoke metaphorically: "I am old, but I hope yet to bear children, who will grow up and people our nation, as we are now to be under the protection of Congress and shall have no more disturbance." The bonds of kinship both promised peace and permitted her to speak for her children: "The talk I have given is from the young warriors I have raised in my town, as well as myself. They rejoice that we have peace, and we hope the chain of friendship will never more be broken."[39]

The political power of Ward and other Cherokee women rested on their position as mothers in a matrilineal society that equated kinship and citizenship. In such a society, mothers—and by extension, women—enjoyed a great deal of honor and prestige, and references to motherhood evoked power rather than sentimentality. Traditionally, Cherokee men attained power through prowess and knowledge; women acquired power by virtue of their ability to bear children. Traditional paths to power endured even as some Cherokee men began to consolidate political power and transform Cherokee political institutions.

Men benefitted materially from fighting as well as hunting, and they used their bounty to gain political power. In the process of enlisting their aid in an expedition against St. Augustine in January 1717, the South Carolina House of Commons appropriated funds to purchase gifts for three visiting Cherokee headmen. Each received "One Gun, one Cutlash and Belt, a Cagg Rum, a Bagg Sugar, a stript Duffield Blanket, a Peece Calicoe and some Strings Beads." The value of these goods was roughly sixty deerskins, or about twice the annual kill of an average Cherokee hunter. Later that year the South Carolina commissioners of Indian affairs gave ten visiting Cherokee headmen blankets, shirts, and pipes "as a Reward for their particular Services, and to incourage them to assist the white men." Often recipients did not even have to be in attendance; they received gifts from the colonial government through traders "in Remembrance of Friendship."[40]

The headmen did not keep all the gifts presented them but used their newfound wealth to extend their influence and bind warriors to their leadership. The three headmen who intended to raid St. Augustine (but never did) asked that some of their goods be stored until their return (they received them anyway), but they promptly took the rum and sugar to their towns "there to assemble the Warriers, and drink the same in a Bowl of Punch, in Commemoration of the English." They also distributed small arms to the warriors who agreed to accompany them. Each of the men who went to England with Sir Alexander Cuming in 1730 received twenty guns, six dozen hatchets, and twelve dozen knives—far more than their personal needs required.[41] The funneling of goods through prominent warriors was an established practice by the 1750s, and all conferences with warriors involved extensive gift giving by the British. Shipments of goods arrived with instructions that they be turned over to warriors for distribution, although many of the items had little to do with military expeditions. In addition to guns and cutlasses, a 1751 shipment to the head warriors of six towns included a variety of clothing and fabrics, beads, earbobs, ribbons, buckles, needles, thread, scissors, combs, kettles, mirrors, wire, and trunks. Adair suggested that the traditional corporate ethic influenced this new system: "They wish some of their honest warriors to have these things, as they would know how to use them aright, without placing their happiness, or merit, in keeping them, which would be of great service to the poor, by diffusing them with a liberal hand."[42] Redistribution now extended beyond basic provisions to luxury goods. Where skins were concerned, women found a way to retain control over redistribution, but this vast array of goods flowed directly from individual warriors to their followers.

Women occasionally did receive goods from colonial officials, although certainly not on a par with warriors. In 1717 the Indian commissioners appropriated funds to provide strouds for nine Cherokee women "who promised his Honour [the deputy governor] to follow their Warrier's Camp" on an expedition against the Yamassees that never materialized. The presence of women on lengthy campaigns was desirable because the warriors could not prepare food, particularly corn, since that was a gender-specific task. Their absence caused problems. In 1740 General James Edward Oglethorpe's provisions for a four-month campaign included "Forty-Eight Thousand pounds weight of Rice, instead of Corn, the Indians having no women with them to Parch or pound their Corn."[43] The direct gifts to women, such as those made during the Yamassee War, were few, and frequently, the woman's relationship to a warrior rather than her own contribution justified the gift. In 1751, for example, the wives of three head warriors received silk handkerchiefs, trunks, and a saddle simply by virtue of their husbands' martial status. Their own status and their worthiness as recipients of gifts depended not on themselves, their lineage, or their clan but on their husbands.[44]

By the late eighteenth century the Cherokees had begun to associate economic and political power. They had become dependent on trade goods, and that dependence brought them into the British sphere of influence. When the colonial authorities began to funnel trade goods through head warriors, the war chief assumed new importance in Cherokee society —he became the source of economic largesse as well as the organizer of war parties. The conjunction of political and economic power was never complete in Cherokee society, but one lesson of the eighteenth century was that political power carried certain other perquisites. Warriors could dispense military supplies and other desirable commodities because they managed foreign policy, and their enhanced economic status strengthened their internal power base. Younger warriors and noncombatants, including women, developed a dependency on warriors in somewhat the same way that people who did not hunt became dependent on those who did.

The Cherokees also came to attach a significance to material goods that they had not felt earlier. Adair had noted that southeastern Indians "are all equal—the only precedence any gain is by superior virtue, oratory, or prowess." But the Cherokees were becoming dramatically less equal, and one of the ways in which this inequality manifested itself was through material goods. The grave had been "heir of all" personal property, but according to Adair, "the Cheerakee of late years, by the reiterated persuasion of the traders, have entirely left off the custom of burying effects with the dead body; the nearest of blood inherits them."[45] The people with access to considerable personal property—warriors and hunters, who normally were the same—consequently enriched their families. The other people who had wealth were traders, and both traders and warriors/hunters were men. Consequently, men rather than women became the source of family fortunes.

These individual fortunes consisted of livestock, clothing, personal ornaments, guns, tools, slaves, and other forms of chattel property. Matrilineages probably still controlled the descent of houses and other improvements, although among the families of traders and perhaps even some warriors, this was changing. The land, however, belonged to neither individual nor lineage but to the nation. In 1779 Alexander Hewatt observed, "No Indian, however great his influence or authority, could give away more than his own right to any tract of land, which, in proportion, is no more than one man to the whole tribe."[46] The realities of eighteenth-century wars with the British and then the United States forced the Cherokees into modifying this caveat. In 1770 the Cherokees relinquished their hunting grounds in Virginia and West Virginia. In 1772 they surrendered the territory east of the Kentucky River, and by a patently fraudulent transaction of 1775, they "sold" their land west of that river. These pre-Revolution cessions involved hunting grounds, but following the Revolution, they gave up title to lands east of the Appalachians that included ancient town sites.[47]

The treaties by which the Cherokees ceded thousands of acres of land—fields and houses as well as forests and streams—were negotiated by men. Women often attended treaty conferences and sometimes addressed the assembly, and as late as 1831 they petitioned the council not to sell or allot their national domain, but the people who signed the treaties were the "headmen and warriors of the Cherokee Nation."[48] The precedent for men, particularly warriors, to conduct negotiations long had been established. Furthermore, military action had resulted in the demand for cessions. Consequently, the warriors' cession of commonly owned land seemed only logical. As we shall see, women continued to head households that retained possession of particular tracts of land and to exercise influence over the disposition of the common domain. Men, however, firmly controlled the new political system that delegated power and centralized authority. Increasingly influenced by materialism and individualism, men saw little need to incorporate women into this system.

War and land cessions precipitated a demographic change that further limited political participation by women. In the 1750s, many Cherokees moved from the lower towns on the headwaters of the Savannah River. War with the Creeks and Chickasaws, who repeatedly attacked these towns, prompted them to relocate. By May 1752 all the lower towns had moved except Estatoe and Toxaway. One group that moved north was attacked by "northern Indians" (probably Seneca or Shawnee), and so most of these people only shifted towns away from the frontier into northern Georgia.[49] They found that region to be a poor refuge. As a center of Chickamaugan resistance to peace with the United States, these towns suffered militia invasions that finally forced pacification in 1794. The people from these towns long bore the psychological scars of their experience. In 1796 Benjamin Hawkins, United States superintendent of Indian affairs south of the Ohio River, visited an area in north Georgia settled by refugees from the lower towns of Tugalo and Keowee. Their collective memory no doubt included the invasions of the Seven Years' War, the Revolution, and the Chickamaugan war, and the stories passed from one generation to the next perpetuated the memory. Hawkins found that these people were terrified at the sight of a white man; women became mute and children hid in fear.[50]

Some towns that were destroyed by invading armies rebuilt in what residents perceived to be less vulnerable locations, but secure location often proved to be elusive.[51] Keowee, for example, had been adjacent to Fort Prince George. After its destruction in the Seven Years' War, the town moved somewhat north, only to be leveled again in the Revolution. One can sympathize with a woman Hawkins encountered in 1796: "She was poor, she said from trouble and difficulty not from want of industry. She had been greatly incommoded by the misunderstanding between the Red and White people. She knew not where to fix down, and this uncertainty continued until it was too late to make corn, she planted some, but too late."[52] Many women shared her sense of hopelessness, a feeling exacerbated by the fear that since they could no longer grow corn, they could no longer be women.

One problem, some Cherokees came to believe, was not the location of towns but the institution of towns. After the American Revolution, many Cherokees who relocated chose not to rebuild their towns. Instead, according to John Norton, they "separated and seated themselves on plantations suiting their fancies or convenience." Norton believed that towns declined because "peace has done away the necessity of living in collective bodies for mutual support."[53] More likely, Cherokees perceived towns to be too vulnerable to invading armies. Towns were a viable defense strategy only as long as warfare consisted of periodic raids by a few warriors. The enormous war parties and even larger armies of the eighteenth century, however, viewed towns as targets. In this new age of total war, isolated homesteads provided far more protection than the towns, which concentrated population and production.

Consequently, Cherokees abandoned some towns altogether. Norton reported that at Great Hiwassee "there are now only a few houses remaining." When Hawkins traveled through the Cherokee country in 1796, he remarked on the disappearance of towns. He "passed through Santa, formerly an Indian town, there was one hut, some peach trees and the posts of a town house." At Little Chota, he found "one small field of corn, some peach, plumb and locust trees." At Quanasee, where the trader Cornelius Daughtery had lived and operated a thriving business for many years, he saw "nothing remaining of the town except the open flats where were formerly the corn fields." Even the towns that Cherokees still inhabited were mere shadows of their former selves: "I saw five houses in view and there were several others in the neighbourhood; it is called Chewayqok; the river is the same name. From appearances there must have been a very large town in the neighbourhood of our encampment last evening, and from thense down to this village." The traditions collected by Butrick in the early nineteenth century insisted that "anciently the Cherokees lived in large towns contiguous to each other, so that the whole nation could be easily convened." But American Board missionaries in 1818 found that the situation had changed radically: "There is no place near us where a large audience can be collected. As the people do not live in villages, but scattered over the country from 2 to 10 miles apart, to collect in any place 20 or 30 who can understand our language, is as much as can be expected."[54]

Vestiges of towns in the form of council houses and ceremonial sites remained in parts of the Cherokee nation, but even in these areas, many Cherokees began to live at isolated homesteads. The assortment of native household structures—granary, summer and winter houses, menstrual hut—gradually gave way to the typical pioneer homestead. Norton commented on the disappearance of the *asi,* or winter house: "Those living along the Tennessee, and in the South Western part of the Nation, seem to think the common log house, a sufficient shelter against the winter cold."[55]

The more recently settled parts of the Cherokee Nation were almost indistinguishable visually from the southern states.

The dissolution of many towns and the depopulation of others had an impact on the kinship system and the lives of women. Traditionally each town had contained several households of each matrilineal clan. Because clan members lived in close proximity to one another, they could offer assistance and protection. Clan members knew if a relative had been wronged or was in need. They could call conjurors for the sick and properly mourn the dead. When people no longer lived together, the traditional role of the clan became far more difficult to maintain. Lineages also changed. Although they might still be neighbors, sisters, their husbands, their children, their mother, aged uncles and aunts, unmarried brothers, and orphaned children of their clan did not normally live together anymore. Families increasingly became "nuclear" along the lines of Anglo-American families with mother, father, and children living in a log cabin. Women no longer shared their work because often there was only one adult woman in the household. The large fields where women had farmed together, according to Hawkins, were "covered with wild onions," and now they tilled small individual plots.[56]

Towns had formed political and religious as well as social units, and when people dispersed, they began to pay less attention to the complex function of towns. People still gathered for ball games and the annual Green Corn Ceremony, but the elaborate ritual life that John Howard Payne's informant remembered from his youth began to wane.[57] The Green Corn Ceremony absorbed some other ritual events, such as the "feast of propitiation and cementation," while other rites, such as those that accompanied spring planting, had almost disappeared from memory by the late nineteenth century, when James Mooney visited the eastern Cherokees.[58] In the twentieth century, Jack and Anna Kilpatrick could only ponder the "apparent paucity of charms applicable to agriculture" when so many formulas existed for hunting, war, courting, sports, and other human endeavors.[59] Unlike those activities, agriculture demanded communal ceremonies, and the decline of towns made such observances increasingly problematic. Equally significant for women were the town council meetings at which they had opportunities to speak to the entire community. Town councils continued to meet into the nineteenth century, but their power disintegrated as the national council composed of men claimed most issues of vital importance for itself.

Eighteenth-century warfare contributed to the demise of towns, the loss of a rich ceremonial complex involving agriculture, the loosening of kinship bonds, and the silencing of women's public political voice. The rise of warriors as a governing body, the delegation of authority, and the centralization of power jeopardized women's status. Furthermore, foreign policy came to dominate Cherokee politics, and gender rather than kinship came to determine political participation. The productivity of a woman's fields and the well-being of her household depended on the skills of warriors on the battlefield and at the treaty conference. Male concerns—war and foreign affairs—still were male concerns, but they threatened to subsume the female domain.

Part 3

"Civilization"

War and trade dominated Cherokee society in the eighteenth century, but by the end of the century, neither seemed to have much of a future. Overhunting contributed to a decline in deer, encroaching white settlements and roaming livestock destroyed the deer's habitat, and other commodities replaced deerskins in trans-Atlantic commerce. The colonial wars that had claimed thousands of lives and had destroyed orchards, fields, homes, and towns, too, seemed to be at an end. Europeans settled their differences or moved to another theater, and British colonists won their independence. The Cherokees, who had participated in European colonial expansion as allies and trading partners, found themselves with an economy geared to trade and a government shaped by warriors. The United States, invigorated by its political reorganization in 1789, had little use for such anachronistic Native societies, and it embarked on an Indian policy designed to accommodate the land needs of its expanding population and the moral imperatives of its republican ideology. The federal government took on the task of "civilizing" the Indians, that is, converting them culturally into Anglo-Americans. Although eighteenth-century changes threatened the marginalization of women politically and economically, "civilization" implied a far more dramatic transformation. Guided by an idealized view of men and women in their own society, reformers sought to turn men into industrious, republican farmers and women into chaste, orderly housewives.

The idea of Indians becoming "civilized" was not a new one. Eighteenth-century writers usually attributed even physical differences between Europeans and Native Americans to culture, a human invention that could be changed, they believed, relatively easily. The Virginian Robert Beverley, for example, maintained that the darker skin of Native peoples came from "greasing and sunning themselves" and that an infant's skin was "much clearer" than an adult's.[1] Europeans explained perceived differences in accomplishment in terms of cultural, not racial, superiority and held out hope that Native peoples could progress to Europe's elevated position. Thomas Jefferson suggested that with time, literacy, and an increase in population, the American Indians might even produce an individual comparable to Isaac Newton.[2]

Scottish social theorists shaped North American interpretations of culture to some extent and provided a framework for understanding Native peoples. Native peoples were "savages" whose cultures were less complex than "civilized" ones. Savage peoples lived off the bounty of the land without investing their labor, whereas civilized peoples were busy, as Robert Berkhofer has phrased it, "transforming nature into property."[3] Savage peoples, according to the learned academicians revered by the early republic, did not farm. Benjamin Rush echoed the Scottish school when he divided all mankind into three groups: "The savage lives by fishing and hunting, the barbarian by pasturage, and the civilized man by agriculture." Agriculture, he believed, was "the true basis of national health, riches and populousness."[4] For Native people to become civilized, they must shift from hunting to farming.

Henry Knox, George Washington's secretary of war, introduced the concept of the federal government as civilizing agent. Lamenting the demise of Native peoples as the European settlers encroached on them, Knox speculated: "How different would be the sensation of a philosophic mind to reflect, that, instead of exterminating a part of the human race, by our modes of population, we had preserved, through all difficulties, and at last had imparted our knowledge of cultivation and the arts to the aboriginals of the country, by which the source of future life and happiness had been preserved and extended." Knox conceded that many thought it "impracticable to civilize the Indians of North America," but he suggested that "this position is probably more convenient than just." Earlier attempts at "civilization" had rested primarily on converting and educating Indians, but Knox suggested a novel approach: "Were it possible to introduce among the Indian tribes a love for exclusive property, it would be a happy commencement of the business." In order to instill in Native peoples a sense of private property, Knox proposed making gifts of livestock to Native chiefs or their wives.[5] While "civilization" involved a radical transformation of Native societies including their government and religion, economic change was the first order of business.

The civilization program became an official part of Cherokee relations with the federal government in 1791 when the Cherokees signed the Treaty of Holston. The treaty provided that the federal government furnish the Cherokees with "implements of husbandry" and send residential agents to give instruction in their use. As a result of this aid, "the Cherokee nation may be led to a greater degree of civilization, and to become herdsmen and cultivators, instead of remaining in a state of hunters."[6] In 1793 the Indian Trade and Intercourse Act committed the United States to providing agricultural implements and draft animals to all Indians and to appointing agents to instruct Native people in their use. The Cherokees, devastated by invasion and impoverished by the decline of the deerskin trade, welcomed assistance. Yet they must have been somewhat bemused by the proffered lessons in agriculture. Not only had Cherokee women been farming for centuries, but many of the crops and techniques used by Euro-Americans came from Native peoples.[7]

In 1796 George Washington outlined the key provisions of the civilization program in a letter addressed to "Beloved Cherokees."[8] In it, he pointed out that "you now see that the game with which your woods once abounded, are growing scarce, and you know that when you cannot find a deer or other game to kill, you must remain hungry." Washington noted that "some of you already experience the advantage of keeping cattle and hogs." He urged other Cherokees to follow their example: "Let all keep them and increase their numbers, and you will have plenty of meat. To these add sheep, and they will give you clothing as well as food." Washington also encouraged commercial agriculture: "Your lands are good and of great extent. By proper management you can raise live stock not only for your own wants, but to sell to the White people." The president recommended the use of the plow to increase production and the adoption of wheat, which he claimed "makes the best bread." To this point, the president's letter is ungendered—it appears to address all Cherokees—but then he turned to the cultivation of fiber crops: "You will easily add flax and cotton which you may dispose of to the White people; or have it made up by your own women into clothing for yourselves. Your wives and daughters can soon learn to spin and weave."

Washington's instructions did not bode well for Cherokee women. Directly addressing Cherokee men, the president implied that animal husbandry and farming were male responsibilities in a "civilized" society. Spinning, weaving, and sewing were women's work. Such expectations threatened the traditional division of labor in Cherokee society and whatever remnants of female autonomy remained. The president assumed that Cherokee men would take up the tasks and adopt the work habits common in the United States while women would become helpmates, mere auxiliaries. In order to convert men from hunters into farmers, "civilizers" had to transform Cherokee conceptions of gender.

Beyond Washington's economic message, however, was an even more ominous signal to Cherokee women: in a "civilized" society women belonged to men, who both headed households and governed the nation. The president addressed Cherokee women only through men: "*your own* women"; "*your* wives and daughters." Washington also hoped to accelerate the political centralization already under way in the Cherokee Nation. He suggested that the Cherokees send representatives to an annual meeting, the forerunner of the Cherokees' National Council, where they could meet with United States agents and "talk together on the affairs of your nation." The president probably did not expect these representatives to include women.

The government's program to "civilize" Indians rested on an image of Indians as hunters who derived their livelihood from vast game preserves. These hunting grounds presented both an obstacle to "civilization" and a boon to those who succeeded in "civilizing" their proprietors. Native people who became farmers presumably would no longer need their excess lands and would willingly cede them for additional aid to improve their farms. Therefore, land cession supposedly benefitted both Native people and white pioneers.

Total expulsion of Native peoples from the eastern United States was an idea that dated back to the purchase of Louisiana in 1803. Thomas Jefferson suggested an exchange of lands in the East for tracts in the West, and he specifically proposed such a scheme to the Cherokees and Choctaws. Jefferson, however, did not press the issue, because he believed that Native peoples would become "civilized," live contentedly on reduced acreage, and blend into American society. Land cessions negotiated during Jefferson's administration provoked intense factionalism as well as creating population displacement, and so some Cherokees expressed interest in moving west, and the federal government encouraged individual families to migrate to what is today Arkansas. Treaties negotiated in 1817 and 1819 provided not only for land cessions but also for voluntary removal to the West. By the 1820s, two to three thousand Cherokees lived west of the Mississippi while approximately sixteen thousand remained in their homeland in the East.

Some Cherokees believed that "civilization" was their best protection against forced removal. Consequently, they spoke English, sent their children to school, and converted to Christianity. They established a Cherokee republic with written laws, a court system, and a national police force. They also tried to conform to Anglo-American notions about appropriate behavior for men and women. Trade and warfare had accentuated traditional roles for men and women, but "civilization" threatened to usher in new roles by making men farmers and women housewives.

The Cherokees who are most visible in the historical record succeeded in this transformation. They reacted to the crises of the late eighteenth and early nineteenth centuries by trying to re-create Cherokee culture and society in ways that accommodated "civilization." As a result, Cherokees laid claim to the title of "most civilized Indian tribe" in America. Although they comprised a minority, the Cherokees who enthusiastically embraced "civilization" dominated Cherokee economic and political life as well as Cherokee history. Not surprisingly, men—particularly wealthy and powerful men—play the lead roles in this history. The documents recording their actions and beliefs usually mentioned women only incidentally. Whereas the history of these men forms a compelling narrative of Cherokee "civilization," ferreting out the experiences of women and using them to create an alternative narrative forces reconsideration of Cherokee culture change, even in a period when it seemed so dramatic.

FIVE

A Changing Way of Life

An Indian policy developed in Washington faced an uncertain future among the people for whom it was designed. The Cherokees, like most other Native people, did not reject the civilization program, nor did they embrace it wholeheartedly. They simply adopted those aspects of the policy that seemed to address their particular set of problems. The result was not always what policy makers had intended. The Cherokees accepted many of the technological innovations offered by government agents, and Cherokee homesteads began to resemble those that dotted the rural landscape of the United States. Where gender was concerned, however, the transformation proved far less successful. Male hunters and female farmers were anathema to "civilization," and since hunting was no longer a viable enterprise, "civilizers" expected men to replace women as farmers. These expectations, however, failed to take into account the durability of gender conventions and the adaptability of Cherokee culture.

Benjamin Hawkins, who resided permanently with the Creeks, was also responsible for implementing the civilization program among the Cherokees.[1] When he visited the Cherokees in the fall of 1796, the men were absent, and so Hawkins spent his time primarily with women. One of his hostesses, a Mrs. Gagg, invited a group of women over to meet him: "They informed me that the men were all in the woods hunting, that they alone were at home to receive me, that they rejoiced much at what they had heard and hoped it would prove true, that they had made some cotton, and would make more and follow the instruction of the agent and the advise of the President."[2] Because "civilization" rested on agriculture and domestic manufactures, tasks women traditionally performed, the women believed that the civilization program validated what they did and promised to help them do their work more successfully on their homesteads.

Women's level of production became apparent to Hawkins when he visited women in the town of Etowah: "They informed me they performed most of the labour, the men assisted but little and that in the corn. They generally made a plenty of corn and sweet potatoes and pumpkins. They made beans, ground peas, cymblins, gourds, watermelons, collards and onions." Furthermore, these women kept livestock. One group of women told Hawkins that they raised "hogs, some cattle, and a great many poultry," and he encountered other women driving cattle to market. Women also had primary responsibility for domestic manufactures. They told Hawkins that "they made sugar, had raised some cotton, and manufactured their baskets, sifters, pots and earthen pans." Again and again they indicated to him their support for "the plan contemplated by the government for the bettering of the condition of the Red people," because they understood the concrete ways in which support for agriculture, animal husbandry, and domestic manufactures could improve their lives.[3]

Women envisioned "civilization" bringing improvement, not profound change. The matters Hawkins discussed with them were perfectly comprehensible because farming, tending livestock, and making utilitarian items had long been part of their world. In some ways, surprisingly little had changed during the preceding century: they continued to farm as their ancestors had for centuries. Metal hoes made the job easier, but the work remained the same. Agricultural production had expanded to include a number of crops introduced by Europeans and Africans. These included watermelons, onions, collards, fruit trees, and even a little cotton.[4] But farming remained women's work.

Cherokee women viewed animal husbandry as an extension of their role as farmers. The Cherokees traditionally did not fence their fields, and so the horses, cows, and pigs that eighteenth-century traders brought into the Nation presented a genuine threat to the crops. Although men complained to whites about damage done by roaming livestock, women actually had the responsibility for keeping the animals out of the fields. This led to a growing familiarity with the animals' habits and needs. By the end of the eighteenth century Cherokee women were well acquainted with the principles of animal husbandry. They also knew how to use such animals. Nancy Ward, the War Woman of Chota who learned to make butter from Mrs. Bean, supposedly introduced the keeping of milk cows. When Hawkins asked "what they wished, in aid of their own exertions," they answered "salt." This request demonstrates that women owned not only milk cows and laying hens but also animals used for meat: "Where they were able to supply themselves plentifully with meat, they were unable to preserve it for the want of salt."[5]

Although a few women already planted cotton, spinning and weaving were new skills for most of them. Lah-to-tau-yie had learned to card, spin, and weave from her English husband, who ordered a wheel from England and made her a loom himself.[6] A few women, such as Sally Waters, who served as Hawkins interpreter, had learned how to spin and weave while living in white settlements, but they normally had not been able to acquire wheels and looms. One woman told Hawkins that "once she had made as much cotton as purchased a petticoat, that she would gladly make more and learn how to spin it, if she had the opportunity." Fabric, however, had been part of Cherokee material culture throughout most of the eighteenth century because men exchanged their deerskins for calico, strouds, duffels, and even finished petticoats and blouses. Although men continued to wear leather leggings, they also wore fabric hunting shirts, and women dressed almost exclusively in the woven cloth for which men traded.[7]

Women seized the opportunity to manufacture their own clothes. As soon as their agent, Silas Dinsmoor, who served as Hawkins's subordinate in the Nation, made cards, wheels, and looms available in 1797, Cherokee women began adopting them. In 1809 a Cherokee man reminisced with Major John Norton about the women's response: "He [Dinsmoor] then addressed our women, and presented them with cotton seeds for planting; and afterwards with cards, wheels and looms to work it. They acquired the use of them with great facility, and now the most of the clothes we wear are of their manufacture." Spinning, weaving, and sewing conformed to women's practice of making clothing, household utensils, mats, and baskets and even dressing deerskins, and it promised to free them from dependence on the declining deerskin trade. Moravian missionaries who visited the Cherokees in 1799 reported that Cherokee women were so eager to make cloth that they carried spinning wheels on their backs from the agency to their homes.[8]

The Moravians, who sought permission to open a school, provide a good description of the Cherokees' domestic life three years after Hawkins's initial visit. One of the Cherokees they visited was John Watts, whose "family is supported mainly by his mother-in-law, the widow of the former chief, Hanging Maw. This old woman is called Grandmother Maw by the whites and is respected as a very sensible and industrious woman." When the Moravians arrived, Grandmother Maw "was breaking corn in a field not far off and putting it in fine baskets woven of reed." At the homestead "there were only women and children" since the men were hunting. At Hiwassee, which was in the process of being abandoned, Kulsathee showed Moravian missionaries "his cotton carding-combs, spinning wheel and, also yarn that his daughter had spun." The Moravians visited the plantation of Betty Martin, the Cherokee wife of a white man. She lived in a hewn-log house with plastered walls and a stone fireplace, furnished with "two bedsteads with bedding, a table of walnut-wood and a closet with tin and china ware." In addition to cotton cards, Mrs. Martin also had a loom. Her fenced cornfields "were plowed and cleared of grass; the wheat had been sown." Mrs. Martin and her neighbors kept "horses, cattle, hogs, fowl, dogs and cats." Their hostess also had "negro slaves that were well clothed." Although Washington's plan had not fully taken hold when the Moravians visited, there were promising signs.[9] Women apparently had embraced its major tenets.

The prosperous farms and industrious work habits described by the Moravians, according to "civilizers," represented the Cherokees' hope for the future, while hunting deer and trading skins reflected the past. Hawkins described the poverty reliance on hunting had brought: "Their men hunted in their proper season and aided them with the skins in providing cloaths and blankets, such as I saw, but this was not sufficient to make them comfortable and the poor old men, women and children were under the necessity of sleeping as I saw them in their town house."[10] Nevertheless, many men persisted in their hunting economy. When agent Return J. Meigs arrived in 1801, he had to settle a hunting party's claim for 123 deerskins, 40 bearskins, 5 small furs, and a buffalo skin that its eight members had left in the hunting grounds the previous year when a group of whites threatened them.[11] Like Hawkins, Meigs discovered that by November the chiefs had "gone to their hunting grounds & will not return for two or three months."[12] Yet hunting days were numbered. By 1808 losses from hunting camps were more likely to be half a bear and some deermeat than a substantial pile of skins.[13] Hunting, however, was one of the things that defined masculinity, and few Cherokee men were willing to forgo it. When a twenty-four-year-old man applied for admission to the school at Brainerd, he requested permission to hunt to clothe himself: he received instead a job on the farm.[14]

The persistence of hunting and the Cherokees' attachment to hunting grounds troubled "civilizers." Thomas Jefferson instructed Hawkins in 1803 "to promote among the Indians a sense of the superior value of a little land, well cultivated, over a great deal, unimproved." Eventually, he hoped, their hunting grounds "will be found useless, and even disadvantageous."[15] When Cherokee men's devotion to the chase momentarily thwarted Meigs's attempt to secure a cession of the Cumberland Mountain region in 1805, he complained: "That land is of no use to them. There is not a single family on it, & the hunting is very poor. Yet those of idle dispositions spend much time in rambling there & often return with a stolen horse which they have afterwards to pay for. In fact it is only a nursery of savage habits and operates against civilization which is much impeded by their holding such immense tracts of wilderness."[16] Meigs summarized the civilizers' major concerns. First of all, hunting promoted idleness rather than the industriousness on which civilization was based. Second, the common ground encouraged a disregard for private property. And finally, "wilderness" stood in direct opposition to "civilized" towns, pastures, and fields. Meigs, Hawkins, Jefferson, and other "civilizers" linked the cession of hunting grounds with the civilizing process. Herdsmen and farmers presumably no longer needed vast forests, and so the United States looked forward to the acquisition of the Indians' "surplus & waste lands."[17]

The hunting grounds were not the only target. When the United States acquired Louisiana in 1803, Jefferson suggested that the land be used to resettle Native peoples from east of the Mississippi.[18] Meigs actively promoted the exchange of the Cherokee homeland for a new country in the west, but most Cherokees opposed the measure.[19] In order to achieve an exchange, the United States had to alter Cherokees' conception of the land. "The Mother Earth has been divided," the Cherokee council asserted in 1801, "one part [to the] whites and the other is [to] the red people where the present have been raisd from their infancy to the years of manhood."[20] For them, their country was more than a commodity to be bought and sold.

Land was not a part of the Cherokees' nascent market economy. They held land in common, and any Cherokee could use unoccupied land as long as it did not infringe on the rights of neighbors. The common ownership of realty enabled the Cherokees to invest in other forms of property, including improvements to realty such as fences and houses, which they did sell to one another. But no Cherokee sold improvements on their part of "Mother Earth" to those on the other part: they strictly curtailed property rights in realty. Ultimately, Hawkins believed "the acquirement of individual property by agricultural improvements, by raising stock, and by domestic manufactures . . . will prepare them to accommodate their white neighbours with lands on reasonable terms."[21] That is, individual ownership of other kinds of property not only "civilized" Indians, but it eventually made them more receptive to the notion that land—like deerskins, fabric, or livestock—was a commodity to be sold. The linkage between land cessions and "civilization" became increasingly apparent as Cherokees committed themselves to the program.

Most Cherokee men, long familiar with the machinations of Euro-Americans, viewed "civilization" with suspicion from the very start. One Cherokee man revealed to John Norton that upon hearing the president's plan, "many of us thought it was only some refined scheme calculated to gain an influence over us, rather than ameliorate our situation; and slighted his advice and proposals." The fact that the president of the United States, who normally sent messages about war and trade, now wanted to talk about farming was enough to make the most gullible Cherokee man suspicious. Consequently, Cherokee men at first chose to ignore the civilization program. As a result, men suffered by comparison to women. John McDonald, an intermarried white man, told Norton that "the females have however made much greater advances in industry than the males, they now manufacture a great quantity of cloth; but the latter have not made proportionate progress in Agriculture."[22] The men's initial lack of enthusiasm and relative failure may well have derived from their assumption that because farming was women's work, "civilization" had little to do with them.[23] For the civilization program to succeed among men, they had to adapt it to Cherokee culture.

Washington and Secretary of War Henry Knox provided an avenue for just such an adaptation: they suggested that the transition to farming be eased by the Cherokees' first becoming herdsmen. Spanish explorers had introduced livestock into the Southeast in the sixteenth century (the Cherokees borrowed their word for cow, *wa'ka*, from the Spanish *vaca*). By the eighteenth century, traders had made livestock familiar, but Cherokee men exhibited little interest in keeping hogs, cattle, or sheep.[24] Instead, they commonly regarded such animals as game. At the abandoned encampment of a hunting party in 1751, colonists found five sheepskins and some beef bones.[25] White backcountry farmers as well as the garrison at Fort Loudoun complained constantly about the loss of livestock to hunting parties.[26] Because livestock usually foraged in the forest until late fall, the Native assumption that these animals were game was not implausible. The Cherokees had no tradition of domesticated animals other than the dog, which they apparently did not eat, and so the distinction between foraging animals that one could kill freely and those that belonged to an individual may have appeared artificial. Even in the towns, domestic animals belonging to traders were not safe. Adair complained that "Indian youth are as destructive to the pigs and poultry, as so many young wolves or foxes" and that their parents did little to control their behavior.[27] Such an attitude did not bode well for the keeping of livestock by men.

By the end of the eighteenth century, Cherokees certainly knew the difference between livestock and game even though their behavior sometimes belied that knowledge. A vegetarian German pietist, who fled ridicule in Pennsylvania in 1795 and took refuge among the tolerant Cherokees, fretted constantly about the Cherokees' lack of regard for God's creatures. He offered to loan one of his milk cows to Cherokee neighbors on the condition that they would not kill it, but according to Moravian missionaries who met him, "the Indians could not agree to the condition." His compassion finally compelled him to provide a cow to an infirm elderly man despite his failure to exact the promise. Upon the old man's death, the vegetarian watched in horror as the heirs barbecued his milk cow.[28]

As late as 1818, visitors to the Cherokees expressed amazement at the way men treated livestock: "It was near sunset when we arrived. When he [the Cherokee host] learned who we were, and saw the obligation he was under to entertain us for the night, he took his rifle as I supposed to shoot some wild game which might be near. But while we were standing in a sort of porch attached to his hut, he discharged it at a cow which was eating grass immediately before our eyes; he only wounded the poor animal, which ran bellowing and frantic about the yard. In this situation, two or three half naked negroes, who stood at the corner of the house to enjoy the bloody spectacle, fell upon the cow with axes; cleaved it to the ground; butchered it immediately, and in two hours after our arrival, part of the very cow which we had found browsing happily on the grass, was stewed for our supper."[29] Clearly Cherokee culture did not readily equip men to care for livestock.

Nevertheless, by the time of Hawkins's visit some men were beginning to raise livestock, and their numbers increased steadily in the nineteenth century. Among the first herdsmen in the Cherokee Nation were white men or the sons of white men. For example, John Candy, who had come to the Cherokee Nation from East Florida in 1783, owned "some fine cattle." But Cherokee men, even traditionalists, also kept stock. One known as The Terrapin, who spoke only his Native tongue, "had raised some cattle of 1,200 lbs."[30] Deer were still fairly plentiful, however, and livestock remained relatively scarce at the turn of the nineteenth century. In 1802, when the agent Return J. Meigs surveyed the boundary between North Carolina and the Cherokee Nation, he paid a dollar apiece for deer while hogs cost between $3.25 and $6.00 each and a single beef brought $16.00.[31]

The Cherokees ceded their last expanse of hunting grounds in a series of treaties in 1805–6. The remaining forests near their towns could not sustain a hunting economy, and so they acquired more cattle and hogs. These domesticated animals competed for food with the dwindling supply of game. White intruders further strained resources by releasing their herds on Cherokee land. In one part of the Cherokee Nation in 1805, more than a thousand head of cattle belonging to intruders grazed on Cherokee land.[32] After a decade of rapidly expanding livestock herds in the Cherokee country, one visitor observed: "Since they have become graziers, the game has nearly disappeared from their country."[33] Cherokee men had found a new use for their "hunting grounds," that is, land they did not cultivate. They simply restocked hunting grounds with cattle and hogs. By 1810 the Cherokees owned 19,500 cattle and 19,600 hogs as well as 6,100 horses and 1,037 sheep, and all accounts suggest that the number was growing rapidly.[34] The male approach to raising livestock, however, can hardly be called animal husbandry.

The work pattern of Cherokee herding did not differ dramatically from that of hunting. The Cherokees, like most southerners, neither penned their livestock during the summer nor put them in barns in winter. Norton observed that "people raise cattle with the greatest facility, and without any further trouble or expence than that of giving them salt. In the winter, they feed in cane brakes, and in summer, they are dispersed in herds in the vicinity of little Salt Licks."[35] In the late fall and winter, the herdsmen simply shot the animals they intended to butcher. The practice appalled visitors accustomed to abattoirs or slaughter pens, but American Board missionaries requested a gun soon after their arrival "on account of the beeves we kill being so very wild that we cannot catch them without shooting."[36]

The process of capturing those animals they hoped to take to market could be nearly as time-consuming as hunting. In November 1802, the chief Doublehead delayed his journey to purchase supplies, he explained, because "I am so engaged hunting and gathering my beef cattle that I expect it will be a moon or two before I can come."[37] This "hunting and gathering" sometimes involved a mad chase through the woods. Daniel S. Butrick, an American Board missionary, could easily have been writing about game in 1818 when he noted that the small attendance at services was "soon a little enlarged by the arrival of a number of men in pursuit of cattle."[38]

If we consider the grazing of cattle analogous to hunting, it is not too far-fetched to regard horse stealing as a substitute for war. Horse theft was not confined to the Cherokees in the late eighteenth and early nineteenth centuries, but the border between the Cherokee Nation and the states proved attractive to Indian and white horse thieves alike. Confusion over jurisdiction, the readiness of the federal government to settle claims for stolen horses, and mountainous terrain made the frontier ideal territory for illicit traffic in horses.[39] Meigs lamented: "It is an undoubted truth that considerable numbers of horses are stolen by citizens & by Indians that never will or can be detected on account of the wilderness country; so that detection is easily avoided. The number of horses carried thru & into this country is almost incredible from Georgia, both the Carolinas, & Kentucky."[40] One Cherokee man told Norton that he had traveled four to five hundred miles to buy horses from the Pawnees.[41] By the first decade in the nineteenth century, horses had replaced deerskins as a medium of exchange: Meigs described them as "a kind of currency."[42] As such, horses helped soften the economic blow from the demise of warfare and trade. When the Moravians called on Kulsathee at Hiwassee in 1799, they discovered that he operated a livery stable: "He has many horses, cattle, hogs, and fowl. The first named he rents to Traders, who give him salt in payment."[43] Kulsathee may no longer have had skins or captives to sell, but he found a perfectly acceptable replacement.

Horse stealing fit well into a male culture that expected men to distinguish themselves on forays against the enemy. After the Chickamaugans made peace in 1794, young men had few other ways in which to demonstrate martial skills, prove their valor, and become men in the traditional sense.[44] Occasionally they undertook expeditions against the Osages, who lived across the Mississippi, but the vulnerability of small war parties far from home, along with the Cherokee agents' injunction against warfare, made the Osage country an unattractive battleground.[45] Stealing horses, however, provided men with some of the same rewards as warfare—it demonstrated prowess and brought profit—and horses became a kind of substitute for the war captives who previously had been sold as slaves. In one episode in 1797, the Cherokees literally equated the two: a Virginia man traded a horse for his brother, who had been taken prisoner by the Cherokees some years earlier.[46] With the opening of a road through the Cherokee Nation, opportunities for theft became more numerous, and thieves became more brazen and less discriminating. Although horses remained the preferred prize, travelers lost hogs, cows, salt, clothing, boats, and slaves.[47] The Cherokee council ultimately had to order return of property "detained" along the road.[48]

Women owned horses and other kinds of livestock, but these animals never became central to women's lives in the way they did to men's: horses, cattle, and hogs brought economic advantages to women but fulfilled no cultural function. Women, however, could not escape the impact of male horse stealing any more successfully than they had been able to avoid the ramifications of war. White horse thieves made little distinction between the property of Cherokee men and women. Granny Maw lost two horses branded HM (for Hanging Maw, her late husband), while a Creek and a white man stole two horses from Sally Hughes.[49] Maw and Hughes were fortunate that they were not injured. An assailant beat one unnamed Cherokee woman and stole her earbobs as well as her horse.[50] Nevertheless, this new kind of frontier warfare claimed relatively few women victims. The vast majority of cases that came to the attention of the agent involved men exclusively. Horses were becoming a new symbol of male culture.

When Cherokee men adapted male imperatives to horse stealing and hunting techniques to herding, they confronted a host of negative European attitudes. White settlers were understandably reluctant to regard the theft of their property as an acceptable alternative to raids by war parties. Horse theft seemed particularly despicable because it inflicted enormous hardship on subsistence-level families and embodied a European folklore of nightriders and highwaymen. Their response to hunting was less visceral. They believed, however, that hunting was at the very heart of Native "savagery" because it permitted men to engage in "sport and pastimes" instead of labor.[51] Benjamin Franklin attributed the failure of colonial efforts to civilize Indians to "the Proneness of Human Nature to a Life of Ease" provided by "the Spontaneous Productions of Nature, with the additions of very little Labour, if Hunting and Fishing may indeed be called Labour when Game is so plenty."[52] Thomas McKenney later suggested that a major obstacle to civilizing the Indian was "the preference he cherishes for sport and pastimes," that is, hunting.[53]

The adaptation of livestock herding to traditional labor patterns and land use left the "civilizers" in dismay. The Indians seemed to be reversing the process of domesticating animals by releasing them into the forest to forage. Although most whites in the South and on the frontier did the same, early proponents of selective breeding objected to the practice and decried its extension to Indians. The Indians' half-wild beasts hardly represented progress or reform. Furthermore, this approach to animal husbandry deprived the Cherokees of the refined products—milk, butter, and cheese—that derived from domesticated animals. The only milk available came from those cows that decided, of their own free will, to come home.[54] Yet missionaries who later tried to set a good example by penning their livestock complained that the animals starved in winter.[55] John McDonald, an intermarried white man, told John Norton why livestock raising was the only part of the civilization program most Cherokee men had accepted: "They raise great herds of cattle, which can be done with little exertion; and the sale of these brings much wealth into the Nation."[56] That is, herding demanded the same kind of "exertion" as hunting and provided the same kind of return. Cherokee herding methods required little of what Europeans considered labor and failed to promote the industrious habits associated with "civilization." Meigs pointed out with some disgust that "the raising & manufacturing of cotton is all done by the Indian women. . . . The Indian men attend to the raising of cattle and swine—this costs them no labour, a thing they will avoid as long as possible."[57] In the eyes of Meigs and other "civilizers," farming constituted labor but herding, like hunting, did not. In their attempt to avoid women's work—farming—men seemed to be avoiding any sort of labor at all.

Men found ways to contribute to agricultural productivity and compensate for the women's labor lost to spinning and weaving without actually farming themselves. In the first decade of the nineteenth century, many of them began to lease or rent land to white families on shares.[58] The council had grave misgivings about the practice since it brought large numbers of white people into the Nation, and expelling them at the end of the year was difficult. In 1808 the council considered banning the practice, but Agent Meigs protested: "I wish you to weigh this matter well before you act because I think you will find that you will again want the help of poor [white] people to raise corn & do other work for you & in a year or two you will do it. All People that ever I know hire poor people to work for them. Some families dont want to hire because they have help enough of their own; but other families have not hands of their own & they ought not to be deprived of having help when they can find it."[59] Meigs clearly saw sharecropping as a way for Cherokees to increase agricultural productivity, but by 1811 he had changed his mind. Instead, sharecropping was a way for Cherokee men to avoid work: "They have no need for white men as croppers because it encourages idleness in Indians."[60] As concern over intruders grew, the practice of cropping declined.

Cherokees found another form of labor in African slaves.[61] Traders had brought their own slaves into the Cherokee country in the eighteenth century, and Cherokee warriors had participated in a frontier slave trade. Like horse stealing, the theft of slaves presented men with an opportunity to remain warriors, and so an illicit traffic in slaves continued well into the nineteenth century.[62] By the early nineteenth century, however, Cherokees also were acquiring slaves for their own use. The transition to slave labor, like that to livestock herding, seems to have been one in which Cherokees invested little thought. When Young Wolf wrote his will in 1814, he explained how he managed to accumulate his estate: "From herding my brother's cattle I recevd one calf which I took my start from, except my own industry, & with cow & calf which I sold, I bought two sows & thirteen piggs sometime after I was abel to purchase three mares & the increase of them since is amounted to thirty more or less & from that start I gathered money enough to purchase a negro woman named Tabb, also a negro man named Ceasar."[63] By 1809 slaves in the Cherokee Nation numbered 583.[64] Although some of these probably belonged to whites employed by or married to Cherokees, most belonged to Indians. According to a census taken in 1825, the number had increased to 1,277, and by 1835 it had reached nearly 1,600. Instead of becoming the yeoman farmers so admired by Washington and Jefferson, most Cherokee men (like Washington and Jefferson) seemed more inclined to adopt the aristocratic planter as a role model. Only a very few ever achieved this goal, but those who did dominated Cherokee economic and political life.[65]

The introduction of slave labor into the economy had a profound effect on Cherokee women and men. Cherokees were in the process of acquiring the racial attitudes of white southerners, and the use of this subject race in agriculture demeaned the traditional labor of women. The fact that slaves cultivated the fields of upper-class Cherokees made all Cherokee men less likely to embrace farming since one risked ignominy by agricultural labor. The use of slaves in farming also challenged women's view of themselves. If growing corn contributed to the gender identity of women, what happened when black men joined or replaced them in the fields? Gradually they saw their traditional role as women compromised.

The extent to which Cherokee men did actually take up the plow is difficult to determine. As early as 1796, The Terrapin was using the plow.[66]

Fields may have become more of a middle ground between men and women in the early nineteenth century as new gender-specific tasks replaced the old. Meigs reported that "the raising of cattle & making cloth are the principal objects." The former of these was men's work while the latter was women's, but neither men nor women, according to Meigs, had any interest in "extending their tillage."[67] The decline in hunting seemed to mandate an increase in agricultural production, and periodic food shortages may have resulted in part from the Cherokees' failure to grow enough corn to compensate for the loss of game. On the other hand, drought seems to have been largely responsible for hunger.[68] Men coped with famine by appealing to the agent for food, but their dependency may have forced them to pay some attention to his admonitions about turning from hunting to farming.

The novelty of the plow, its status as a gift of the federal government, the example of white men, and the association of the plow with horses may have led increasing numbers of Cherokee men to became directly involved in farming. More than likely, however, men adopted the new technology of plow agriculture while women continued to perform more traditional tasks, such as hoeing, associated with farming. Men requested plows from the agent, but these petitioners were headmen who spoke for their towns rather than for themselves.[69] Gender-specific association with plows is contradictory: Meigs's assistant requested a plow for Arthur Burns, "one of the most indefatigable and industrious men," while Bartlet Robbins "was sent by Nancy Falling to the Blacksmith's to have some plough irons sharpened."[70] Lists of goods being sent from the agency to various Cherokee towns included hoes, women's traditional farming implement, as well as the more innovative plow.[71] Often hoes substantially outnumbered plows, but plows cost four times as much and required the services of a blacksmith to remain usable.[72] By 1811 there were about five hundred plows in the Nation, perhaps one for every four families.[73]

Horses provided an obvious link between men and farming, but in the early years of plow agriculture, some question remains about the use of the horse. When Meigs wrote to his supplier, William Cocke, in 1802 to request a shipment of plow irons, he gave specific instructions for how they were to be constructed. The Indians had learned how to make wooden parts for the specified plows, thereby reducing the cost of implements to the government. Meigs pointed out that the plows "must be very light [because] they have not teams for heavy ploughs." The relatively few orders for equivalent numbers of harnesses, collars, traces, and other paraphernаlia needed to put a horse in the row suggests that the Cherokees may first have used push plows or manually pulled plows. By the 1820s, however, most Cherokees had hitched horses to their plows.[74] Missionary Daniel Butrick wrote that "a horse is their chief dependence for raising support for their families," and when his own mount ran away, he had difficulty borrowing one because the Cherokees had all of theirs in the fields.[75] In 1821, missionaries introduced oxen, which seem to have been common elsewhere in the South, but horses remained the draft animal of choice.[76]

Men probably held the reins. Traditionally men helped women prepare fields and plant corn, tasks for which plows were intended. After planting, women took over the care of the crops. As a result, men appeared idle during much of the year. As late as 1828, over thirty years after the inauguration of the civilization program, missionaries complained that men did not fully occupy themselves with farming: "Every family has a corn field, plough & horse or horses, to till it. They keep cows & hogs—raise horses & beeves—The women spin & weave—In general old & young are decently clad in cotton cloth of their own making—especially on the Sabbath. The season of raising corn is a time of general industry with both men & women & perhaps we may say with most of the women, the year round. But as agriculture is extended only to raising corn, potatoes, & cotton (except with a very few, lately, a little wheat) the men have not a sufficient stimulous to keep up their exertions after the corn is laid by—This is a very great evil, both as it tends to demoralize, & also to keep them poor. The women are evidently going before the men; & we think this (at least in a great degree) is owing to their being more constantly employed."[77] As long as men confined themselves to plowing the fields, little hope existed for keeping them "constantly employed." Albert Gallatin complained that "although the men may to some extent have assisted the women in the cultivation of the ground, the greater part of the labors still fell upon the latter."[78] He did concede that the Cherokees had, in a limited way, "become an agricultural nation, meaning thereby that state of society, in which the men themselves do actually perform agricultural labor." But even among the Cherokees, he estimated, only one-third of the men farmed.[79]

On the surface, the civilization program seems to have reversed the eighteenth-century trend that concentrated economic power in the hands of men at the expense of women. Nineteenth-century observers agreed that men lagged behind women in adapting to the new economic order.

But a market economy underlay the civilization program as surely as it had the deerskin trade. The Cherokees were never going to be able to create the agrarian republic of yeomen farmers envisioned, but not practiced, by Jeffersonians. The economic expansion of the United States drew the Cherokees into a maelstrom from which they could not have escaped even had they been so inclined. As it was, the Cherokees had long ago adapted their political and economic institutions to the demands of an international market. The vast majority of Cherokee men and women had little desire to withdraw.

The women with whom Hawkins spoke had a sophisticated understanding of their own economic subservience. They knew that male ascendancy derived largely from the market. Consequently, they shifted the conversations with Hawkins from production to marketing. The women who told Hawkins about their agricultural production added that "if they could be directed how to turn their labour to account like the white people, they should be contented."[80] Cherokee women had no complaints about their role as farmers. What they wanted was an opportunity "to turn their labor to account"—that is, to market what they produced.

The obstacles confronting these would-be entrepreneurs were considerable. Hawkins heard their complaints: "I was here informed of some of the difficulties and hardships which these poor people are subject to. They sell the fowls grown, 2 for 2½ yards of binding worth 2 cents, a bushel of corn for a quart of salt and sometimes a pint, and the woman had just returned from the [white] settlements, a journey of 17 days. She carried a bushel and a half of chestnuts on her back and gave them for a petticoat."[81] This woman, like most Cherokees, needed to buy salt, clothing, and other goods, and so she had to sell at whatever price she could get.

Often Cherokees could find no market at all for what they produced. A group of women complained "that they would make corn enough but that they never could sell it."[82] One of their difficulties was the absence of a substantial internal market. Since most Cherokee households farmed, corn had little market value. Those Cherokees who had no corn usually had no means to pay for it.[83] Drought tended to touch all Cherokees equally so that when Cherokees needed to buy corn, no one had corn to sell.[84] Scattered white farmsteads near the Nation's borders offered poor markets, and the distance to larger white settlements coupled with the hardships of travel posed problems for women who had to tend house and mind children as well as farm.[85] The Creeks briefly offered women an opportunity to enter the market: by 1809, Cherokee women were swapping them cloth for cattle.[86] War soon interrupted the trade, however, and Creeks acquired their own spinning wheels and looms.

Textiles had always been an important part of the trade between Europeans and Native peoples. As the supply of deerskins that Cherokees exchanged for textiles declined, they might have begun to rely exclusively on women's domestic manufactures, but they did not. Women possibly could not keep up with demand, but more likely, men were unwilling to compromise their commercial role in Cherokee society. Participation in commerce had come to define masculinity as much as war or hunting, and factory-made textiles were part of the material culture dominated by men and non-Cherokees. Textiles became a trophy for young men no longer permitted to go to war, and whites along the frontier complained bitterly about the loss of their best bedding.[87] Textiles came to play a major role in the financial diplomacy called annuities, the federal government's annual payment for land previously ceded. In 1801 the chiefs notified their agent, Meigs, that they no longer wanted their annuity paid in goods "not of substantial use," in particular silk stockings, gold lace, damask tablecloths, morocco shoes, and ostrich feathers. Instead, they wanted "blankets, strouds & coating." Meigs added in his instructions to the supplier, "Some fine Cloth is always expected for the Chiefs."[88] The government factory at Tellico Blockhouse in eastern Tennessee stocked a substantial array of textiles and supplied those Cherokees who had money to spend or credit to command.

Despite the competition from factory-made textiles, Cherokee women continued to increase their production. By 1809 they had 1,600 spinning wheels and 467 looms in a total population of just over 12,000. Gideon Blackburn, a Presbyterian missionary, estimated the potential output of Cherokee women to be 584,684 yards of cloth a year.[89] Blackburn, of course, did not account for the hours that women had to spend in other activities. While the potential is staggering, the more modest actual production of perhaps half Blackburn's estimate was substantial.[90] Cherokee women, however, never adequately matched the competition. In 1804 the federal government completed a road across the Cherokee Nation, which reduced shipping costs by almost one-half, and presumably the cost of textiles declined. The government factory closed in 1811, but Cherokee merchants filled that commercial vacuum and continued to market fabric made outside the Nation.

Competition to women's manufactures came from unlikely sources. Missionaries, who arrived in large numbers in the decade following the closing of the government factory, competed with both domestic producers and local purveyors of fabrics. Ann Paine, a New Englander who visited missionaries in 1820, noted that "many of the Cherokee women are skillful in spinning cotton which they manufacture into cloth, but the Mission is much benefitted by the sale of cloth and garments from the charity boxes. For these the Cherokees give money and articles of produce; and they are sold with considerable proffit as it would not do for the Missionaries to undersell the Cherokee Merchants, at whose stores common shirt factory is sold at 50 cts per yard—A common factory shirt from the boxes is sold for two dollars."[91] Missionaries also bartered textiles for beef and occasional labor.[92] In addition to marketing textiles, the mission participated in production, although on a more limited basis. The girls at one mission school made quilts from old cloth. The quilts brought six or seven dollars each from the Cherokees and "please them very much."[93]

Women's difficulty in participating in the market stemmed from far more than the industrial revolution. Cherokees had well-established mechanisms for commerce that proved remarkably persistent. Rooted in part in ancient cultural traditions that entrusted men with foreign relations and women with domestic ones, these mechanisms had adapted to an international market economy in the eighteenth century. Men were at the forefront of the deerskin trade in part because men obtained the skins, but also because men dealt with outsiders—that is, with European traders and emissaries. For women suddenly to have entered this world would have disrupted a long-established protocol. Women certainly sold corn, livestock, and even textiles, but the primary responsibility for marketing rested with men. The Cherokees simply adapted established patterns of behavior to new circumstances. Women continued to be women according to old definitions, and men continued to be men.

Within the context of the civilization program, men served as the intermediaries between women and the federal government and as conduits for most of the tools and implements that the agent made available to the Nation. Requests for cotton cards, spinning wheels, looms, and corn hoes normally came from men.[94] Sometimes women directly instigated these requests. Pathkiller and Toochalee prefaced their application for wheels and cards with the words, "These women came to me to write them a few lines to you."[95] Doublehead made a particularly poignant plea when he wrote to Meigs: "I have to solicit of you in behalf of two poor middle aged women living here, who have begged me to make the application having large families composed entirely of girls, that you will be so good as to forward them by me three small wheels and three pairs of cards, the familys are very poor and have no other means but their industry to cloth themselves and show much anxiety to learn the usefull arts, they are deprived of the aid of any man in their family having no man in either."[96] One of the things these women needed a man for was to appeal to the agent for tools.

As intermediaries, men also often marketed commodities associated with women. When Meigs participated in surveying the boundary line between North Carolina and the Cherokee Nation in 1802, he purchased sweet potatoes, cabbage, corn, and even "Indian bread" from men.[97] Of the eighty-seven receipts Meigs issued to his suppliers, only three—for two chickens, forage, and "provision"—were to women. Women's total direct income from the survey was only $3.75.[98] This does not mean, of course, that women did not produce some of the commodities that Meigs bought from men or profit indirectly, but women did not sell the product of their labor, at least not to Meigs. While women remained important producers in Cherokee society, men became the entrepreneurs.

In 1801 several headmen from towns along the Tennessee River visited Hawkins: "They stated the improvements made in the products of the country; that a total change had taken place in the habits of the nation since the introduction of the plan for their civilization." Even more significantly, these men requested Hawkins's aid. They told him "that a desire for individual property was very prevalent, and that the current of conversation now was how to acquire it, by attention to stock, to farming and to manufactures."[99] These men viewed "civilization" in strictly material terms: it was a way to obtain "individual property." With the end of the deerskin trade and colonial wars, men had lost an acceptable way to express the aggressive, competitive, individualistic male culture that had shaped their lives. Similarly, the lustre faded on symbols of that lifestyle—guns, war trophies, items of personal adornment. Now they saw an opportunity to reorient male culture toward the acquisition of "individual property," and property became an emblem of success.

In the first decade of the nineteenth century, business opportunities abounded in the Cherokee Nation, and intermarried white men and their sons as well as native Cherokees eagerly took advantage of these. The agent employed a blacksmith to repair tools, but the demand for his services was such that several Cherokees went into partnerships with smiths. Similarly, the demand on the public miller led individual Cherokees to construct their own grist- and sawmills and to employ skilled white men to run them.[100] By 1804 the business of the National Council was business.

The council granted five-year leases for "houses of entertainment" along the Cumberland Road through Cherokee territory and issued permits to blacksmiths, wheelwrights, millers, a cooper, and saltpeter makers. Apparently agreeing with Meigs on the importance of education in transacting "the ordinary business required in civilized life," the headmen also issued permits to a schoolmaster and Moravian missionaries on the condition that the latter focus on education.[101]

The completion of the 220-mile-long road between Augusta, Georgia, and Nashville, Tennessee, opened other possibilities for men to profit. Individual Cherokee men, in partnership with whites, obtained contracts for taverns and ferries, a turnpike company was organized for the maintenance of the road and then subcontracted its obligations, and a Cherokee applied for the mail contract.[102] The Georgia road proved so successful in facilitating commerce that the Cherokees built another 300 miles of wagon roads at their own expense.[103] In addition to their income from these enterprises, according to Meigs, "they have no inconsiderable quantity of cash in circulation which they receive annually for the sale of cattle and swine."[104] James Vann, in fact, had sufficient cash in 1805 to be robbed of $3,500.[105]

Just as many Cherokee men failed to become great warriors, not all Cherokees shared equally in the spoils of economic expansion. In 1809 Meigs wrote to the secretary of war: "A spirit of industry does by no means pervade the general population. The greatest number are extremely poor from want of industry. The hunting life is here at an end: but a predilection for the hunter state pervades a great part of the Cherokees."[106] These Cherokees, he believed, should move west of the Mississippi. Meigs defined "want of industry" as the refusal of "the men to labour in the Fields with their own hands."[107] But even wealthy Cherokee men did not "labour." They merely had the capital, inherited from white fathers or acquired through trade, horse stealing, or official position, to invest in other kinds of labor. As town chiefs and members of the National Council, prominent men had the power to award themselves contracts and permits or to receive gifts, bribes, and private reservations from the federal government.[108] These men adroitly used their capital and political positions to increase wealth and the symbol of success, individual property.

The statistical table Agent Meigs sent to the secretary of war in 1809 indicated a remarkable change in Cherokee material culture. "The Cherokees," he asserted, "[have] prospered by the pastoral life and by domestic manufactures." Livestock abounded and spinning wheels whirred throughout the Nation.[109] In more fundamental ways, however, Cherokee lives remained remarkably untouched: the Cherokees had adapted "civilization" to their own expectations of men and women. Cherokee women used the civilization program to embellish their culture, but they did not transform it. Certainly, women added new crops, cotton in particular, and new skills such as spinning and weaving, but they continued to farm, keep house, and tend children just as they always had done. Similarly, men's culture retained the basic ethic of eighteenth-century hunting and warring. Aggression and competition, however, found expression in the rapidly expanding market economy. The deerskin trade had educated men far more than women in European economic practices and values, and the industrial and market revolutions and the civilization program made that knowledge increasingly valuable. Unlike the deerskin trade of the eighteenth century, the emerging "civilized" economy generated substantial Native wealth, considerable internal inequality, and a host of problems that the Cherokees had never before had to confront. As the first decade of the nineteenth century drew to a close, Cherokees had to resolve complex issues involving the individual ownership, state protection, legitimate enhancement, and just inheritance of property. Men and women shared many of the same concerns about both real and chattel property, but their property interests were rooted in different gender conventions: individual property reflected male culture while common ownership of realty formed the basis of women's culture. The Cherokees' attempt to reconcile the corporate ethic of farmers and the competitive ethic of entrepreneurs gave rise to the Cherokee republic.

SIX

Women in the Early Cherokee Republic

Cherokee clans traditionally fulfilled the basic responsibilities of government: through retribution and retaliation, they maintained order and provided defense. Leadership rested with those of proven ability, and women as well as men participated in decision making. A centralized Cherokee government originated in the late eighteenth century out of the need to coordinate foreign policy and to protect the entire nation from violence provoked by the actions of individual warriors. In 1794 the last belligerent Cherokees made peace with the United States, and the Cherokee political agenda shifted from war and peace to property, a chief concern of the "civilization" program. The Cherokee republic, with written laws and constitution, centralized authority, and delegated power, emerged from this agenda. Property concerned men and women, but culture and history conditioned them to think about property in different ways. In Cherokee law, different kinds of property embodied different values, which found expression in gender. Protection of individual rights characterized the Cherokees' approach to personal property. Hunters and warriors had embraced individualism far more strongly than farmers who worked as a group on land shared by their matrilineage, and consequently, personal property expressed male values. Commonly held real property, on the other hand, reflected the corporate ethic that governed women's lives. As the Cherokees created their republic in the early nineteenth century, they struggled to reconcile these two value systems and to create a code of laws in which individual and community, private and public, men and women balanced each other.

Pressure for cessions made the Cherokees wary of the civilization program, particularly aspects that dealt with property. In 1806 Agent Meigs told the Cherokees that the president wanted "to have every man enjoy his own property, [and] to make estates by industry." Meigs cited the president's wishes as evidence that the federal government did not intend to dispossess the Cherokees, and he pointed out that individual ownership of realty meant that "it will not be in the power of any Council to sell your farms as has hitherto been the case."[1] The Cherokees, however, decided that individual temptation to sell land outweighed the likelihood of cessions by the council, and so they rejected individual, fee simple titles for landholders.

Instead of recognizing land as a commodity, the Cherokees developed a bifurcated system of property holding. They individually owned personal items, livestock, slaves, and improvements such as houses or fences that a person erected on the land, but the land itself, as well as natural resources, belonged to the Nation.[2] The civilization program, with its emphasis on agriculture, quite unintentionally confirmed and enhanced the value of commonly held land while it encouraged commerce and the acquisition of substantial personal property. The program also enabled the Cherokees to construct a political system that protected both commonly held real estate and privately owned improvements and chattels. Indeed, property became the major concern of the Cherokee republic, and in attempting to protect both private and common property, Cherokee government intersected the lives of women in profound ways.

Women as well as men had a vested interest in the protection of private property and the preservation of the common domain, but the relationships of men and women to these two species of property were not exactly the same. Women traditionally had been the farmers in Cherokee society, and they remained stationary while men hunted, traded, fought, and negotiated. Cherokees associated women with the earth and its bounty. When the Cherokee council referred to "Mother Earth" in 1801, they gendered their homeland.[3] Such reference was not common, but the crops that took root in the earth had a clear cosmological association with women through Selu, whose blood soaked the ground and germinated corn. Men had no such mythical connection to the land: when Kana'ti discovered his wife's death, he became a wanderer who never returned to his homeland.[4] Like Kana'ti, men went abroad in search of game while women stayed home, hoed their corn, and became Selu's heirs. Women made particular plots theirs by farming them. Since the women of a matrilineage normally worked together, the land belonged to the matrilineage that used it, and through their maternal kin succeeding generations of women inherited their right to farm it. Consequently, women had a profound interest in the Nation's land and genuine concern about any proposed cession or change in land tenure. Farming—and by implication land use—helped define them as women just as hunting—and the abandonment of homeland that it entailed—defined men.

With the end of colonial wars and the decline of the deerskin trade, men began to reorient male culture toward the acquisition of "individual property" through commerce.[5] The United States government encouraged this shift. In 1806 Agent Return J. Meigs told the Cherokees that President Thomas Jefferson wanted them "to carry on business to buy & sell & to transact all your affairs like men who possess property of their own."[6] The definition of individual property, however, was not always clear: for a while, leading men used the Nation's annuity—annual payments by the federal government for previously ceded land—to pay off individually acquired debts.[7]

Cherokee women as well as men owned private property. Clothing, jewelry, and items of personal use traditionally belonged to an individual, and the Cherokees so closely associated these things with a person that they interred such items with the owner's corpse.[8] Through eighteenth-century trade, Cherokees acquired an enormous array of goods, many of which had considerable value, and by the time of the American Revolution, the Cherokees had largely given up the practice of burying valuable trade goods, like guns or hoes, with the deceased.[9] In this trade, men accumulated far more than women because they procured the deerskins that served as currency in the trade, and they used deerskins to purchase guns and ammunition, which they held individually. Men also gained greater familiarity with the European concept of private property, and so men had a somewhat clearer view of European rules that regulated it.

The hoes and kettles that men provided women probably belonged to households rather than individuals and passed from one generation to the next in a matrilineage. As a result, women tended to have less knowledge of or interest in private property than men. Their central role and permanent residence in matrilineal households made the distinction between what belonged to the family and what belonged to the individual less important. Nevertheless, they could not escape the broader changes that their new material culture entailed and the questions that it raised. Precisely which things belonged to an individual, or to a household, or to the Cherokee people as a whole? What rules governed the sale of goods? Who inherited them? Because women and men often viewed their new material wealth differently, they sometimes had very different answers to these questions.

Livestock provides a good example. For women, animal husbandry was an extension of their role as farmers; for men, herding substituted for hunting, and rustling sometimes replaced warfare, particularly among restless young men. The agent's records reveal controversies between men and women over livestock that suggest ideological as well as personal conflict. For example, when William Bright returned a horse he had hired from Nelly Crittenden, he compensated her for an injury to the horse's back. Her husband later took the horse to Bright's farm and demanded payment for the useless animal. Bright was absent, but his wife agreed to exchange the horse for a cow and calf. The horse subsequently recovered and wandered back to the Crittendens' farm. At this point Nelly Crittenden refused to give it up. Then the horse died, and she seized Bright's gun at a ball game in payment for the horse.[10] Crittenden's apparently irrational behavior probably resulted from her attempt to deal with a new form of property in a traditional way. Husbands and wives normally held separate property in Cherokee society, and so the payment to the husband may not have compensated Nelly for the horse. No wonder she refused to give up the horse a second time. But why did she demand payment after the horse died? Perhaps she believed compensation in addition to that originally paid was due, or perhaps she believed that Bright killed the horse through some nefarious means. In any event, William Bright and Nelly Crittenden were not operating on the same assumptions about property rights and justice.

The traditional Cherokee judicial system based on retribution and clan vengeance seemed inadequate to deal with new species of property, particularly when it involved the ambiguous legal relationship between Cherokees and neighboring whites. John Black, a white man, bought a cow from a Cherokee named Willnoi about 1806. Nancy Maw claimed that the cow had been stolen from her. Black offered to sell the cow back to Willnoi so that it could be returned to its rightful owner, but Willnoi refused. After five years of trying to resolve the dispute, Maw simply drove the cow and its increase, now a total of five cows, to her house, but Black took them back.[11] Maw had no legal evidence that the cows were hers, and the Cherokees had no formal courts in which she could seek justice from Willnoi. When she retrieved her cows, she acted according to traditional Cherokee jurisprudence, but old ways did not resolve new problems.[12] The Cherokees had to devise new ways for dealing with their changing world.

In 1808 Thomas Jefferson wrote to the Cherokees that "once you have property, you will want laws and magistrates to protect your property and person."[13] Jefferson's suggestion came a little late, for the Cherokee council already had acted. As early as 1797, the council, according to Hawkins, "appointed some warriors expressly to assist the chiefs in preventing horse stealing."[14] The Lighthorse, as the Cherokees often called their national police force, operated only sporadically until 1808, when the council authorized the organization of "regulating parties . . . to suppress horse stealing and robbery of other property . . . and to give their protection to children as heirs of their father's property, and to the widow's share."[15] The council's attention to property in what is often regarded as the Cherokees' first written law reflects the interests of the men who composed that body. So did the laws they subsequently enacted: a substantial proportion of them dealt with protection of private property and regulation of the economy.[16] Such matters remained central to Cherokee men, particularly those with political power, and only peripheral to the preponderance of Cherokee women. Nevertheless, the actions of the council often had a profound effect on individual women and on the underpinnings of Cherokee women's status.

Through its laws, the republic usurped many of the prerogatives of clans and undermined the principle of matrilineal kinship. In particular, the inheritance practice established by the council and given the protection of the Lighthorse in 1808 dramatically reordered traditional lines of descent, which had been strictly matrilineal. Although the inheritance of property had normally been of little consequence to the Cherokees, since they lived at the subsistence level and buried personal items with the dead, this new inheritance law threatened to reorder descent and to replace maternal blood ties with paternal material ties. A subsequent law in 1825 compounded the problem by providing that the property of both men and women who died intestate be divided among their children and surviving spouse.[17] Those who wrote wills, an innovation, were the very people least likely to follow traditional practices, and so on paper, the transformation became universal.

Such a change is exactly what the "civilizers" had in mind. In Jefferson's 1806 message, Meigs told the Cherokees, the president instructed them "to leave their property when they are called away to their children."[18] Meigs and other outsiders regarded the Cherokee practice of matrilineal descent as cruel to widows and children. Under matrilineal descent, a man's belongings went to his blood relatives, usually brothers and sisters, while his wife and children, who were not blood relatives, received nothing. According to Meigs, such inheritance practices "left [the wife and children] destitute unless she had some property which she brought to the family or acquired by her industry afterwards."[19] Of course, Meigs exaggerated. Women had their own property, separate from that of men, and common ownership of land meant that they were never landless, although they conceivably could lose the improvements their husbands claimed. Nevertheless, the great fortunes that were emerging in the early nineteenth century belonged to men, and many of these men wanted to bequeath their wealth to their children. For example, Doublehead, a Chickamaugan warrior who enthusiastically embraced capitalism, left his property to two sons and two daughters (their mother had died earlier) when he was killed in 1807 for his unscrupulous dealings.[20] Such a radical change in inheritance patterns created a number of problems. Meigs, one of the executors of Doublehead's estate, had to struggle to preserve the bequest intact.[21]

Two estates settled soon after the enactment of the law further demonstrate the confusion and strife that resulted when wealthy men left wills providing for dispersal of their estates contrary to customary practices. When James Vann died in 1809, he bequeathed his household furnishings to his wife Margaret and the remainder of his substantial estate to his favorite son, twelve-year-old Joseph. The will left his other children nothing and his wife homeless. The executors presented the will to the National Council, and the council, according to Moravian missionary John Gambold, "empowered them to make some amends to Vanns other children as likewise to the widow, and have likewise decreed, that the Widow shall have Liberty to live in her late husbands House, as long as she pleases." What seemed equitable to the executors and council, however, did not please some of Vann's relations, particularly his sisters. Those in charge of administering the estate "found such rude opposition from them" that one "resolved to resign his Executorship at the next Council."[22] The dispersal of Vann's property contrary to matrilineal descent set off a family feud in what was already a contentious lot.[23]

The oral will of William Shorey, who also died in 1809, precipitated a similar family squabble. Shorey, son of a white Tory who had married a Cherokee woman, supposedly dictated a will to his great-nephew John Ross. To his two young daughters, Alcey and Lydia, he left four slaves, cattle, and horses, which he instructed his sister, Anne McDonald, to divide between them when they reached adulthood. He bequeathed two slaves to his sister, part of an island to her grandson John Ross, and another slave to her grandson-in-law. He made the following provision for his eldest daughter Elizabeth (Bessey) Lowry: "I have given her horses, cattle, &c that goes under her name to the amount of three hundred dollars lawful money which property she has received all [I] intend she will get."[24] Elizabeth, however, took charge of her sisters, according to Anne's husband John, "with a view to obtain the property." Elizabeth conceded that Shorey might have engaged in musings about such a distribution of his estate when he was drunk, but she claimed that Shorey "never menched nothing of the kind when he was sober" and that he left no written will to that effect. She even produced Shorey's widow (not mother to the girls) to verify her assertion, but the McDonalds countered that the widow "had quited Shoreys bed & board without any just cause long before his decease." This case also ended up before the council, which found in favor of McDonald.[25]

Shorey's will demonstrates the difficulty of interpreting a specific inheritance exclusively along the lines of one system or the other. His bequests to his sister and her grandson (her daughter's son) were fully in accord with matrilineal descent, and Elizabeth Lowry's behavior toward her sisters probably was consistent with a matrilineal kinship system. Elizabeth, Alcey, and Lydia, however, may not have shared the same mother, in which case the eldest sister's behavior is inconsistent. Shorey, in any event, did not conform to the principles of matrilineal descent when he exhibited such concern for the welfare of his young daughters. Traditionally they would have become the charges of their mother's clan members. What all this points to is enormous confusion over the rules governing inheritance. And the effect of this confusion was an erosion of the matrilineal clan system that earlier had ordered descent without question or controversy.

The Cherokee council's attempt to reorder descent coincided with an assault on a major function of clans—personal protection through blood vengeance. Traditionally matrilineal clans had the responsibility for avenging the deaths of clan members. The principle of retaliation also extended to those believed to be responsible for accidental deaths and, after the institution of the Lighthorse, to those who killed other Cherokees in the performance of their official duties. "Civilizers" objected to the "vile principle of retaliation" and urged the Cherokee council to take action to prevent its implementation.[26] They believed that the government alone had the responsibility for protecting life and for punishing those who took life. For an extra-governmental body such as a clan to assume such responsibilities was, in their view, barbarous.

The council first acted against blood vengeance in 1797. In the presence of Benjamin Hawkins "they did . . . pronounce, after solemn deliberation, as law, that any person who should kill another accidentally should not suffer for it, but be acquitted; that to constitute it a crime, there should be malice and an intention to kill."[27] In these chaotic times, enforcement of such a provision proved impossible. In 1802 Meigs complained "that a man and woman supposed to be of Mr. Runions family in your neighborhood have been killed by an Indian of the name of the *Dirt Bottle* (alias) Catah Cookee, the Uncle of Sam who was killed by accident by a Mr. Runion in July last."[28] Many Cherokees, like Sam's uncle, still believed that they had a sacred duty to avenge the deaths of clan kin, whose spirits could not be dispatched until they had done so, and council pronouncements to the contrary had little effect. Not long after Dark-Anse killed Hen-and-Chickens in 1802, a chief told Meigs that "the murderer Indian had now paid the Debt that way one must pay & that he was gone above."[29]

When retaliation crossed the boundary between Cherokees and whites, disparities in the two legal systems threatened peace along the frontier. Meigs confronted enormous obstacles in getting state authorities to bring white murderers to justice and in convincing Cherokees to restrain themselves from seeking vengeance. He had some satisfaction in 1804 when a council at Eustenaulee announced that "we shall be glad to hear that no retaliation has taken place" against white North Carolinians for the murder of a Cherokee child and the wounding of his father. But the council also wanted affirmation of judicial parity: "These acts of your bad people towards us will not be the means of spoiling the treaties existing between the United States and as therefore we hope you will act well on your part towards us."[30] The refusal of white juries to convict those who had murdered Cherokees, however, made Meigs's task of keeping peace particularly difficult and jeopardized cooperative projects such as the Georgia road.[31] Ultimately, the United States resorted to the payment of compensation to the families of murdered Indians, a practice that continued until 1820.[32]

The Cherokees took a major step toward creating a government along Anglo-American lines in 1810 when "the various clans or tribes which compose the Cherokee Nation, have unanimously passed an act of oblivion for all lives for which they may have been indebted." The clans also agreed that in the future, "no satisfaction shall be demanded for his [the victim's] life from his relatives or the clan he may belong to." Furthermore, the same rules applied within a clan: if one member of a clan intentionally killed another, "he shall be accounted guilty of murder and suffer accordingly."[33] The Cherokee government rather than a Cherokee's family now assumed responsibility for punishing murder and, by implication, for protecting a person's life. Meigs saw this as a great advance over clan retaliation in which "the passions are aroused to revenge rather than to do Justice which should be the object of punishment."[34] Nevertheless, a most sacred duty had passed from the matrilineal clan, an extended kin group that included women and conveyed membership through women, to the exclusively male council. The role of matrilineal clans in protecting a person's life had invested enormous social, political, and spiritual power in families and in women. Rendering clans powerless had a corresponding effect on women.

The council evolved as the Cherokees' political organization moved toward the centralization and delegation of power. In the eighteenth century prominent headmen from various towns found it advantageous to negotiate jointly with Europeans and to exercise control over young warriors whose actions threatened the accords they had made. Foreign policy, both negotiations and war, was the business of men, and so informal national councils that responded to eighteenth-century exigencies were composed of men—in particular, war chiefs.[35] After the American Revolution, circumstances changed and so did the composition of the council. The sons of intermarried white men began to take seats alongside the sons of warriors. The council's admission of the descendants of traders, Tories, and other white men who had settled in the Cherokee country and married Cherokee women reflected two distinct realities of Cherokee life. First, because their mothers were Cherokee, the matrilineal Cherokees considered these men to be Cherokee, not mixed-bloods or "half-breeds," as whites saw them. Second, in a period of increasing contact with the United States and its citizens, bilingual and bicultural men possessed the expertise essential to a new Cherokee way of life and commanded the kind of respect that prominent warriors had when their skills were in demand.

The specter of land cession created its own divisions within the Cherokee Nation, and concerted action seemed more desirable than ever before. With a major cleavage between Lower and Upper towns in the first decade of the nineteenth century, Cherokees struggled to establish a representative body that had the authority to speak for the Nation and the power to enforce its decisions. Finally, in 1809 the Cherokee republic, with a centralized government that exercised expanded, delegated power, emerged from a crisis generated by land cession and political corruption. The council established an executive committee to manage the affairs of the Nation; the National Council, which met each fall, had the right to ratify or revoke the committee's actions.[36] Such an action seemed reasonable since matters frequently arose that demanded attention before the National Council's annual meeting. Subsequent Cherokee political history involves the refinement and elaboration of the 1809 structure, and an act in 1817 provided for the general election of a Standing Committee to make decisions—except land cessions—when the council was not in session.[37] The consequence of this process toward centralizing and formalizing political power, however, was to distance women further from politics.

Town councils seem to have been the venue for women's participation in government. When American Board missionary Daniel Butrick visited Turkey Town in 1824, he noted in his journal that women, men, and children attended the local council meeting.[38] Few accounts of such meetings survive because outsiders did not normally attend local council sessions, and in any event, Cherokees rarely deliberated in front of non-Cherokees. The Moravians who observed negotiations over the Georgia road in 1803 noted that whenever the Cherokees needed to discuss their position, they withdrew from the presence of whites and "met secretly." The Moravians also implied that the Cherokees recognized distinct interest groups; in this case, "the young warriors" deliberated as a body.[39]

Further evidence of how women participated in government comes from Arkansas, where many Cherokees had moved following land cessions. In 1820 missionaries requested permission of a council of "the chiefs and head men" to open a school. After hearing the missionaries' formal presentation, "the chiefs then retired from the council-house; and in a few minutes, returned." They invited the missionaries to establish their school, and each member of the council shook their hands. The interpreter then told the missionaries "that a number of women wished to give us their hands also." The missionaries were happy to oblige the women: "We turned to the side of the council house, and received in succession, the hands of two rows of women, who had been sitting without, in the rear." It does not require too much imagination to speculate where the men had gone when they "retired from the council house." They probably had consulted the women, who had a direct interest in the education of their children.[40]

In the late eighteenth and early nineteenth centuries, political power in the Cherokee Nation shifted from local councils to the national government, in part because the threat of war and then land cessions demanded concerted action, but also because towns themselves lost much of their traditional significance and power. The "civilization" program had encouraged Cherokees to "scatter from their towns and make individual improvements," and the Cherokee council encouraged this demographic change by prohibiting settlement within a quarter mile of another person.[41] Living on widely dispersed farms, the Cherokees ceased to regard the council house as the focal point of their communities or local councils as important institutions in their lives. Furthermore, some missionaries prohibited converts from entering local council houses out of fear that religious rituals or bacchanalian debaucheries took place there, and the injunction prevented converts' participation in local government.[42]

This waning of town councils had enormous significance for women. Town councils had permitted women some indirect participation in national government, since town councils determined representatives to the National Council and served as courts. In 1820 the National Council further undermined the authority of local town councils by creating eight judicial districts and providing for the election of four delegates to the National Council from each district; in 1821, the council established a national superior court to hear appeals from the district courts.[43] This new male structure virtually eliminated women from any role in choosing representatives, arbitrating disputes, or meting out official justice. Finally, in October 1826 the General Council of the Cherokee Nation called for an election of delegates to a constitutional convention and nominated candidates. The council provided that "no person but a free male citizen who is full grown shall be entitled to a vote," and recommended only men as delegates. Not surprisingly, the constitution adopted by the convention excluded women from holding office and denied them the franchise.[44] The constitution did not explicitly prohibit women from participating, but it limited the privileges of citizenship to "free male citizens."

The men who dominated the constitutional convention and the Cherokee national government may have been elected, but their wealth and lifestyles were hardly representative of those of the Cherokee people. They patterned themselves after the white planters who played a major political role in the surrounding states. As early as 1809, Major John Norton, a visiting Mohawk, observed that a relatively small group of Cherokees aspired to leadership positions on the basis of "real or imaginary talents" or "because they have wealth."[45] The twelve signers of the constitution who can be located on the roll made in 1835 in preparation for removal owned 355 slaves, approximately 23 percent of all those in the Cherokee Nation, and at least seven had received reservations—private tracts within ceded territory that the federal government conveyed to chiefs willing to negotiate. The twelve farmed an acreage four times the average for Cherokee heads of household and produced five times as much corn and six times as much wheat as other Cherokees.[46] Most of these men had adopted the gender conventions as well as the economic values of white planters. In 1818 Charles Hicks, who became principal chief in 1827, described the most prominent men in the Nation as "those who have kept their women

& children at home & in comfortable circumstances."[47] John Ross, the first (and only) principal chief elected under the new constitution, sent his daughter Jane to the Moravian Female Academy in Salem, North Carolina, for her education, and a visitor to the home of Ross's brother Lewis remarked that his wife and daughters dressed "in English stile" with "leghorns—crapes—silks—and . . . many ornaments."[48] Trained and treated like elite women in the non-Native South, these women had connections to the new locus of power in the Cherokee Nation, but they were the Cherokee women least likely to attempt an exercise of power themselves.

The exclusion of women from formal political bodies had far less potential for diminishing their power, prestige, and status than the early elimination of women from the major functions of government—protection of property and person. Those who promoted "civilization" accepted the proposition "that security of person and property, is the basis of all our rights, and is the chief cause of our civilization."[49] By establishing a Lighthorse company to protect property and transferring punishment for murder to the national government, the Cherokees presumably took a giant step toward "civilization." Both of these actions, particularly the latter, excluded women from participation in the judicial system. Women presumably no longer personally sought return of stolen livestock. Nor did women have a hand in quieting "crying blood." Now they were supposed to go through male intermediaries to whom they were not necessarily related. By reordering inheritance and depriving clans of coercive authority, the council seriously undermined the matrilineal kinship system on which women's traditional status partly rested.

The council struck three other blows to matrilineality. In 1819 council action restricted white men to one wife and "recommended that all others should have but one wife hereafter."[50] In 1825 the council flatly outlawed polygamy.[51] Although whites generally considered polygamy degrading to women, multiple marriage as practiced by many polygamous Cherokees tended to strengthen matrilineality and the bonds among women. Cherokee men usually married sisters and traditionally lived in their wives' households; if their husbands separated from them, the women kept their children and property. Such families were a far cry from the patriarchal families Anglo-Americans—and some Cherokees—considered ideal. Cherokee John Ridge described objections to polygamy in the context of a more general attempt by the council "to pass a law regulating marriage," which had failed. The other regulation apparently embodied Christian notions of marriage with its emphasis on "morality among men, the same among women & a respect for their characters & matrimonial happiness"—that is, institution of the patriarchal family and restrictions on sexual autonomy.[52]

Also in 1825, the council severely compromised matrilineality when it extended Cherokee citizenship to "the children of Cherokee men and white women, living in the Cherokee Nation as man and wife," and made them "entitled to all the immunities and privileges enjoyed by the citizens descending from the Cherokee race, by the mother's side."[53] The Cherokees had a long history of intermarriage between Cherokee women and white men. In the first decade of the century, many people, including Meigs, had advocated intermarriage as a way to promote rapid acculturation. In 1808 he defended his position to Chulisa and Sour Mush: "You say I encouraged marriages between white men & Cherokee women. I always have and shall do it because your women are industrious & because I conceive that by this measure civilization is farther advanced than in any other way having always considered the whole human race as brothers."[54] Cherokees had little objection to Meigs's proposal, but matrilineality presented a major obstacle to the reverse—the intermarriage of Cherokee men and non-Cherokee women. Cherokee citizenship stemmed from clan membership, and the recognition of children with non-Cherokee mothers as Cherokees required suspension of the principle of matrilineal descent. In 1824 Shoe Boots, a prominent warrior, asked the council to do just that when he requested that his children by his African-American slave be granted Cherokee citizenship. Demanding that Shoe Boots "cease begetting any more children by his Slave woman," the council nevertheless extended citizenship to the children.[55]

The marriage of John Ridge, son of the prominent Major Ridge, probably prompted the council's far more sweeping action that effectively divorced citizenship from matrilineal kinship. In 1825 young Ridge married a white woman whom he had met while a student at the Foreign Mission School of the American Board of Commissioners for Foreign Missions in Cornwall, Connecticut. Outside the Cherokee Nation, enthusiasm for intermarriage with Indians had waned considerably by the 1820s. Ridge's marriage and that of his cousin Elias Boudinot to another daughter of Cornwall in 1826 touched off riots in New England, acrimony in a number of newspapers, and cowardice in the American Board, which closed the Foreign Mission School.[56] Many missionaries in the field, however, still supported the concept of intermarriage. American Board missionary William Chamberlain told Major Ridge that he "was willing that the young people of different nations should marry where they pleased."[57] For some individuals, the Cherokee law merely removed an obstacle to marriage to white women; for the Cherokees as a people, it further devalued matrilineal kin ties.

Finally, in 1826 the council prescribed a penalty of fifty lashes for "any woman or women whatsoever, who shall be found guilty, before any of the courts of justice, of committing infanticide during her or their state of pregnancy."[58] The evidence for Cherokee practice of abortion or infanticide is murky. In 1805 missionary Gideon Blackburn asserted that women aborted pregnancies so that they could accompany husbands on hunting expeditions.[59] Although such a reason presumably no longer existed, a report from Dwight Mission in 1829 implied that infanticide continued among the Cherokees who moved to Arkansas.[60] At this time, however, mission periodicals were rife with lurid accounts of female infanticide in India, and it is possible that the council passed this provision to placate missionaries, who tended to lump "savage" peoples together and assume that they all observed the same customs.[61] Nevertheless, the Cherokees traditionally had a clear concept of the world becoming overcrowded, and so they may indeed have used abortion to limit population or infanticide to eliminate weak or deformed infants.[62] In any event, the council found cause to intrude into what certainly would have been solely a woman's prerogative. Women once had controlled entry into the Cherokee world. Now the council, composed exclusively of men, had assumed that authority.

The provision that abolished clan vengeance in 1810 came not from the council, but from "the various clans or tribes which compose the Cherokee Nation." At that point, neither individuals nor representatives of Cherokee towns made up the Cherokee Nation: clans did. By 1828, however, highly acculturated Cherokees such as Elias Boudinot, editor of the *Cherokee Phoenix,* regarded clans as anachronisms that held merely antiquarian interest. In 1829 he penned an essay, "Indian Clans," in which he described the clans' chief function: "This simple division of the Cherokees formed the grand work by which marriages were regulated, and murder punished." The former he found innocuous enough, but the latter he judged "savage and barbarous." Boudinot assured his readers that twenty years earlier, the Cherokees had abolished clan vengeance and "from that time, murder has been considered a governmental crime." In order to educate those who did not know the rules governing revenge and to demonstrate how far the Cherokees had progressed, he listed the major principles of the abandoned system:

The Cherokees as a nation, had nothing to do with murder.
Murder was punished upon the principle of retaliation.
It belonged to the clan of the murdered to revenge his death.
If the murderer fled, his brother or nearest relative was liable to suffer in his stead.
If a man killed his brother, he was answerable to no law or clan.
If the murderer (this however is known only by tradition) was not as respectable as the murdered, his relative, or a man of his clan of a more respectable standing was liable to suffer.
To kill, under any circumstance whatever, was considered murder, and punished accordingly.

These laws, Boudinot told his readers, had been "rigorously executed" in the past, but in the new Cherokee republic, they had become merely "vestiges of ignorance and barbarism."[63]

Boudinot noted in his article that clans were matrilineal—"a child invariably inheriting the clan of his mother"—but he did not dwell on the implications. In fact, matrilineality meant that a child's mother and her kin were the ones responsible for protection and vengeance, not the child's father or paternal relatives. Although men may have been the ones who normally exacted vengeance, the connection to avenging kin was solely through women and women were equally members of the clan to whose responsibility vengeance fell. When clans ceased to perform that function, however, Cherokees looked to the Lighthorse companies and the national government, male institutions in which women had no role, for their security. Indeed, the only function of clans that still had some relevance for Cherokees, according to Boudinot, was designating ineligible marriage partners—members of one's own clan and members of one's father's clan. Even this custom reportedly was declining: "But it has scarcely perhaps never been violated, except within a few years. Now it is invaded with impunity, though not to an equal extent with other customs of the Cherokees." Clans had become more like social clubs than judicial arbiters.

United States agents and Protestant missionaries had considerable influence in the early Cherokee republic, and Cherokee laws clearly reflect their views. When the Cherokees established a national police force, reordered inheritance patterns, abolished clan vengeance, extended Cherokee citizenship to descendants of intermarried white women, disfranchised women, and made polygamy and infanticide illegal, they won the approval of these powerful forces. This is not to suggest that the council was insincere in passing these measures. Indeed, many council members embraced the major tenets of the civilization program. The question that remains, however, is to what extent average Cherokees adopted such a redefinition of gender. Gender, the way in which cultures define appropriate behavior and roles for men and women, is deeply ingrained. Did the Cherokees reject old conventions in the space of several decades? Probably not, but documenting the persistence of old patterns of behavior presents substantial problems. The Cherokees and non-Cherokees who left records supported the civilization program, and in order to avoid damaging the Cherokees' image as a progressive, "civilized" Native people, they probably both ignored and hid those Cherokees whom they regarded as recalcitrant.[64]

The evidence, however, points to remarkable cultural persistence. The marriages of Ridge and Boudinot, for example, provoked considerable controversy among Cherokees as well as among New Englanders. When an American Board missionary questioned Major Ridge about the source of the opposition, "He said that those who opposed were of the lower class of people [and] that they were generally those who on account of their ignorance were very much prejudiced against the white people."[65] But there had never been any opposition when white men married Cherokee women, perhaps because the clan affiliation, citizenship, and ethnicity of children from such unions were not in doubt. When white women married Cherokees, matrilineal descent, to which many Cherokees still apparently adhered, made the situation quite different. Furthermore, opposition to Cherokee men taking non-Cherokee wives sometimes extended beyond "the lower class," presumably traditionalists, to the most highly acculturated Cherokees in the Nation. Although John Ross descended from interracial unions (in which wives were always Cherokee) and married a white woman himself in 1844 following the death of his Cherokee wife, he had "warmly opposed two such [intermarriages] in his family, and consented to a third because he believed opposition would do no good."[66]

While the council's extension of citizenship to the children of non-Cherokee women undermined matrilineal kinship, legislation did not expunge official recognition of citizenship based on clan affiliation. As late as the 1830s, the Cherokee Supreme Court recognized this earlier, but apparently still valid, legal tradition when it confirmed an eighteenth-century adoption of the Deer Clan. A white trader, Sam Dent, had killed his Cherokee wife, but he avoided clan vengeance by purchasing an African-American slave, Molly, whom the Deer Clan accepted and adopted in the place of the woman who had died. When a white woman claimed Molly and her sons, Edward and Isaac Tucker, as part of her inheritance, the council refused to countenance her claim and reaffirmed the citizenship of the mother and sons by virtue of Molly's adoption into a Cherokee clan.[67] In this case, clan adoption took precedence over other considerations, including racial prejudice, an attitude that many Cherokees had adopted as they acquired black slaves. Although the council had outlawed miscegenation involving people of African descent,[68] the race of the petitioners did not compromise their clan ties, despite the fact that those ties came through the adoption of an African American.

Many Cherokees continued to attach considerable significance to clans and looked to clans rather than the national government to provide order and protection. Long after the enactment of national laws against blood vengeance, missionary Daniel Butrick reported that the perpetrator of an assault "was now gone to avoid the revenging brother."[69] When Noochorwee of Aquohee received a reprieve from his death sentence for murder in 1829, the council felt compelled to place him "under the protection of the laws of this Nation," presumably because the victim's relatives presented a genuine threat to his life.[70]

The perpetuation of blood vengeance, as well as other traditional practices the council had attempted to eliminate, is difficult to document except by the almost total absence of violations in the judicial record. The Cherokee national government, for example, executed no one for murder until 1827, and the condemned man in this case was a Creek, not a Cherokee.[71] Furthermore, apparently the only prosecution for polygamy came in 1829 when Elizabeth Hildebrand Pettit filed suit against her white husband, who reportedly had a wife and several children in Missouri. The council ruled that he should relinquish his farm in the Nation to his wife and pay her five hundred dollars.[72] Either the Cherokees were exceptionally law-abiding or a dual system of jurisprudence existed in which some people, perhaps most, applied customary methods of social regulation to a traditional code of behavior and others followed the laws of the republic.

Perhaps the viability of matrilineal clans and the persistence of traditional gender conventions help explain a crosscurrent in the male council and its law code. While most laws undermined the position of women, other laws actually acknowledged and protected matrilineal kinship and the property rights of women. The 1817 "Articles for Government," which provided for the election of a Standing Committee, included as the fourth article, "The improvements and labors of our people by the mother's side shall be inviolate during the time of their occupancy."[73] Two years later, in the first act restricting polygamy, the council, contrary to the laws of surrounding states, formally established the right of married women to their property when it provided that "any white man who shall marry a Cherokee woman, the property of the woman so marry, shall not be subject to the disposal of her husband, contrary to her consent."[74] In 1828 the council amended the law concerning the dispersal of the estates of people dying intestate so that "the nearest relatives of the deceased shall have the right to recommend to the Circuit Court of the District in which the deceased lived, such person or persons as they shall choose, administer on the estate."[75] By failing to define "nearest relatives," the council permitted families flexibility to follow the kin rules of their choice. In 1829 the council extended protection of married women's property by prohibiting seizure of a woman's property for debts incurred by her husband.[76]

The provisions protecting married women's property probably affected most Cherokee women, but the number who held property separate from their husbands is difficult to determine. Spoilation claims from the War of 1812, including petitions from women who lost horses, cattle, and hogs as well as pots, plows, and fire irons, suggest that property ownership by women was widespread.[77] John Ridge observed that traditional Cherokee women tended to be more likely to have property separate from their husbands: "Property belonging to the wife is not exclusively at the control & disposal of the husband, and in many respects she has exclusive & distinct control over her own, particularly among the less civilized."[78] Even after removal and the Civil War, a United States congressional report noted that "it is not uncommon among full-bloods for the women to own most of the stock, and generally as much as their husbands."[79] Among less traditional Cherokees, women also owned considerable property independent of their husbands. When Elias Boudinot prepared to travel in the North before returning home from school in Connecticut, his mother asked the American Board administration in Boston to provide him with the necessary funds on the assurance that she would reimburse the Brainerd Mission with the proceeds from the sale of some of her livestock. Brainerd missionary Ard Hoyt assured the board, "She has cattle, & hogs that will soon do for pork."[80]

Some women's property included slaves. Of the 209 slaveholders in the Cherokee Nation in 1835, 20 were women; of 1,592 slaves, 129 belonged to women.[81] When Rachel Ratcliff made a will in 1821, her wealth consisted primarily of slaves:

I will and devise unto Kitty Ratliff, my half sister, daughter of Nancy Ratliff, one negro girl named Mary; the daughter of my old wench named Dinah—also I gave to my half sister Kitty Ratliff one negro Boy named Johnston, son of said Dinah my old wench—Secondly, I gave and Bequeath unto my other half sister Charlotta, Second daughter of Nancy Ratliff, one negro Girl called Eliza, daughter of my said old wench Dinah, also one negro Boy named Williamson, son of said wench. Thirdly I gave and bequeath unto my half Brother Robert Ratliff, Son of Nancy Ratliff, my negro woman named Dinah, also my negro boy named Taney, Fourthly I gave and bequeath unto my aforesaid half sister Kitty Ratliffe all my body Apparel of every description for her use exclusively.[82]

Women also owned improvements to real estate, received reservations under treaties in 1817 and 1819, and had their estates valued when they emigrated.[83] Perhaps a third of the names listed on the 1835 removal roll as heads of household are those of women.[84] Although men and women may have had different attitudes toward and concerns about property, property holding extended to both, although somewhat unequally.

Although clans may have continued to resolve disputes over property, women, like men, relied on the mechanisms of the Cherokee national government to protect their interests. In 1819 Betsey Broom, Mrs. Lesley, and four men complained to the National Council about infringement of their right to operate a turnpike. The council found in their favor and also recognized the obligations of the Widow Fool to maintain the road leading to her ferry.[85] The council ordered return of an improvement that Elizabeth Pack had purchased from Charles Hicks when a white man took "forcible possession . . . under pretext of having married a Cherokee wife."[86] Women appealed their cases to the Cherokee Supreme Court, although not nearly as often as men, and they consistently won cases against men in which farms and improvements were contested.[87] They also won a majority of cases involving ownership of slaves and livestock.[88] Other kinds of property for which women attempted to establish ownership or right to compensation before the Supreme Court include glassware and ostrich feathers.[89] Three women recorded the emancipation of their slave Prince and swore to "defend him against the claim or claims of any other person or persons," and Mary Stedman recorded a bill of sale in which she conveyed title to fourteen slaves—three generations of a family—as well as cattle, horses, and a wagon to Joseph Vann for $4,020.[90]

The United States government generally acknowledged and honored Cherokee law regarding married women's property rights. When Meigs attempted to sort out whether Cow, the husband, or Cooester, the wife, held title to an improvement, Cherokee law and custom shaped his decision: "I should be clearly of the opinion that Cooester could not be treated as the 'Head of a Cherokee family' were it not for the fact that she was the Mother of children by a former husband—and for the Cherokee law—that such children are not subject to the control of the second husband. The relation of husband and wife sits loosely upon them.—The families of each by a former marriage, acknowledge them *separate authority,* and their property is *separate.*"[91] The distinction between spouses' property extended to slaves as well as improvements.[92] In 1836 James Vaught sold to General Isaac Wellborn slaves his Cherokee wife, Catherine, had inherited from her father. She protested, and United States soldiers returned the slaves to her. Wellborn demanded trial in a Georgia court, which would have recognized her husband's title to the slaves, and an Alabama court ordered the slaves' return to Wellborn, but federal authorities recognized and protected Catherine Vaught's right to the slaves under Cherokee law.[93]

Marriage between white men and Cherokee women made protection of women's property rights, particularly those of married women, crucial. Whereas many whites and Indians married for legitimate reasons, some unscrupulous men took Cherokee wives solely for the purpose of gaining control of their property. Under the laws of the states surrounding the Cherokee Nation, a woman's property passed to her husband when they married, and many whites hoped to use matrimony to secure Cherokee land or, during enrollment for removal, payment for improvements. For example, Townsend, a white man and member of the infamous Georgia Guard, married the niece of a Cherokee named Oldfields, who had fled the chartered boundaries of Georgia after he got into trouble with the guard. Oldfields left his house and other improvements in the care of White Path, and they remained secure until Townsend, claiming that Oldfields had transferred title to his niece, broke in. One doubts both Townsend's honesty and his affection for Oldfields's niece: records reveal that "on the eve of his marriage he consulted a justice of the Superior Court of Cass County, Georgia, to know whether he could have these improvements valued as his property provided he married the girl."[94] In cases such as this, protecting the property rights of married women helped secure the common domain as well as individual claims.

The Cherokee national government's commitment to the preservation of common title to realty was perhaps the most important way that the early Cherokee republic embodied a feminine ethic in its legal code. All

Cherokees had once had strong communal values, but the deerskin trade and military alliances of the eighteenth century had promoted individualism on the part of Cherokee men. The "civilization" program emphasized similar values and encouraged individual acquisitiveness, particularly by men. By contrast, the selfless, nurturing, supportive role of women, extolled by "civilizers," enhanced the traditional corporate values of Cherokee culture. Land, and common title to land, was the physical expression of these values, and commonly owned land served as a check on the individualism and commercialism that increasingly characterized Cherokee male culture—at least the culture of the male elite who controlled the affairs of the Nation.

Meigs had hoped that the civilization program would lead Cherokees to "place a value on their land"—that is, to regard land as a commodity to be bought and sold.[95] For those men who engaged successfully in commerce and amassed individual wealth, the commodification of land seemed a logical step. But a more communitarian ethic rooted in traditional Cherokee culture and preserved in women's roles ultimately prevailed, even in the male National Council. A series of actions confirmed common title to realty and restricted the sale of improvements. The Cherokees adopted Articles of Government in 1817 "in order to deliberate and consider on the situation of our Nation, in the disposition of our common property of Lands, without the unanimous consent of the members of Council in order to obviate the evil consequences resulting in such course."[96] In 1822 the council vowed "not to dispose of even one foot of ground."[97] Three years later, the council clarified Cherokee property law "for the better security of the common property of the Cherokee Nation."[98] The constitution, unlike the United States Constitution, included the boundaries of the Cherokee Nation in its very first article and affirmed that "the lands therein are, and shall remain, the common property of the Nation."[99] In 1829 the council committed to writing "a law [which] has been in existence for many years, but not committed to writing, that if any citizen or citizens of this Nation shall treat and dispose of any lands belonging to this Nation without special permission from the National Authorities, he or they, shall suffer death."[100]

In order to protect commonly held land, the council restricted private property rights. In particular, it passed laws restricting the sale of improvements belonging to those who chose to emigrate.[101] The personal impact is apparent in the disposition of Dark Horse's estate. He bequeathed his property to his four sons, but two had emigrated. The court decided that only the two remaining in the east were entitled to the inheritance. The importance of preserving intact the common domain, in which women had a special interest, took precedence over the individual property rights so often championed in the National Council.

Although we know nothing about women's views on most measures passed by the council, we do know how they felt about land cession and the allotment of land to individuals. They had no formal role in the National Council, but on at least three occasions, Cherokee women petitioned that body—not as holders of individual property but as women. In 1817 the United States sought a large cession of Cherokee territory and removal of those who lived on the land in question. A group of Indian women met in their own council, and thirteen of them signed a message to the National Council. They recognized the source of their power: "The Cherokee ladys now being present at the meeting of the Chiefs and warriors in council have thought it their duties as mothers to address their beloved Chiefs and warriors now assembled." Referring to the members of the National Council as "our beloved children," they established their familial connection to the Cherokee homeland: "We have raised all of you on the land which we now have, which God gave us to inhabit and raise provisions. . . . If a father or mother was to sell all their lands which they had to depend on, which their children had to raise their living on, which would be bad indeed." They adamantly opposed cession and removal: "We have understood some of our children wish to go over the Mississippi, but this act of our children would be like destroying your mothers. Your mother and sisters ask and beg of you not to part with any more of our lands."[102]

The next year, the National Council met again to discuss not only another cession but also the possibility of allotting Cherokee land to individuals, an action the United States government encouraged as a preliminary step to removal. Allotment destroyed common ownership of land by dividing the Nation into parcels and assigning individual ownership to each parcel. Once again, Cherokee women reacted. As mothers, they affirmed their relationship to the land and to common title: "The land was given to us by the Great Spirit above as our common right, to raise our children upon, & to make support for our rising generations." Lest the council forget the proper order of relationships, the women addressed the members again as "our beloved children, the head men & warriors" and urged them "to hold out to the last in support of our common rights." As Cherokees, "the first settlers," and as mothers, these women "claim[ed] the right of the soil" and voted unanimously "to hold our country in common as hitherto."[103]

The effect of the women's protests in 1817 and 1818 is difficult to determine. In 1817 the Cherokees ceded tracts of land in Georgia, Alabama, and Tennessee, and in 1819 they made an even larger cession. In negotiating these treaties, the council resisted general allotment, in which all territory would have been divided into individually owned tracts, but both treaties contained provisions for some allotments to individuals including council members. Following the treaties, however, the council strengthened restrictions on alienation of improvements to the common domain. Furthermore, the Cherokees gave notice that they would negotiate no additional cessions—a resolution so strongly supported that the United States ultimately had to turn to a small unauthorized faction, led by men who had white wives, in order to obtain the minority treaty of 1835.[104]

Even in this final removal crisis, Cherokee women voiced their opposition to land cession. Influenced by government agents and Protestant missionaries, the women of two Cherokee communities felt compelled to preface their petition: "Although it is not common for our sex to take part in public measures, we nevertheless feel justified in expressing our sentiments on any subject where we feel our interest is as much at stake as any other part of the community." The language may have been more polished and the tone more deferential, but the message echoed earlier petitions: "We sincerely hope that there is no consideration which can induce our citizens to forsake the land of our fathers of which they have been in possession from time immemorial." New conventions stressed men as the fathers of the Nation, but once again, women described a familial bond to the land. As mothers, they argued against any action that would "compel us, against our will, to undergo the toils and difficulties or removing with our helpless families hundreds of miles to unhealthy and unproductive country."[105] Some fathers, however, had begun to rely on their own judgment rather than respect the will of the community, and this time, the "consideration" was sufficient for them to sell their homeland.

In December 1835, a small group of men who had no official standing signed the Treaty of New Echota, which provided for an exchange of the Cherokee homeland for territory west of the Mississippi and for the removal within two years of the entire Nation to this new country. As in other Cherokee land cessions, no women's names appear on the document, but women as well as men suffered the consequences of the Treaty of

New Echota. In late spring 1838, federal troops began rounding up Cherokees and imprisoning them in stockades in preparation for their removal west. A high death toll and pleas of Cherokee leaders persuaded President Martin Van Buren to delay removal to the winter of 1838–39, when the Nation moved west on what has become known as the Trail of Tears, a terrible experience shared by men and women.

On one level, women in the early Cherokee republic experienced steady exclusion from political life, but on another level, women's views and women's values remained essential to Cherokee national identity and public policy. Recognition and protection of common land concerned all Cherokees, but it held special meaning for women. Where the blood of the first woman, Selu, had soaked the ground, corn and beans sprang. Whenever Cherokee women tilled the fields and harvested the land's bounty, they affirmed their identity as women. Furthermore, common title to the land validated traditional Cherokee values of community and cooperation. Even as commerce and individual wealth had become increasingly important to Cherokees, particularly men, in the late eighteenth and early nineteenth centuries, most women continued to embody those traditional values and maintain their ties to the soil. In the end, common land proved to be an important defense against dispossession. As a result, women's roles and women's concerns remained central to the Cherokee republic.

SEVEN

Selu Meets Eve

The Cherokee republic's usurpation of many of the responsibilities of clans and its restrictions on women's autonomy coincided with an external ideological assault on the Cherokee concept of womanhood. Cherokees had always regarded women as different from men—just as Kana'ti, the first man, provided game, Selu, the first woman, provided corn and beans—but each enjoyed a distinct arena of power and each complemented the power of the other. The new view of womanhood promoted by policy makers, agents, and missionaries also recognized difference, but the roles ascribed to women left them in a distinctly subservient, largely powerless position. Christianity emphasized a hierarchy that placed men above women, and the growing romanticism of the period imbued the Protestant theology with intense emotionalism. Barbara Welter has called the idealized view of womanhood pervading middle-class American culture in the early nineteenth century the "cult of true womanhood."[1] Characterized by purity, piety, domesticity, and submissiveness, a true woman occupied a separate sphere apart from the ambition, selfishness, and materialism that permeated the man's world of business and politics. Her proper place was the home, which she made a haven from the outside world through her piety, morality, and love. Openly submissive to men, a true woman influenced them subtly through her purity and piety. When Thomas L. McKenney, the clerk in the War Department responsible for administering Indian affairs, wrote about the benefits of transforming Native society, he noted that only through "civilization" could the Indian woman "rise into her high distinction and shine out in all her loveliness, heaven's best gift to man"—that is, become a true woman.[2]

Just as the true woman embodied secular and religious ideals, the transformed Cherokee had to be both "civilized" and Christian. The task of accomplishing both objectives fell largely to missionaries. In 1799 Moravians sought permission, ultimately granted, to open a school. The missionaries of this pietist German sect labored alone, except for schools operated by the Presbyterian Gideon Blackburn from 1803 to 1810, until Congregationalists and Presbyterians (supported by the interdenominational American Board of Commissioners for Foreign Missions) arrived in 1816, to be followed shortly by Baptists and Methodists. Heavily influenced by the evangelicalism of the second awakening, these missionaries, many of whom were from the Northeast, sought to transform the world as well as win souls.[3] Consequently, they linked the spiritual salvation of the Cherokees to their worldly transformation.

For early-nineteenth-century reformers and philanthropists, the two were inseparable, an assumption deeply imbedded in evangelical discourse.[4] In the fictional dialogue of a missionary tract, a man asked his niece how "missionary experiments" proposed to accomplish the salvation of American Indians. She replied: "By educating the rising generation,—proclaiming the Savior's dying love, and diffusing a knowledge of the arts of civilized life."[5] The subjects of "missionary experiments" also linked teaching and preaching. A young woman from the American Board's Brainerd Mission wrote to a correspondent: "I think the missionaries are doing a great deal of good: if it were not for them, these children, that are here, would be without any knowledge of God, and now the most of them can read and write."[6] Missionaries in the field reported evidence that only confirmed the connection: "They appear to advance in civilization first in proportion to their knowledge of the gospel."[7] Various missionary societies argued, in chicken-and-egg fashion, which came first, but few evangelical Christians maintained that the two were independent.[8]

Missionaries undertook cultural transformation with religious zeal. When missionary Daniel Butrick received ordination in Boston, the officiating minister charged the candidates not "to improve the Indian language but to make the Indians English in their manners,—their religion, and their language." Although Butrick tried to learn Cherokee, he accepted the basic premise that all Anglo-American ways were preferable to Cherokee ways. In 1818 he joined other missionaries in the following observation: "The Natives already understand the art of raising corn & keeping cattle in the wood, but they have never experienced the advantage of pasture, fields & meadow. . . . If we had sufficient help to extend our agricultural business on the above plans, our example might be followed." They encouraged the raising of wheat, a "civilized" (i.e., European) crop, rather than corn, and concluded that "the condition of the people in the vicinity is much better" when local farmers began to grow "small grain." Butrick sought imitation in small things as well as large. Several years later, he wrote to his Boston headquarters for assistance in teaching some Cherokee women to plant flower gardens, a horticultural genre that had no Cherokee precedent.[9] The desire to help Cherokee women "improve" their homes extended beyond ornamental gardens. Ladies' missionary societies sent the Indians gowns, shirts, vests, stockings, and bed and table linens, "for it was thought by many that the sooner civilized habits were formed, in domestic arrangements, the better."[10]

Reverend Jedidiah Morse, like many advocates of this policy, believed that reformers should focus their efforts specifically on women: "It is essential to the success of the project of the Government, that the female among our native tribes, be raised from its present degraded state, to its proper rank and influence. This should be a *primary* object with the instructors of the Indians."[11] The elevation of Native women promised several results. First of all, civilization and Christianity would improve the lot of the women themselves, whom most missionaries regarded as "merely menial servants, and not honoured to be in company with men."[12] Second, through a woman's influence, her husband might be "led to acknowledge the reality and excellency of true religion."[13] Many evangelicals believed that "the noise and tumult of the active world often drowns the 'still small voice' of the Gospel, which sounds in the ear of the man of business," and so a special responsibility to reach them fell to women, "who do not mingle in the bustle and hurry of the world, who are required to a more quiet, though not to an unimportant sphere."[14] Finally and most important, women who "nurse and nourish every one that cometh into the world" had a unique opportunity to train their children, since God had given them "authority over the mind in its most pliant state, paramount to every other."[15]

Missionaries in the early stages of their ministry, however, usually considered it more practical to short-circuit "degraded" mothers and attend directly to children, whose habits had not yet been fixed. Except for the Methodists, missionaries preferred to teach children in boarding schools, where they had "the influence of example as well as precept," and to limit vacations, which "greatly retarded" their progress. In 1819 President James Monroe visited the American Board's Brainerd Mission and praised "the plan of instruction; particularly as the children are taken into the family, taught to work, &c." This was, the president believed, "the best, & perhaps the only way to civilize and Christianize the Indians."[16] Consequently, the little girls who attended the mission schools lived with the missionaries' families and followed a regimen designed to produce chaste, pious, submissive housewives.

Mission schools provided an elementary education for girls as well as boys. Either single women or the wives of male missionaries usually taught the girls, but all students studied the same academic subjects, which included reading, writing, spelling, arithmetic, geography, and history, as well as, by the late 1820s in some schools, the syllabary Sequoyah had developed for writing Cherokee. Examinations took place annually at the American Board schools, and the young scholars' parents attended. The teachers questioned students in their academic subjects as well as Bible history, catechism, and hymns, and "the girls showed specimens of knitting, spinning, mending, and fine needlework."[17] Missionaries had great confidence in their students' ability to learn. A Baptist missionary remarked that "though their skin is red, or dark, I assure you, their mental powers are white."[18] American Board missionaries concluded that "they are as bright & promising as any children of equal number we ever saw collected," and they managed to convey this conviction to the children, who sometimes doubted their abilities. Nancy Reece, a student at the American Board's Brainerd Mission, wrote to one of the school's benefactors: "When Miss Ames tells the two white girls they have done well, we often say they can do well, because they are white girls, though she says people at the North think that the Cherokees have as good a genius to learn if it was only cultivated. And I think they have."[19]

Mastery of the domestic arts was an essential part of the girls' education because, according to one missionary, "all the females need is a proper education to be qualified to fill any of the relations or stations of domestic life." The children at the mission schools performed a variety of tasks, and the division of labor approximated that in a typical Anglo-American farming family. The boys chopped wood and plowed fields, and the girls milked, set tables, cooked meals, washed dishes, sewed clothing, knitted, quilted, did laundry, and cleaned the houses.[20] This was far from the traditional division of labor in which women farmed and men hunted or, in its more recent rendering, engaged in commerce, but the missionaries regarded it as their duty to teach the Cherokees "that the raising of corn and otherwise managing the plantation belong to the male sex."[21] When Adam Hodgson visited Brainerd in 1820, the missionaries told him "that many of the Indians evinced, at first, an indisposition to labour in the field, especially as the females were entirely exempted from the task. . . . One of the Chiefs offered to find a slave who should work all day, if the Missionaries would excuse his son from agricultural labour between school-hours; but he was easily convinced of his mistakes, and apologized for his ill-judged request."[22] Just as boys did not want to farm, some girls objected to doing laundry, cooking meals, and scrubbing floors. Missionaries endeavored to convince them that "the charge of the kitchen and the mission table" was not degrading but was instead a "most important station," which taught them "industry and economy."[23]

Because their families were wealthy, some students were not accustomed to menial labor. Their objections to such work, therefore, derived from class as well as culture. Missionaries expressed anxiety over the first female students who lived with the mission family at Brainerd: "They had been accustomed to somewhat different living, from what we could give our numerous family."[24] No evidence suggests that missionaries accepted only children whose parents were wealthy—indeed, they often took in poor children and orphans—but the presence of Cherokees of substantial means provided considerable relief to the financially strapped missions. At very least, missionaries expected parents to be able to provide some of their children's clothing. Conforming to a traditional hospitality ethic, the parents of students usually shared produce and even cash with the missionaries.[25] Although the Baptist missionaries warned about dependence on contributions, they nevertheless based a proposal for two new schools on the ability of people in each locale to provide some support: "At M'Nair's, if a good teacher could be procured, the neighbouring families would contribute about $100 a year. The people at Notley met a few weeks ago, and agreed, if the Board would establish a school there, that they would contribute 500 lbs. of pork, and 120 bushels of corn."[26] The results of wealthy Cherokees' generosity were clear: the American Board reported that its school at Haweis, "owing to the respectable girls they have boarding with them, is now in a very flourishing state."[27]

Many missionaries thought that the best way to convert the Cherokees was first to convert their leaders, and consequently, they sought the children of the elite as students.[28] American Board missionaries frequently referred to the official positions of men they met or described them as "principal men of the town."[29] Along with family connections—such as "mother of Catharine," "is a widow," "has a lovely family"—American Board church rolls usually noted ancestry—"is a half-breed," "is a Cherokee," "is a black woman of Mr. Ross's," "is a white man." Rolls occasionally included a category, "Pedigree," in which they noted whether church members were middle class, lower class, or from a "respectable family."[30]

Missionaries may well have been more conscious of social and economic distinctions than were the children at the mission schools. In an attempt to improve the grooming habits of one young woman, Ann Paine "offered as a motive her obligation to set a good example to her nation as the daughter of their chief. . . . She never appeared more mortified than in hearing of her superiority of birth."[31] Through such admonitions, missionaries imparted to students an awareness of and concern with status.

Missionaries recognized the need to minister to all Cherokees, but most made only halfhearted attempts to do so. When the Baptists received permission to open a mission among the most culturally conservative Cherokees, American Board missionaries' relief that someone else was going to serve "the most ignorant and uncultivated" area was almost palpable.[32] Instead, missionaries usually preferred to establish satellite stations in places like Taloney where they could not set up a model farm or board children because "nearly or quite all the good land in this neighborhood is improved by men who value property."[33] Daniel Butrick noted "the great diference between the social classes within the Cherokee Nation" and criticized his fellow missionaries for their reluctance to minister to "the great body of these people." Instead, he charged, missionaries preferred to live like the Cherokee elite and "thus fix their marks entirely beyond the reach of all the common Indians."[34]

This sensitivity to ancestry, acculturation, and class extended to children at American Board mission schools, who were described as "full," "mixed," or "of the [mission] family."[35] At least some missionaries, however, do not seem to have equated ancestry and intellect. The Baptist Evan Jones found that "those who understand English improve as fast as any white children I have met with. . . . The full breeds also learn those things in which they have equal advantages, fully as fast as the others." Any apparent slowness on their part he attributed to "the dark and tedious business of spelling and combining sounds which they cannot articulate, and which convey no ideas to their minds."[36] A student at Brainerd also had an explanation for differences in performance: "We have twenty one Cherokee girls in our school but only six are full Cherokees. Some are learning very fast, I think all try but some have not so good a genius as others."[37]

Missionaries did link prosperity and Christianity, primarily because they believed Christian values of self-restraint and discipline brought material rewards, whereas the indolence associated with "savagery" condemned one to poverty. In writing about the family of Samuel Mills, a Cherokee man who had joined the church at Brainerd, the missionaries extolled their industry: "Their wealth was good as could be expected considering the degraded state from which they are raised."[38] More generally, they believed that nothing "but the Christian religion ever made men more comfortable in their outward circumstances."[39]

The great advantage of teaching Cherokee girls of all classes "industry and economy" was the influence they might exert in their own homes. One young woman wrote to northern benefactors: "We have the opportunity of learning to work and to make garments which will be useful to us in life." Another girl expressed gratitude that missionaries had taught the students "how to take care of families [so] that when we go home we can take care of our mothers house." A missionary assessed the impact of their work: "We cannot expect that the influence of these girls will have any great immediate effect on their acquaintance—but I believe in each case it is calculated to elevate the families in some degree, with which they are connected." Although missionaries and students expected the domestic arts learned in the mission schools to improve the parental home, they believed that the primary benefit would be to the homes the young women themselves established. Missionary Sophia Sawyer specifically hoped to "raise the female character in the Nation" so that "Cherokee gentlemen" could find young women "sufficiently educated for companions."[40] In 1832 missionaries reported with satisfaction that the girls who had married "make good housewives and useful members of society."[41] Missionaries rejoiced when they united in matrimony young couples of "industrious habits & reputable behavior" who were "very decent and respectable in their moral deportment."[42]

Achieving "moral deportment" at the mission schools was no simple matter, but missionaries considered the teaching of middle-class sexual mores to be one of their chief responsibilities. According to some reports, they enjoyed success. In 1822 American Board missionaries reported: "Mr. Hall thinks that the moral influence of the school has been considerable. . . . The intercourse between the young of both sexes was shamefully loose. Boys & girls in their teens would strip and go into bathe, or play ball together naked. They would also use the most disgustingly shameful language, without the least sense of shame. But, when better instructed, they became reserved and modest." To maintain decorum, the missionaries tried to make certain that girls and boys were never alone together: "When the girls walk out any distance from the house they will be accompanied by instructors." Male and female students normally attended separate classes. When Sophia Sawyer became ill in 1827, she reluctantly sent the small girls to the boys' school, but she taught the larger girls in her sickroom. Miss Sawyer so feared for the virtue of the older girls that she asked the governing board "could not the boys at Brainerd be at some other school[?]" The Moravians did resort to separate schools. The American Board, however, simply put locks on the bedroom doors.[43]

Even with the precautions, difficulties arose. In 1813 the Moravians recorded in their journal: "After prayer we directed our talk toward Nancy, indirectly admonishing her to abstain from the lust which had gripped her. She seemed not to have taken it to heart, for instead of mending her ways continues to heap sin upon sin." Nancy Watie, along with her cousin Sally Ridge, later moved to an American Board mission. Their fathers, David Watie and his brother Major Ridge, were prominent in the Cherokee Nation, and they left strict instructions that their daughters be supervised constantly and their purity preserved. A problem arose when teenage boys in the neighborhood began calling on the two girls at the mission. At first, the young people decorously sat in front of the fire under the watchful eyes of the missionaries, but soon the conversation shifted from English to Cherokee, which none of the chaperons understood. Suspecting the worst, the missionaries ordered the suitors to "spend their evenings in some other place." A year later, however, the missionaries reported that despite their care, the girls "had given themselves up to the common vices."[44]

The missionaries did not, of course, intend to cloister the young women to the extent that they did not meet suitable young men. Sophia Sawyer observed: "Like all females they desire the admiration of men. They can easily be shown that the attention, or good opinion of men without education, taste, or judgement is not worth seeking, & to gain the affection or good opinion of the opposite character, their minds must be improved, their manner polished, their persons attended to, in a word they must be qualified for usefulness." Attracting the right young men was permissible and even desirable.[45] John Ridge asserted that among young Cherokee men, "a large a number are of fine habits—temperate and genteel in their deportment. The females aspire to gain the affection of such men & to the females we may always ascribe the honor of effecting the civilization of man."[46]

To this end, the appearance of female students demanded the attention of the missionaries. By the late eighteenth century, Cherokee women had universally adopted the modest skirts, blouses, and shawls commonly worn by Anglo-American women, but the missionaries' objectives extended beyond merely covering nakedness. Ann Paine related the source of her dissatisfaction with the young woman of whom she tried to make an example: "Altho' her parents supplied her with good clothes, she was careless and indifferent about her appearance.—I often urged her attention to these things and . . . told her how the young ladies of the North were taught to govern their manners and tempers and of their attention to personal appearance." Paine soon had "the satisfaction of witnessing her rapid improvement." Four years later, Sophia Sawyer complained about the female students in general: "I have had to punish several times to break bad habits respecting cleanliness in their clothes, books, & person—I found them in a deplorable situation in this respect. The largest girls I had in school were not capable of dressing themselves properly or of folding their clothes when taken off." Sometimes concern for the students' appearance went beyond clothing. One girl wrote a correspondent: "Mr. Ellsworth told me I had better alter my voice. He said I spoke like a man."[47]

In addition to a neat, feminine appearance, respectable men presumably admired piety in young women and probably expected the women to be more pious than they themselves were. The missionaries clearly believed that the female students in mission schools were more serious about religion than were the male students, and they encouraged this emotion. Student Nancy Reece wrote to her northern correspondent that "after work at night the girls joined for singing a special hymn Mr. Walker wrote for them & then go to worship services." Several of the girls wrote about their spiritual lives. A ten-year-old confided in a letter that "some of the girls have been serious about their wicked hearts and have retired to their Chambers to pray to God. . . . I feel as though I am a great sinner."[48] The piety of the young women at the mission station was manifest in other ways. They organized a society to raise money to send missionaries into heathen lands. The American Board agreed to pay them for clothing they made, and they sold their handwork to local Cherokee women with the proceeds going to mission work.

Concern for the spiritual lives of Cherokees extended well beyond the mission schools. Missionaries held regular services, met privately with potential converts, and even itinerated throughout the Nation on horseback. Women as well as men were involved in this ministry. William Chamberlain requested a "woman's saddle" for his wife so that she could visit her "female neighbours" with a Cherokee woman as interpreter: "It might be the means, of carrying the gospel to some poor, but precious soul."[49] Conversions were slow at first: the Moravians labored nearly a decade before they baptized their first convert, Margaret Vann. But after the arrival of other denominations, the pace of conversions picked up. Although salvation presumably brought joy, the conversion process was painful and difficult. First of all, missionaries had to convey concepts alien to Cherokee thought—in particular, original sin and human depravity.[50] Missionaries revealed both amazement and horror at the ignorance of the people to whom they ministered. The Baptist Evan Jones wrote: "They are altogether ignorant of God, and of the nature of their own souls. They have no idea what will become of them after death: and though they do acknowledge a Creator, they are totally unacquainted with any of his attributes: hence they have no motive to stimulate them to virtue, or to deter them from vice; and their own corrupt passions are their only guide."[51] One man told American Board missionaries that he "thinks he never did anything wrong" while another "appeared to have no idea of forgiveness."[52] When missionaries at Brainerd asked a woman who had brought her children to school "if she was a sinner, she replied, No. After a lengthy conversation, she changed her mind."[53] Similarly, slaves belonging to Cherokees did not know they were sinners until the missionaries told them. Consequently, missionaries "endeavored to explain & enforce the doctrine of total depravity."[54] When Cherokees ultimately comprehended "the sinfulness of man;—the sufferings of the Saviour—& forgiveness through him," they became anxious and unhappy.[55] One woman had "singular feelings" on her way to plant beans: "She felt very bad and sat down on a log."[56] After a conversation with missionaries, another woman "wept & desired to know more" while another "suffered much from fear."[57] Although conversion presumably brought relief and rejoicing, little evidence for those emotions appears in mission records.

The cult of the Virgin, which made Catholicism attractive to many Native women, had no parallel in Protestantism, but many missionaries sought ways to make the message of Protestant Christianity relevant to women. The official organ of the Baptist Foreign Mission Board published an article entitled "To Christian Mothers" emphasizing the importance of Mary to all women: "A woman now elevates not only her own sex, by the favour of Heaven; but also renders conspicuous in the annals of the world, a descendant of that royal family that once reigned over Israel." Mary, however, was not the only heroine of the Christian story: "Christian women, your praise and your fame, your zeal, your affection, and even your courage, shine with so much resplendence in the New Testament history, as to throw the more distinguished of our sex, very much, into the shade. . . . Women were the last at the Cross, and the first at the tomb of their great and mighty Saviour."[58] Missionaries stressed the role of mothers and the promise of reunion with children who had died: "The little group that now clusters around you are destined for immortality. . . . In that other world to which you are going, you may through grace say, 'Lord Here am I, and the children thou hast given me.'"[59]

Sects that practiced infant baptism normally extended the sacrament only to children of converts, and so missionaries emphasized that the conversion of parents entitled their children to God's grace. If parents did not convert, missionaries usually declined to baptize their infants even if the parents wanted them to do so.[60] On occasion, a child led a parent to salvation or the death of a child prompted conversion. The American Board mission among the Cherokees in Arkansas reported that the conversion of a woman, previously reviled for her "masculine and ferocious disposition," resulted from "an afflictive providence, in the removal of a dear child by death" and "some reproof for her inordinate weeping" by a surviving child who had converted.[61] In some cases, conversion and baptism became family affairs as parents received baptism along with their children. Sally Fields, for example, was baptized with her four children.[62]

When missionaries achieved the conversion of women, they encouraged these women to express their piety in acceptable ways: "Your usefulness to the church is not curtailed by the apostolic injunction, which allots to you that silence and submission, which comport with that modesty and diffidence, which are now, and ever have been, the highest ornaments of the female character."[63] Once a month, neighboring women gathered at American Board missions for prayers "that missionary labors may be blessed." A missionary reported with satisfaction that "the females have a praying society which is well attended, and they begin to do something by way of benevolence."[64] In Arkansas, where some Cherokees had moved following land cessions in 1808–10 and 1817–19, missionary Cephas Washburn reported the organization of a female temperance society.[65] Despite the "apostolic injunction," women also assumed a very public role in the Christian ministry as interpreters. Lydia Lowry, who attended mission school and married Milo Hoyt, son of an American Board missionary, often interpreted sermons.[66] Neither Cherokees nor missionaries apparently saw such practice as unusual, although a headman did object to thirteen-year-old Sally Ridge translating a sermon, because of her youth.[67]

Of the several hundred Cherokee women who attended mission schools, joined churches, and lived pious lives, the best example of "true womanhood" was Catharine Brown. She was sixteen or seventeen years old when she arrived at Brainerd Mission. She had some European ancestry, and although she had grown up in a fairly traditional Cherokee household, she spoke and read a little English. The missionaries reported that despite the absence of Christian influence in her childhood, "her moral character was ever good." Her biographer added: "This is remarkable, considering the looseness of manners then prevalent among the females of her nation, and the temptations to which she was exposed, when during the war with the Creek Indians, the army of the United States was stationed near her father's residence. . . . Once she even fled from her home into the wild forest to preserve her character unsullied." When she applied for admission to Brainerd, the missionaries hesitated because they feared that she would object to the domestic duties required of female students. They later recalled that she was "vain, and excessively fond of dress, wearing a profusion of ornaments in her ears." Catharine "had no objection" to work, however, and shortly after her admission, her jewelry disappeared "till only a single drop remains in each ear." After joining the mission family, Catharine became extremely pious: "She spent much time in reading the Scriptures, singing, and prayer." She attended weekly prayer meetings and helped instruct the younger girls in the Lord's Prayer, hymns, and catechism. In 1819 Catharine received baptism. Her intellectual achievements were also remarkable, and soon the missionaries sent her to open a female school at the Creek Path mission station. There she fulfilled not only her spiritual and educational responsibilities but also her domestic ones. Visitors reported: "We arrived after the family had dined, and she received us, and spread a table for our refreshment with the unaffected kindness of a sister." When her father proposed to take the family to Arkansas, Catharine was appropriately submissive. Although she did not want to go, she acquiesced to his wishes and prepared to leave for the West. Catharine's health, however, was fragile. She became ill, and "as she approached nearer to eternity her faith evidently grew stronger." In July 1823, "this lovely convert from heathenism died."[68]

Few women in the Cherokee Nation could equal Catharine Brown or, at least, her memory. Most did not seem to want to. They preferred their traditional religion, which did not distinguish between the physical and spiritual worlds, which emphasized harmony and balance, and which placed the needs of the community above those of any individual. Those Cherokees who converted to Christianity became part of a hierarchical religion that promised little control over the physical world (that is, illness and weather), defined relationships to the natural world and other human beings in terms of dominion and submission, and placed responsibility for salvation, behavior, and success squarely on the individual.[69]

The gendered language of evangelicalism clearly revealed the patriarchal structure of Christianity; the articles of faith adopted at the beginning of the Brainerd missions affirmed, "We believe that God created man holy in his own image; and that by disobedience he lost his primitive purity, and became wholly sinful."[70] The Baptists were more explicit about the source of sin in the world: "It originated in the brain of our wayward mother from the fumes of the forbidden fruit."[71] In their ministry to women, American Board missionaries did not obfuscate this particular: "I pointed out the first deviation from virtue, & set a bad woman before them in the most horrid light I was capable."[72]

Eve's surrender to temptation had little parallel in Cherokee mythology, and interestingly, Cherokees never adapted the story of the fall to their own purposes in the way they transformed the biblical account of the creation to prove that Indians were God's chosen people.[73] An elderly Cherokee man, however, shifted responsibility for the fall when he related Cherokee traditions to missionary Samuel Worcester: "The first man plucked the fruit of the forbidden tree; he looked on it—it was fair; he smelt it—it was fragrant; he tasted—and was ruined."[74] Historian William McLoughlin has suggested that the Cherokees did not normally tamper with Eve because she met the needs of an increasingly male-dominated society, but an alternative explanation may be that the concept of women bringing evil into the world was so foreign that no good use could be found for it unless it was re-gendered. Selu gave people corn and beans; Eve took an apple and gave them sin. Why would anyone want to abandon the Corn Mother?

In fact, relatively few Cherokees apparently did. In 1830 Samuel Austin Worcester asserted in the *Cherokee Phoenix* that "the greater part of the people acknowledge the Christian religion to be the true religion," but Worcester's figures did not support his conclusion: just over one thousand people (including resident whites and African-American slaves) out of a total Cherokee population that exceeded fifteen thousand belonged to churches.[75] The percentage of unchurched among neighboring whites did not differ substantially from Worcester's accounting of the Cherokees, but rejection of Christianity and adherence to traditional religious beliefs and values, rather than mere indifference to membership, probably explain the reluctance of many Cherokees to join churches. Furthermore, one missionary maintained that "one half of all who have been added to this church have been suspended from it."[76] While illicit sex was often the reason, other unacceptable activities contributed to the high rate of suspensions. These ranged from drinking and quarreling to participation in traditional rituals such as ball games and all-night dances, both having strong ties to Cherokee religion.[77] Rejection of Christianity does not seem to have been any more prevalent among women than among men, but other aspects of Christian missions indicate a more gendered response.

The Cherokees had considerable enthusiasm for mission schools, but they were far more likely to send their sons than their daughters. Few were as outspoken as the man who advised a couple accompanying their five children to Brainerd "that it would do no good to send their daughters to school," but lagging enrollments spoke volumes: more boys than girls attended mission schools.[78] In part, fewer female students resulted from the difficulty in providing teachers. Overworked women missionaries suffered frequent illnesses, and missionaries only reluctantly permitted girls and boys, particularly teenagers, to attend school together. But some evidence suggests that an increase in spaces available to young women would not have enlarged their classes. John Ellsworth of the American Board reported on the enrollment of young women: "We have had but one application when we have not recd the child—& this one we may still receive." By comparison, he pointed out, "we could receive many more boys if we would."[79] Two months later, he wrote, "We have had no applications of late to receive girls," and speculated "that the girls school is losing rather than gaining ground."[80]

While problems within the missions may account for the discrepancy between male and female enrollments, several other factors also interfered with attendance. Some Cherokee families required the labor of daughters. Brainerd student Sally Reece wrote to a benefactor: "Sister Polly wants to come to school. But Mother cannot spare her."[81] In 1822 the mission at Brainerd faced a crisis because both parents and missionaries needed the children to plant. A spring vacation made truancy unusually tempting, and so the next year, missionaries moved the vacation to August.[82] Since women continued to be associated with farming in most families, a daughter's absence may have been keenly felt. Furthermore, some Cherokee parents (like many non-Cherokee parents in early-nineteenth-century America) may have regarded education as more appropriate for their sons. In 1824 mission teacher Sophia Sawyer suggested that "the Cherokees think much more of their sons than of their daughters."[83] A more likely explanation is that parents believed that commerce and politics, the pursuits of men, demanded an education, whereas farming and housekeeping did not.[84]

On the other hand, some daughters simply may not have wanted a mission education. Cherokee children enjoyed astonishing freedom, and if they did not want to attend school, parents almost certainly did not intervene. American Board missionaries complained: "The children attend school or stay at home as they choose. The parents try to convince them, & they say 'What more can we do? We have tried all we can to persuade them to stay.' . . . The continuance of the child depends entirely on his own wavering mind."[85] Missionary attempts at discipline had predictable results. Polly Wilson confided to the corresponding secretary of the American Board: "When I was reproved I thought that I would run away from school."[86] The fear of such a response haunted parents and apparently impeded the early Moravian missionary effort: the Cherokees told them that "they would send us no children for fear we might abuse them and they would run away and get lost in the woods."[87]

The workload at the missions probably contributed to the reluctance of girls to attend school. Polly Wilson revealed that "when they asked me to work I used to think it was very hard and that I was obliged to work for the good of the missionaries."[88] At home, women presumably did tasks that needed to be done, but they did not work merely to work, that is, they placed no value on the labor itself. On the other hand, missionaries abhorred indolence and sought to fill every minute of the day with productive activity: "When not employed in the dining room & kitchen, they are employed in sewing, sweeping making beds, &c."[89] The most disagreeable arrangement was that sought by Mrs. Chamberlain: "Her plan was to have the Cherokee girls do all the labour, & herself superintend." Needless to say, "the girls did not like to work with her, because she never took hold herself."[90] Most female missionaries, however, worked very hard, and their example may well have aroused among Cherokee girls serious misgivings about Anglo-American housewifery.[91]

Cherokees defined women in terms of their relationship to the land and their role in families. Missionaries regarded men as the appropriate providers for families and attempted to eliminate the role of women as farmers. They also sought to restructure the place of women in families. In the missionaries' worldview, the domestic sphere belonged to women but husbands and fathers headed the household. Furthermore, except in the case of death, this patriarchal household was permanent: men and women had no freedom to separate and remarry. Even among those Cherokees interested in mission education, Cherokee domestic relations failed miserably to conform to the missionaries' standards. Marriage, missionaries maintained, "was formerly but little known. The Cherokee once took as many wives as he pleased but did not support them or have the command of the children."[92] At mission schools, they constantly confronted the problem of female autonomy and even precedence in dealing with children. Those at Brainerd wrote: "We also had some trouble from one parent bringing a child and the other taking it away, where the father & mother do not now live together. We have now three children who were brought here by their father, a halfbreed of some education, who have two mothers, & neither of them have for some time lived with their father. He has another wife, & they have other husbands. The mother of two of them came for the purpose of taking them from the school, & told us the mother of the other was coming for hers soon. . . . The mothers among this people are considered as having a right to the children in preference to the fathers."[93]

Missionaries had considerable evidence for the persistence of matrilineal kinship. Mothers often brought children to schools and checked on their welfare.[94] When missionaries sent expressly for one boy's father, he did not come; the boy's mother came instead.[95] Sometimes, maternal uncles visited their sisters' children, and children often looked to brothers or maternal uncles, the appropriate kinsmen under a matrilineal system, for the means to continue their education.[96] The wife of Judge John Martin, for example, enrolled her own daughter and, acting in her husband's stead, his niece in the school.[97] Fathers also enrolled children and visited them, but rarely did a father's will regarding children prevail over that of the mother and her relatives. One father, for example, came at his wife's behest to retrieve their daughter for the family's emigration to the West. The child did not want to leave, and so he permitted her to remain. In the end, however, she went west with the family as her mother had wished.[98] Missionaries quickly learned to consult mothers. When preparations were being made for John Ridge, whose father advocated acculturation, to attend the Foreign Mission School in Cornwall, Connecticut, the missionaries specifically "enquired if his mother was willing. She expressed great desire to have him go."[99]

Cherokee marriages frequently did not conform to missionary expectations in other ways. Missionaries found polygamous and serial marriages particularly troubling. Most nineteenth-century Anglo-Americans agreed with Louis-Philippe's assertion that polygamy "renders women contemptible in men's eyes and deprives them of all influence" and ignored the possibility that polygamy, particularly the sororal polygamy primarily practiced by Cherokees, might strengthen the bonds among women and contribute to a high status for women. Instead, they believed that only monogamous marriages enhanced a woman's status because these "serve exclusively to heighten the affections of a man."[100]

The extent of polygamy among the Cherokees in any period is uncertain, but in the early nineteenth century, the polygamous unions of prominent Cherokees made the continuation of the practice quite obvious. Although the Cherokee elite accepted many tenets of western "civilization," some balked at abandoning the practice of polygamy. The chief justice of the Cherokee Supreme Court was only one of several Cherokee leaders who had more than one wife, but these marriages usually differed from traditional ones in which a man lived with his wives in their house. James Vann's two wives, who were sisters, lived on his plantation, where "they were busy spinning and weaving cotton."[101] He had a number of slaves who clearly belonged to him, he employed a white overseer and herdsman, and in about 1804 he built an elegant brick mansion. When wives were not related, polygamous members of the elite usually headed more than one household for which they assumed responsibility. However, most members of the elite accepted the desirability of monogamous unions, encouraged others to enter into these, and sent their children to mission schools where they were taught that polygamy was immoral.

In practice, religious denominations confronted polygamy in different ways. Moravians apparently allowed converts to keep more than one wife: among the people who regularly attended their services at Springplace were "Caniguijaka and his two wives."[102] The Moravians, like the Methodists, had an intermediate step to full admission and therefore permitted more latitude than did the American Board and the Baptists, who required a man "to separate himself from all but the first." Aware that some of their major Cherokee supporters were polygamists, the governing body in Boston advised American Board missionaries to be "prudent and kind" when dealing with this "tender subject" and to instruct polygamous converts "in the nature and design of marriage, the original institution, and the law of Christ, that they may act with an enlightened conviction of duty." This directive, however, did not completely resolve the issue, as Daniel Butrick explained: "It is not uncommon for a Cherokee when he takes two wives to take two sisters & contract with them both at the same time; and as this contract is considered the marriage & not any subsequent conduct, we should not know which to have him put away."[103]

Charles Reece perhaps represents the missionaries' worst nightmare. Before his conversion in 1817, Reece "had three sisters for his wives at the same time." He had married them simultaneously, and it was his situation that prompted American Board missionaries to seek further instructions from Boston. One had died before Reece sought admission to the church, but the other two presented a real conundrum since neither had precedence over the other. Reece himself ultimately solved the problem: he left them both and took yet another wife. Missionaries attributed Reece's abandonment of the sisters to "the insolence of their mother." According to the missionaries, he "left a good plantation, & a valuable stock of cattle, for them and his children" and began "anew in the world." Despite his conversion to Christianity, Reece behaved in a very traditional Cherokee manner: he considered the land and its bounty as well as the children to belong to his wives and their mother, not to him. His behavior led the missionaries to conclude: "This illustrates a striking trait in the Indians character. If they have differences with each other, they will not contend, but agree to separate."[104] Despite this apparently rational solution to domestic strife, missionaries could not condone separation and divorce, particularly with the ease to which Cherokees were accustomed. As for Reece, by the time of removal, he seems to have entered into yet another liaison. Charles Hicks, Cherokee principal chief for a brief time before his death in 1827, was accused and then cleared of "criminal intercourse" with a young woman. Sometime after this incident, she confided to an elderly woman that Reece was the father of her two children. Reece publicly confirmed his paternity when he provided transportation for her and her family during removal.[105]

In Christian marriages, men were the heads of household, but many of the families missionaries visited appear from the records to have been matrilineal and matrilocal. When Daniel Butrick itinerated, he usually identified the people with whom he stayed. A surprising number of them were women, and many lived in extended households: two women he first met at Major Ridge's house lived together with their grandmother; Mrs. Pack and her mother shared a house; the Widow Broom "informed her brother of our arrival"; and only half a mile separated the houses of convert John Timson's aunt and sister. Furthermore, the congregations that gathered to hear him preach often reflected matrilineal kin groups: at the home of convert John Arch's mother, for example, he found "his brother, uncles, sisters, &c. assembled."[106] On one trip, Butrick decided to take with him T. Basel, a student and assistant at Taloney, because "he expressed a desire to visit his friends, especially his uncle in the Valley Towns, . . . [but] on our arrival at Brainerd, he visited his sister, who persuaded him to assist her in raising corn, as she had no help."[107] Basel's attachment to his uncle and his sense of obligation to his sister epitomized matrilineal kinship. While these people may have been interested in the Christian message on some level, they do not seem to have been likely to transform their domestic relations. Similarly, the Moravians reported that "our neighbour Tussewallety, and his wife Ajosta, together with her sister, brother-in-law and uncle Cananthoah, came hither with the express design of hearing something about God."[108] A twentieth-century anthropologist could cite no better example of a matrilineage.

Among a few Cherokees, indissoluble monogamous marriages held some attraction, and American Board ministers occasionally remarried in a Christian service couples who had lived for years in "a family capacity."[109] The explanation for the couples' desire to be united in a public Christian service may lie in the demographic changes that preceded the ideological shift in the Cherokee Nation. New family situations often had failed to provoke new responses. The increasingly isolated nuclear families that had replaced large extended kin groups and close-knit villages in many parts of the Nation could not always accommodate and support divorced spouses and dependent children.[110] Unaccustomed to providing for their wives and children, some men simply abandoned them. These fathers were not "deadbeat dads" in the modern sense: their traditional culture did not obligate them to their children. The development of nuclear families apparently had, in some cases, severed the ties to mother's brother and extended family without forging bonds between fathers and children, husbands and wives. In the war on "savagery," women and children suffered collateral damage. According to Ann Paine, "this has been a source of much sorrow to the poor Cherokee women some of whom I saw deserted, dejected with orphan children to provide for."[111] Christian marriage vows promised some protection against such a situation.

Sometimes abandoned women turned to missions for succor. Brainerd agreed to admit the eight-year-old daughter of "a poor Cherokee women, whose husband has taken another wife & left her."[112] Another woman, who had been married to a white man, brought two children to the mission when her husband "burned up her house, destroyed all her furniture, sold her cattle & horses, & she was left destitute."[113] Before the upheavals of the late eighteenth and early nineteenth centuries, of course, the matrilineages would have taken care of these children. Maternal uncles would have provided much of the support and guidance that missionaries expected of fathers while children would have remained in the houses of their mothers and maternal kin. Mission schools provided a viable alternative. Missionaries recorded that the destitute mother of two "appeared thankful that she could find so good a home for her children."[114]

Men may have continued to feel responsible for their sisters' children, but here too they often experienced conflict between traditional obligations and the realities of nineteenth-century life. Brothers, living in nuclear households with their own wives, could not readily take in sisters, nor could other married sisters in their own narrowly defined households necessarily provide shelter. In some cases, missions helped Cherokee men fulfill traditional obligations. When a missionary asked a man who accompanied his deserted sister to enroll her children at Brainerd what he should do if the father tried to take the children, the brother gave the missionary a piece of paper, presumably a note to his brother-in-law: "Show him this and he will not take them."[115] This man clearly felt a sense of responsibility for his sister and her children, and he used his traditional authority to solve the problem of their abandonment in a novel way.

One of the most effective ways for missionaries to break down Cherokee family structure was for them to become the surrogate parents for children and to create a new Christian family that replaced the extended matrilineal kin network. The mission and the church became a child's family instead of the clan.[116] The missionaries' reluctance to permit children to return home for vacation served to strengthen this new social organization. Furthermore, missionaries publicly identified children with Christianity and the missions by renaming them. Cherokees also renamed people, and so the practice was not new to them, but Cherokee names derived from a distinctive trait or an episode in a person's life. Mission names came from benefactors and tied children to the broader Christian commonwealth.[117] At times, missionaries sounded like agents for discriminating collectors. A Baptist missionary wrote to the corresponding secretary: "I have succeeded better than I expected in getting suitable children to be named after those worthy persons who requested it, viz. We have a little girl named Elizabeth Greene; She is about 8 years of age, and very promising. We have also a Howard Malcolm, and we expect in a few days to have a Benjamin Stanton."[118] In contradiction to their advocacy of patriarchal families, missionaries made little effort to promote the use of paternal surnames. As a result, Cherokee siblings sometimes did not share surnames. Elias Boudinot, for example, took the name of the president of the American Bible Society with the approval of missionaries, but his siblings used Watie, their father's name. The Christian family took precedence over both traditional extended families and western-style patriarchal ones.

Families experienced two other challenges, one recently acquired and the other deeply entrenched in Cherokee culture. An American Board missionary identified "the vices which prevail" as "intemperance and fornication."[119] Cherokees, United States policy makers, and philanthropists had long recognized alcohol abuse as a problem within the Cherokee Nation. Indian Trade and Intercourse acts addressed the problem, and in 1819 the Cherokees passed their own regulations.[120] In general, alcohol abuse seems to have been related to public gatherings, in particular, ball games, all-night dances, and council meetings. Social drinking often degenerated into drunken brawls, and so the council prohibited alcohol consumption at these events.[121] The Cherokees continued to be sensitive to the issue, but alcoholism does not appear to have been any more significant a problem among the Cherokees than among non-Indians on the southern frontier. Nevertheless, episodes of drunkenness proved painful for many Cherokees, particularly for the women who became victims of abusive husbands. Most Cherokees enjoyed peaceful domestic relations, perhaps because they simply separated instead of fighting, but alcohol often served as a catalyst for violent behavior. The Moravians, for example, related how Trunk "in a drunken rage viciously abused his wife and would have killed her had it not been for the Negro Harry who tore him from her and bound him. She then fled to the woods with her children."[122]

By the late 1820s, abuse related to alcohol was becoming far more common. In 1830 Georgia extended state law over the Cherokees and thereby suspended both United States and Cherokee laws regulating alcohol. Rum merchants poured into the Cherokee Nation, and many Cherokees, with emotions ranging from anger to despair, tried to drown their sorrows in the bottle. Once again, wives often suffered the brunt of abuse. Zillah Haynie Brandon, a white woman whose family moved into the Cherokee Nation in 1835 and displaced a Cherokee household, observed her neighbors: "The women I believe were chaste and very civil, but their husbands would drink to drunkenness, and were very cruel when under the influence of fire water. . . . When they got drunk from home and their deathlike yells were heard by their families, they would look as if the cords of their souls were torn asunder, they would stand outside their houses weeping and looking so doleful, that it would move any heart, not possessed of a demon, to pity." On one occasion, Brandon gave refuge to a woman whose husband pursued her with his gun and threatened her life.[123]

As the removal crisis intensified and federal troops arrived in 1838, women fell victim to alcohol in other ways. Daniel Butrick recorded the following episodes: "The other day a gentleman informed me that he saw six soldiers about two Cherokee women. The women stood by a tree, and the soldiers with a bottle of liquor were endeavoring to entice them to drink, though the women, as yet were resisting them. . . . A young married woman, a member of the Methodist society was at the camp with her friends, though her husband was not there at the time. The soldiers, it is said, caught her, dragged her about, and at length, either through fear, or otherwise, induced her to drink; and then seduced her away, so that she is now an outcast among her own relatives."[124]

Missionaries associated drinking and "fornication," and in some cases, the two probably were connected, but Cherokees had always enjoyed an astonishing degree of sexual freedom. Difficulties in maintaining sexual propriety in mission schools stemmed as much from Cherokee tolerance of sexual experimentation as from adolescent hormone surges. To the missionaries' dismay, their vigilance and discipline often had little effect on restructuring sexual rules. One missionary wrote with anguish about the fall of one former student: "There is a young woman in the neighborhood who has been at Brainerd, how long I know not; but long enough to learn to talk English tolerably well but is now as degraded an Indian as any in the place. She has been a member of this church but lately was suspended for prostitution." Even more troubling was the frequency of such behavior: "This is not a solitary instance of misconduct in those who have been in mission families after leaving for myself I believe a majority have conducted worse than the above named person."[125] Daniel Butrick concurred, but he blamed white intruders for enticing former students who could speak English to gamble, drink, and commit other sins: "Much of the labour and expense of the mission schools have been wrested into the service of sin. On this account the philanthropist is often lead to regret that any Cherokee has been taught the English language."[126] Missionaries provide considerable evidence, however, that illicit sexual relations also took place between Cherokees. They often suspended church members—male and female—for having "criminal intercourse." Even the Baptists, who managed to forge a syncretic religion incorporating some aspects of Cherokee culture, insisted on chastity and on the sanctity of marriage. In familial relations, missionaries left little room to wiggle. For women, of course, the restrictions on sexuality further compromised their autonomy and, in practice, placed control of their sexuality in the hands of fathers before marriage and husbands afterward.[127]

Missionaries along with United States agents mounted an assault on Cherokee culture that had profound repercussions for women. In the years immediately preceding removal, the culture's viability, particularly in the religious realm, is difficult to document. Cherokees were far less enamored of the missionaries' religion than of the education they offered. The early debate over admitting Moravians centered on their preaching, and the chiefs nearly expelled them for their delay in opening a school.[128] Years later, American Board missionaries noted that as soon as some children expressed seriousness about religion, their parents removed them from school for an extended visit.[129] In the mid-1820s, a more concerted opposition to the missionaries arose. Sermons critical of council houses where local council meetings as well as religious rituals took place prompted overly zealous converts at Taloney to burn down the council house, an action that led to threats of retaliation and encouraged open hostility toward missionaries. The growth in public antimission sentiment coincided with political resistance to the National Council's move toward constitutional government, and Cherokee leaders took immediate steps to stop it.[130]

We know relatively little about the Cherokees' opposition to change and their preservation of traditional culture. Cherokee leaders were generally committed to acculturation, personally and corporately. Cognizant of the importance of public opinion beyond the boundaries of the Nation, they also tried to project the image of a Cherokee Nation "bursting the fetters of ignorance" and becoming "civilized and happy."[131] Furthermore, missionaries, who provide perhaps the best written documentation for the cultural history of the period, scrupulously avoided dances and ball plays, primarily because they associated these activities with drunkenness (and the near nudity of ball players offended them). Nevertheless, references to these events pepper mission journals.[132] Traditionally known as the "little brother to war," ball plays were essentially ritualized warfare accompanied by many of the same ceremonies as those associated with war. Women participated in the rituals preceding these games: they sang special songs and performed dance steps designed to weaken the enemy. Women did not actually play this game, but they did engage men in another type of ball game that was strictly social.[133] Male and female teams competed in throwing a leather ball at a goal mounted on top of a pole, and the close contact of scantily clad men and women led missionaries to oppose these games as well as the more religiously oriented male games.

Dances also had both ceremonial and social significance. Most Cherokee dances honored various spirits or commemorated important events while some, such as the Booger Dance, were farcical.[134] The most significant dance was the Green Corn Ceremony. In the early years of Brainerd, missionaries unwittingly aided the observance of the Green Corn Ceremony by scheduling summer vacations to coincide with this event. Not quite grasping its religious significance, missionaries naively wrote: "Many parents have fixed this season of the year to take their children home to visit, it being the time when green corn & watermelons are plenty—a sort of feasting time with many among this people."[135] Soon they became more knowledgeable and promptly reorganized the school schedule.

To the dismay of missionaries and highly acculturated Cherokees, some people continued to observe scrupulously "the old custom of a sacrifice and dance before they eat green corn or beans." When Charles Reece—who, as we have seen, held on to other traditions—served a group of Cherokees some green beans before they had conducted this ritual, "several immediately remonstrated, accusing him of great wickedness. He laboured in vain to convince them of their error—As he and one of his old neighbors sat down to eat, the others all refused to partake, and left the field."[136]

A belief in witchcraft endured despite attempts by Cherokees and missionaries to stamp it out. Witches were human beings who acquired special powers that they used for evil purposes.[137] Members of an American Board church sheltered in their home a "poor and desolate woman" and her ten-year-old son whose "near relatives were slain for the supposed crime of witchcraft."[138] In Willstown, the site of an American Board mission, "a man was shot . . . (a very inoffensive old man) having been accused by some one of being a 'witch' despite the fact that the Cherokees had outlawed punishing those suspected of witchcraft."[139] Witches used their power in evil and selfish ways. In particular, witches sought to extend their own lives by appropriating the life force, centered in the liver or heart, of others. Consequently, very old people sometimes fell victim to charges of witchcraft because they had lived beyond what Cherokees considered to be a normal lifespan. Cherokees also frequently attributed misfortune to witchcraft and sought to counteract evil spells with the help of conjurors.

Religious practitioners remained active in less dangerous ways than witchcraft. A Cherokee as highly acculturated and concerned with public opinion as John Ridge wrote to Albert Gallatin that "there [are] yet among us [those] who pretend to possess powers of milder character, such as making rain, allaying a storm or whirlwinds—playing with thunder & foretelling future events."[140] Ridge referred to conjuring, which was the way in which traditional Cherokee religion intersected people's lives most frequently and intimately.[141] Conjurors possessed a range of skills from determining the appropriate name for a baby to resolving marital problems.

Cherokees also turned to the spiritual realm in the treatment of disease. In the Western worldview, disease has a physical cause and its treatment rests with science, not religion. To Cherokees, however, the spiritual and physical realms were not separate, and consequently, illness had spiritual causes and cures. Medicine and religion were indistinguishable. Missionaries correctly connected medicine men and women with religion and opposed their practices, usually in vain. At Taloney, one of the Cherokees' most highly acculturated communities located along the federal road, most children played hooky from school because "a conjurer had called all the town together to conjure away the measles."[142] Missionaries found such adherence to traditional beliefs especially troubling when it involved people connected to the mission. When one student was ill for two or three months, for example, her parents refused medicine from the missionaries, much to their consternation, and relied instead on traditional practices.[143]

For some women, conjuring was a way for them to express traditional familial relations and exercise their prerogatives. An American Board missionary visited the family of convert Alexander Sanders daily when his children were ill, "but his wife being so much in favour with the old practice with the sick, prevented my doing any thing for the poor sick children."[144] One mother tried to practice traditional medicine on her son within the confines of the Moravian mission, perhaps as much to confirm her link to him as to heal him. When the grandchild of Charles Hicks, a Moravian convert and prominent national leader, became ill, the female relatives of the child's mother, who had attended mission school, insisted on conjury, and Hicks was powerless to prevent it.[145] Even women who found the Christian message attractive were reluctant to give up conjuring, a public expression of religious belief that had no parallel for women in Christianity. One woman, who "had for years been a conjuress," sought religious instruction, perhaps to increase her power. She traveled twenty miles for baptism, but the minister refused her because "she expressed unwillingness to renounce conjuring." Ultimately understanding the exclusive nature of Christian beliefs, she reapplied for baptism several months later, but this time "she was fully determined never to practice it again"—or at least, so she said.[146]

Any attempt to determine how "civilized" or how traditional the Cherokees were in the years immediately prior to removal is likely to be fruitless. Cherokee society was enormously complex in this period, and Cherokees themselves combined old and new ways in an infinite variety. Nevertheless, one can say with some certainty that despite the claims of Cherokees and missionaries at the time and scholars in subsequent years, Cherokee culture was not dead. Perhaps it was not even dying. Samuel Worcester, an indefatigable defender of the success of Cherokee "civilization," responded to the Cherokee David Brown's published claim that in his Nation, "the female character is elevated and duly respected." Quoting a line from Brown's letter that had been omitted—"It is the mass and common people that form the character of a nation"—Worcester insisted that benefactors who "lend their aid in raising their Cherokee sisters from *degradation*" needed to know that the "evil" had not "ceased to exist."[147] In other words, the "mass and common" women refused to abandon their own ways of doing things and adopt the values and lifestyle that missionaries advocated. Selu had met Eve, but she had not surrendered.

Conclusion

Cherokee women lived in a changing world. Trade and war disrupted their lives in the eighteenth century, and the United States' "civilization" program tried to restructure their world in the nineteenth. Like all historical change, the transformation of Cherokee society was neither constant nor uniform. Some Cherokees—both men and women—embraced change. They turned to the acquisitive individualism of nascent capitalism, limited the body politic, and converted to the evangelical Protestantism that offered theological justification for individualism and hierarchy. They came to regard respectable men as "those who have kept their women & children at home & in comfortable circumstances" and respectable women as those who exercised influence instead of power.[1] Perhaps not all Cherokees who adopted the new beliefs prospered, but since these Cherokees defined success in terms of material gain, many of them did. The wealthiest Cherokees tended to be powerful men: they understood the Anglo-American political system, promoted its adoption by the Cherokees, and dominated the government of the Cherokee republic. While their daughters and wives may have continued to enjoy considerably more autonomy than elite Anglo-American women, they usually did not approach any sort of gender equity.

On the other hand, many Cherokee women as well as men continued to adhere to a traditional belief system that linked the spiritual and physical worlds into a coherent balanced whole, emphasized the importance of community and harmony, and sanctioned the autonomy, complementarity, prestige, and even power of women. Their cultural conservatism, however, does not mean that change completely bypassed these Cherokees. Many traditional Cherokees moved away from their towns, adopted new technologies, voted in national elections, perhaps sat in councils (if they were men), attended Protestant revivals, and sent their children to school. But they tried to fit new ways into an old system of understanding the world and their place in it. Among these Cherokees, cultural persistence, including traditional constructions of gender, is at least as significant as change.

If Cherokee history had unfolded in a vacuum, the magnitude and direction of change for women would have been quite different, but Cherokees lived on the frontiers of aggressively expanding empires that precipitated much of the change. War and disease decimated the Cherokee population, the Cherokees bought peace with land cessions, trade sucked them into a world economic system over which they had no control, and "civilization" promised a loss of culture, sovereignty, and land. Most of these changes reoriented men's lives far more profoundly than they did those of women. Europeans, after all, considered women powerless and made fewer demands of them. Consequently, many women continued to hoe their corn, raise their children, and exercise traditional kinds of power just as they always had.

Because the activities of women have not usually constituted what we think of as "history," the women themselves have slipped from view. The story of removal, for example, is the story of men: an Indian-fighting president, fire-breathing state governors, land-hungry farmers, vicious militiamen, and traitors who defected and signed a removal treaty squared off against an unflinching Cherokee chief, countless patriotic Cherokee delegations to Washington, a terrorized Cherokee citizenry, and righteous missionaries imprisoned for civil disobedience. Despite their apparent absence, however, women played a role in this drama. Their association with the land and their opposition to selling it strengthened the Cherokee concept of and commitment to common landholding as well as the Nation's refusal to negotiate removal. Furthermore, the persistence of traditional women's roles attracted the attention of removal proponents and, for them, became emblematic of the failure of the "civilization" program, the recalcitrance of the Cherokees, and the immutability of race. Women's economic role, their autonomy, the organization of their families, and the remnant of political power that they retained challenged Anglo-American notions of order and propriety.

Anglo-Americans found the economic productivity of women especially troubling. Carroll Smith-Rosenberg has described the way in which postrevolutionary essayists rendered middle-class white women sexually powerless and economically unproductive: the early republic depicted women as consumers, not producers.[2] Contrary to this idealized republican woman, Native women farmed. Furthermore, the sexual division of labor in most Native societies assigned farming *primarily* to women and exempted men from many of the most arduous tasks, such as hoeing. In the minds of Anglo-Americans, the most appropriate analogy for such an arrangement, in which one person performed most of the labor and another enjoyed the fruits of that labor, was slavery. For republicans, slavery was the very antithesis of liberty, and they had employed the imagery effectively in articulating the revolutionary cause: the British king, they charged, had attempted to enslave them by depriving them of their property through taxation without representation. And yet many in the early republic held slaves.[3] This tension between slavery and freedom characterized early American history and provided a vocabulary to describe the status of Native women. Therefore, it is not surprising that the Jeffersonian Albert Gallatin, in his "Synopsis of the Indian Tribes," should adopt the imagery: "Women are everywhere slaves and beasts of burden."[4]

Women had been the farmers in Cherokee society long before Europeans arrived in America. Indeed, Native agriculture was widespread east of the Rockies, a circumstance that defied Anglo-American categorizations of human societies that described "savage" hunting and gathering cultures as less complex than "civilized" ones in which people farmed. Since Native Americans were savages in the eyes of the learned academicians revered by the early American republic, they were not supposed to farm. But the evidence pointed to an agricultural base for most Native economies within the boundaries of the United States. The Lewis and Clark expedition of 1804–6 provides a good index to the extent of agriculture. In his instructions to the explorers, Jefferson requested specific information on the Native peoples they encountered, including "whether they cultivate or not." Until Lewis and Clark met the Sioux on the northern plains, they noted "cultivates Corn, Beans &c. &c." for all the nations they described, and even one band of Sioux grew some corn.[5] Clearly, "savages" *did* farm. How could Euro-Americans reconcile what they saw with what they were supposed to see?

Many responded to this unnatural arrangement by adjusting the facts to fit. Commentators, even those who had observed Native cultures or had read extensively in firsthand accounts, simply ignored the importance of agriculture to Native subsistence and exaggerated people's dependence on hunting.[6] Lieutenant Henry Timberlake, who purchased corn from Native women, described the Cherokees in his *Memoirs* strictly as hunters.[7] In *Notes on the State of Virginia,* Thomas Jefferson wrote that "all the nations of Indians in North America lived in the hunter state and depended for subsistence on hunting, fishing, and the spontaneous fruits of the earth." Almost as an afterthought, Jefferson added "a kind of grain which was planted and gathered by the women . . . is now known by the name Indian corn."[8] Others merely belittled the economic importance of agriculture or blurred the distinction between gathering wild foods and farming. Robert Beverley extolled the fertility of the southern colonies where "none of the Toils of Husbandry were exercised by this happy People; except the bare planting a little Corn, and Melons, which took up only a few Days in the Summer."[9] Few Euro-Americans ever fully appreciated the contradiction embodied in their depictions of Native peoples as hunters while they themselves cultivated Native crops using Native techniques. Racism may well have led whites to denigrate Native crops in general, but the sex of the farmers prompted them to minimize the relative importance of agriculture in Native societies. The fact that women farmed, rather than men, permitted Euro-Americans to shape their view of Native culture to conform to their own cultural parameters.

The dismissal of agriculture as a major feature of Native economies had enormous implications for Native people. Agrarianism was a significant component of republican ideology in the early years of the United States. Republicans idealized the yeoman farmer, and they regarded a patriarchal family, living on its own land and supported by its own labor, as the bedrock of the republic.[10] Benjamin Rush, like most of his contemporaries in postrevolutionary America, believed that agriculture was "the true basis of national health, riches and populousness."[11] These ideas helped shape a particular view of the nation's future that Jeffersonians articulated. It was only a short step from extolling the virtues of those who tilled the soil to bemoaning the inadequacies of those who presumably did not.

By the 1820s, politicians who sought the removal of eastern Indians, including the Cherokees, to land west of the Mississippi River cited the failure of Native people to farm as justification for dispossessing them. Basing their argument on the widely accepted jurisprudence of eighteenth-century theorist Emmerich de Vattel, politicians maintained that no people had a right to land they did not cultivate. The needs of farmers took precedence over those of hunters.[12] Georgia Governor Wilson Lumpkin summarized the position of those who demanded immediate removal: "I believe the earth was formed especially for the cultivation of the ground, and none but civilized men will cultivate the earth to any great extent, or advantage. Therefore, I do not believe a savage race of heathens, found in the occupancy of a large and fertile domain of country, have any exclusive right to the same, from merely having seen it in the chase, or having viewed it from the mountain top."[13] Lumpkin's gendered language should not be ignored. Cultivation of the soil by men constituted legitimate ownership of land: minimal farming by mere women did not entitle one to possession.[14]

At the same time, ideology was beginning to define quite distinct roles for men and women in American society. The cult of domesticity arose from industrialization and the separation of home and industry, and it made the home and domestic virtues the province of women while men came to be associated with the capitalistic values of the new industrial order.[15] Societies in which women worked outside the home became suspect: Jefferson, for example, suggested that heavy labor by women indicated extreme poverty.[16] Others attached more profound meaning to the Native division of labor in which women seemed to do most of the work. "There can be no hesitation in asserting," Albert Gallatin wrote in his long discourse on Native peoples, "that the labor necessary to support a man's family is, on the part of the man, a moral duty; and that to impose on woman that portion, which can be properly performed only by man, is a deviation from the laws of nature."[17] The real problem with Native societies, according to Gallatin, was that women instead of men did the farming.

Policy makers had tried to convert men into farmers who would no longer need the "surplus & waste lands" they used for hunting grounds.[18] When he became president in 1801, Thomas Jefferson endorsed the program because he believed that its success would bring land cessions: "The extensive forests necessary in the hunting life will then become useless, and they will see advantage in exchanging them for the means of improving their farms and increasing their domestic comforts." What Jefferson and others regarded as an economic change, however, involved a far more profound transformation that called into question fundamental values and beliefs.[19] Not surprisingly, many Native peoples resisted "civilization." Gallatin complained that "although the men may to some extent have assisted the women in the cultivation of the ground, the greater part of the labors still fell upon the latter."[20] He did concede that the Cherokees had, in a limited way, "become an agricultural nation, meaning thereby that state of society, in which the men themselves do actually perform agricultural labor." But even among the Cherokees, he estimated, only one-third of the men farmed.[21] By the time of the election of Andrew Jackson in 1828, many lamented the failure of the civilization program, even among the Cherokees, and pointed to the suffering of Native peoples who refused to save themselves from destruction. Regrettably, concluded Lewis Cass, a key figure in Jackson's administration, "distress could not teach them providence, nor want industry."[22]

The proclaimed failure of the civilization program came at a convenient time. The southern states in the 1820s had become insistent that the Native peoples within their bounds be moved west of the Mississippi. Long recognized as a solution to the "Indian problem," removal hinged on acquisition of Native title to remaining lands in the east.[23] But most Native people, including the Cherokees, had no desire to sell their land and move to an unknown country. Proponents of removal, therefore, advanced the claim that Native peoples dependent on hunting had no more right to political independence than they had to the land itself. James Hall wrote: "We cannot believe that the mere fact, that a wandering horde of savages are in the habit of traversing a particular tract of country in pursuit of game, gives to them the ownership and jurisdiction of the soil, as sovereign nations."[24] The solution, of course, was to bring Native peoples under the jurisdiction of the United States and remove them beyond the chartered boundaries of states. Those who did not move to public land in the West should be subject to the laws of those states in which they resided. Those who did move should submit to the "paternal authority" of the United States.[25] Under United States tutelage, they could learn the civic values, nurtured at home and embodied in institutions, that Anglo-Americans considered appropriate to good government.

Anglo-Americans engaged in heated debate over the nature of good government and the appropriate extent of its powers in the early years of the republic, but most agreed that the family was government in microcosm and was the incubator of a republican citizenry. Political ideology and rhetoric employed familial imagery (i.e., the father of his country, the founding fathers), and republicans believed that family polity had enormous influence on government. An unregulated family life could not be expected to produce civic virtue; chaos within the family translated into anarchy within the state.[26] Missionaries saw the failure of parents to control their children, which they phrased as "the want of parental government," not merely as a family matter but as an issue of national concern.[27] One of the primary objectives in establishing boarding schools among the Cherokees was to "impart to them that knowledge which is calculated to make them useful citizens." In order to accomplish that and other objectives, "the children should be removed as much as possible from the society of the natives," that is, their parents.[28] Once again, the Cherokees did not live up to unrealistic expectations. After decades of boarding schools, Albert Gallatin still insisted: "The Indians, as individuals, have preserved a much greater independence than is compatible with a more advanced state of civilization. They will hardly submit to any restraints."[29]

While republicans feared arbitrary and autocratic government, they also recoiled in horror at the specter of no government. For critics of the Indians, no government was precisely what Native peoples seemed to have. In his justification for removing eastern Indians, Lewis Cass wrote: "Government is unknown among them; certainly, that government which prescribes general rules and enforces or vindicates them. The utter nakedness of their society can be known only by personal observation. The tribes seem to be held together by a kind of family ligament; by the ties of blood, which in the infancy of society are stronger as other associations are weaker." Euro-Americans might employ familial imagery and pay homage to the "father of his country," but family could not substitute for government among a "civilized" people. Nevertheless, extended families—clans—continued to have some role in Cherokee government as late as the 1830s. Terrible abominations, Cass charged, resulted when responsibility for law and order rested with families, in particular, "retaliation on the next of kin." Reliance on family for protection and justice meant that Native peoples failed to establish the fundamental institutions of "civilization."[30] Shifting governmental responsibilities from clans to a republican state, of course, eliminated women from participation in the protection of person and property, but for Cass and others, such a consequence only provided additional incentive. Women, they believed, had an entirely different role to play in a republic.

The concept of republican motherhood placed on women considerable responsibility for inculcating republican values and linked female private virtue, defined as purity and piety, to the male civic virtues of independence, reason, moderation, and productivity. According to historian Linda Kerber, "responsibility for maintaining public virtue was channeled into domestic life."[31] The sexual autonomy enjoyed by Cherokee women, therefore, had political ramifications: James Adair described the Cherokees' lack of laws against adultery as "petticoat-government"—that is, the failure of men to control women's sexuality elevated women to positions of power over men, an unnatural political hierarchy.[32] While sexual purity supposedly liberated women in the same way that political independence and economic autonomy liberated men, sexual freedom, according to Europeans, degraded women, jeopardized civic order, and subverted republican values. What Euro-Americans perceived as the absence or blatant disregard of marriage vows by Native peoples had profound significance far beyond the individuals involved. Such behavior bespoke an absence of rules, violated the social contract, and threatened to reduce humans to the level of animals. The Iroquois historian Cadwallader Colden, for example, regarded matrilineality as "the natural course of all animals" because men had no proprietary interest in their offspring.[33] "Civilized" man had moved beyond this "natural course" and had adopted laws, both civil and religious, that bound fathers to children and husbands to wives.

An anonymous treatise suggested that the best way to civilize the Cherokees and make them good citizens was to regularize familial relations: "The morality which it is the part of education to inculcate, refers principally to our relation with others. It teaches us to respect the rights both of person and of property of every individual. The first personal relation in the order of nature, and the nearest which individuals can have, is that of husband and wife; which gives rise to the next, of parent and child. Here our own moral obligations have their origin and flowing as from a fountain, stream and branch in the order of our duties, connecting individuals, and families, and nations, and generations. As I have before said, neither of these relations subsists among the Cherokees. The father does not know his child nor consequently the child his father. Reformation must therefore begin by instituting marriage as a solemn inviolable contract."[34]

Contracts, of course, are legal agreements normally used to secure some form of property—to bind sales of property or to specify payment (in some sort of property) for services. Describing marriage as a contract implies proprietary rights, and indeed the absence of a binding marital contract suggested to this author and others profound ignorance of individual property and the rights associated with its ownership. Anglo-Americans pointed to familial relations as evidence that Native peoples lacked a fully developed concept of property and property holding. These people seemed so devoid of any notion of property that men did not enjoy an exclusive proprietary interest in their wives, certitude of the paternity of their wives' offspring, or control over their children. The absence of property and proprietary rights was at the very heart of Native "barbarism."[35]

Property created citizens. The essayist Samuel Stanhope Smith found that the "circumstances . . . which render the relinquishing of his native region a much less sacrifice to the savage, than to the citizen" included the presumed fact that only the citizen "is attached to his country by property." On the contrary, "a savage can hardly be said to have a country."[36] James Hall maintained "that the insecurity of property, or rather the entire absence of all ideas of property, is the chief cause of their barbarism," and he insisted that civilization could be accomplished only by teaching Native peoples "notions of property."[37] In the early nineteenth century, the most alarming development among Native peoples, particularly the Cherokees, was their elaboration and codification of land tenure based on the principle of common ownership. This process occurred in virtual contradiction to the goals of the civilization program, which was intended to produce private ownership of realty.

Furthermore, restrictions on the transfer of property distinguished between Cherokees and non-Cherokees; that is, a Cherokee could purchase improvements within the Nation but a non-Cherokee could not. Cass complained: "In the civil polity of the Cherokees, and, we believe, of the Creeks, as now established, there seems to be a severalty of property among themselves, regulated we know not how, and a community of property with respect to the federal and state governments."[38] The Cherokees had managed to secure their land base by preventing its piecemeal alienation. While the practicality of common ownership under the circumstances is obvious, such efforts had roots in the communal values of traditional Cherokee culture, now expressed most clearly by women, rather than in the individualistic, acquisitive values of the male elite who instituted these measures.

Cass and others who wanted the Indians out of the Southeast conceded "that individuals among the Cherokees had acquired property, and with it more enlarged views and juster notions of the value of our institutions, and the unprofitableness of their own." But, Cass charged, "this change of opinion and condition is confined, in a great measure, to some of the half-breeds and their immediate connextions." Slave labor and commerce along the federal road had enabled them to amass fortunes, but "the great body of the people are in a state of helpless and hopeless poverty." Cass attributed their situation to "improvidence and habitual indolence," which in the coded language of the nineteenth century meant cultural conservatism.[39]

Proponents of removal blamed the Cherokees' refusal to negotiate with the federal government on the wealthy, who did not want to lose the estates they had established in the Southeast, and hatched a variety of schemes to discredit or banish particularly obstinate members of the elite so that they could no longer manipulate the mass of Cherokees.[40] Benjamin Curry, the United States agent for enrolling Cherokees to go west voluntarily, even suggested to the Georgia legislature that "where a man had two wives, and one could be induced to enrol, that all the improvements should be valued to her, and that she should be protected in the removal of all negro slaves on the farm on which she lived, or she should have the disposal of them to whom she wished."[41] While the Georgia legislature never seriously considered this idea, other measures enabled Georgians to dispossess most members of the elite. Such schemes, however, illustrate the profound ignorance of advocates for removal.

Even before his arrival in the Cherokee Nation in 1830, a visitor from Connecticut heard that the Cherokee elite had thwarted the will of the majority: "Almost every one who spoke of this removal, intimated that the private members of the nation, and the full Cherokees especially, were willing and even anxious to go, but were kept back, by the influence of their chiefs, and of the whites living among them." After spending time among the Cherokees, however, he came to a different conclusion: "I was repeatedly informed, both by full Cherokees and by others, that most of those who had enrolled to go to the Arkansas, were either white men having Indian families, or halfbreeds, and that but very few full Cherokees had enrolled. This class are evidently the most opposed to a removal."[42] Most Cherokees did not regard their homeland as a commodity to be sold. Only those Cherokees who were likely to have patriarchal families—"white men . . . or halfbreeds"—seemed interested in going west in 1830, and when a small group of Cherokee men illegally signed a removal treaty five years later, several of them had non-Cherokee wives.[43]

Opposition to removal found strength and sustenance in the traditional culture of Cherokee women. Their association with the land and common title to it as well as their centrality to family and community quietly challenged the men who accumulated vast wealth, acted out of self-interest, and asserted political authority over other Cherokees. But the institutional changes implemented by these men had largely eliminated women from public action. They seemed to retreat into the shadows, and while they exerted considerable moral force during the removal crisis, they had even less power to resist removal than the male leadership whose authority the federal government subverted. In the winter of 1838–39, the main body of the Cherokee Nation moved west to join earlier emigrants. They left behind in the remote mountains a small remnant, the Eastern Band of Cherokee Indians. They also left the land that had soaked up Selu's blood, but they carried with them the spirit of Selu. A distinct Cherokee women's culture survived removal, rebuilding, civil war, reconstruction, allotment, and Oklahoma statehood.

The reemergence of Cherokee women onto a public stage at the end of the twentieth century is testimony to the endurance of that culture. Service to community rather than individual achievement still distinguishes Cherokee women and brings them acclaim. In 1985 Wilma Mankiller succeeded a male banker as principal chief of the Cherokee Nation of Oklahoma. She rose to prominence as a community organizer who worked with isolated and impoverished Cherokees.[44] In 1995 the Eastern Band of Cherokees in North Carolina impeached an allegedly corrupt chief who had used the office for personal gain and replaced him with Joyce Dugan, a teacher who had served as superintendent of schools.[45] These women did not become chiefs by succeeding in business or law; they became chiefs because they embodied the values of generations of Cherokee women, values apparently still honored and respected by men and women alike. The story of Cherokee women, therefore, is not one of declining status and lost culture, but one of persistence and change, conservatism and adaptation, tragedy and survival.

NOTES

INTRODUCTION

1. Janet D. Spector, "Male/Female Task Differentiation among the Hidatsa: Toward the Development of an Archaeological Approach to the Study of Gender," in *The Hidden Half: Studies in Plains Indian Women,* ed. Patricia Albers and Beatrice Medicine (Lanham MD: University Press of America, 1983), 77–100; Joan M. Gero and Margaret W. Conkey, *Engendering Archaeology: Women and Prehistory* (Oxford: Basil and Blackwell, 1991); Margaret Scarry, ed. *Foraging and Farming in the Eastern Woodlands* (Gainesville: University Press of Florida, 1993).

2. For example, see Carolyn Niethammer, *Daughters of the Earth* (New York: Collier Books, 1977); Mark St. Pierre and Tilda Long Soldier, *Walking in the Sacred Manner: Healers, Dreamers, and Pipe Carriers—Medicine Women of the Plains Indians* (New York: Simon and Schuster, 1995); Virginia Giglio, *Southern Cheyenne Women's Songs* (Norman: University of Oklahoma Press, 1994); and Steven Wall, *Wisdom's Daughters: Conversations with Women Elders of Native America* (New York: HarperCollins, 1993). A good guide to older autobiographies can be found in Gretchen M. Bataille and Kathleen Mullen Sands, *American Indian Women: Telling Their Lives* (Lincoln: University of Nebraska Press, 1984). Since publication of that work, a number of Native women have written or dictated autobiographies, including Mary Crow Dog and Richard Erdoes, *Lakota Woman* (New York: Harper-Harper-Collins, 1990); Mark St. Pierre, *Madonna Swan: A Lakota Woman's Story* (Norman: University of Oklahoma Press, 1994); and Wilma Mankiller and Michael Wallis, *Mankiller: A Chief and Her People* (New York: St. Martin's Press, 1993).

3. The best description of ethnohistorical methodology remains James Axtell, "Ethnohistory: An Historian's Viewpoint," in *Ethnohistory* 26 (1979): 1–13.

4. Janet D. Spector, *What This Awl Means: Feminist Archaeology at a Wahpeton Dakota Village* (St. Paul: Minnesota Historical Society Press, 1993), 73–75.

5. Vernon James Knight, "Tukabatchee Archaeological Investigations at an Historical Creek Town, Elmore County, Alabama, 1984," Office of Archaeological Research, Alabama State Museum of Natural History, University of Alabama, Report of Investigations 45, July 31, 1985, 116–19.

6. A good example is in Ella Cara Deloria's ethnographic novel, *Waterlily* (Lincoln: University of Nebraska Press, 1988), 87.

7. For example, see Amelia Rector Bell, "Separate People: Speaking of Creek Men and Women," *American Anthropologist* 92 (1990): 332–45. For a study of the linguistically disparate ways men and women dealt with culture change, see James T. Carson, "Native Americans, the Market Revolution, and Culture Change: The Choctaw Cattle Economy, 1690–1830," *Agricultural History* 71 (1997): 1–18.

8. Waheenee said that Hidatsa women "thought that the corn plants had souls, as children have souls, and that the growing corn liked to hear us sing, as children like to hear their mothers sing to them." Gilbert L. Wilson, *Waheenee: An Indian Girl's Story Told by Herself* (1927; reprint, Lincoln: University of Nebraska Press, 1981), 94.

9. For a variety of practices relating to childbirth and menstruation, see James Axtell, ed., *Indian Peoples of Eastern America: A Documentary History of the Sexes* (New York: Oxford University Press, 1981).

10. Thomas Buckley, "Menstruation and the Power of Yurok Women: Methods in Cultural Reconstruction," *American Ethnologist* 9 (1982): 47–60.

11. Charles Hudson, "James Adair as Anthropologist," *Ethnohistory* 24 (1977): 317; James Adair, *Adair's History of the American Indians,* ed. Samuel Cole Williams (Johnson City: Watauga Press, 1930), 130–31, 198. Adair also probably had a Cherokee wife and descendants.

12. Bernard Romans, *A Concise History of East and West Florida* (1775; reprint, Gainesville: University of Florida Press, 1962), 40–43. Romans conceded that "in married women, incontinence is severely punished," but other Europeans noted that even a breach of marital vows sometimes went unpunished and that husbands on occasion loaned their wives to others. See Theda Perdue, "Native American Women: Old World Perceptions, New World Realities," in *Native Americans in the Early Republic,* ed. Frederick E. Hoxie and Ronald Hoffman (Charlottesville: University Press of Virginia, 1998).

13. See Regna Darnell, *Readings in the History of Anthropology* (New York: Harper & Row, 1974); Robert E. Bieder, *Science Encounters the Indian, 1820–1880* (Norman: University of Oklahoma Press, 1986); and Robert F. Berkhofer, *The White Man's Indian: Images of the American Indian from Columbus to the Present* (New York: Alfred A. Knopf, 1978).

14. Henrietta L. Moore, *Feminism and Anthropology* (Minneapolis: University of Minnesota Press, 1988), 197; Alison Wylie, "Gender Theory and the Archaeological Record: Why Is There No Archaeology of Women?" in Gero and Conkey, *Engendering Archaeology,* 31–54.

15. Alice B. Kehoe, "The Shackles of Tradition," in Albers and Medicine, eds., *The Hidden Half,* 53–77.

16. Patty Jo Watson and Mary C. Kennedy, "The Development of Horticulture in the Eastern Woodlands of North America: Women's Role," in Gero and Conkey, *Engendering Archaeology,* 255–75.

17. Guy Prentice, "Origin of Plant Domestication in the Eastern United States: Promoting the Individual in Archaeological Theory," *Southeastern Archaeology* 5 (1986): 103–19.

18. Angie Debo, *The Road to Disappearance: A History of the Creek Indians* (Norman: University of Oklahoma Press, 1941). Debo relied largely on the work of anthropologist John Swanton for information about the traditional role of women. Women had an even more insignificant role in Henry Thompson Malone's *Cherokees of the Old South: A People in Transition* (Athens: University of Georgia Press, 1956).

19. Carolyn Thomas Foreman, *Indian Women Chiefs* (Muskogee OK: n.p., 1954).

20. James Axtell, "Colonial Americans without the Indians: Counterfactual Reflections," *Journal of American History* 73 (1987): 981–96.

21. Joan Wallach Scott, "Gender: A Useful Category of Historical Analysis," *American Historical Review* 91 (1986): 1053–75.

22. Sherry B. Ortner, "Is Female to Male as Male Is to Culture?" in *Woman, Culture, and Society,* ed. Michelle Z. Rosaldo and Louise Lamphere (Stanford: Stanford University Press, 1974), 67–88.

23. Mona Etienne and Eleanor Leacock, eds., *Women and Colonization: Anthropological Perspectives* (New York: Praeger, 1980). Other examples are Alan Klein, "The Political Economy of Gender: A Nineteenth Century Plains Indian Case Study," in Albers and Medicine, eds., *The Hidden Half,* 143–74; Carol Devens, *Countering Colonization: Native American Women and Great Lakes Missions, 1630–1900* (Berkeley: University of California Press, 1992).

24. Nancy Shoemaker, "The Rise or Fall of Iroquois Women," *Journal of Women's History* 2 (1991): 39–57; Shoemaker, ed., *Negotiators of Change: Historical Perspectives on Native American Women* (New York: Routledge, 1995).

25. Laura F. Klein and Lillian A. Ackerman, eds., *Women and Power in Native North America* (Norman: University of Oklahoma Press, 1995).

26. Richard A. Sattler, "Women's Status among the Muskogee and Cherokee," in Klein and Ackerman, eds., *Women and Power,* 214–29.

27. William N. Fenton, "Indian and White Relations in Eastern North America: A Common Ground for History and Ethnology," in *American Indian and White Relations to 1830: Needs and Opportunities for Study* (Chapel Hill: University of North Carolina Press, 1957), 21–22.

28. Charles Hudson, *Knights of Spain, Warriors of the Sun: Hernando de Soto and the South's Ancient Kingdoms* (Athens: University of Georgia Press, 1997), 11–30, 190–99. Also see Marvin T. Smith, *Archaeology of Aboriginal Culture Change in the Interior Southeast: Depopulation during the Early Historic Period* (Gainesville: University Press of Florida, 1987).

29. Hudson, *Knights of Spain,* 417–26. For disease, also see Alfred W. Crosby Jr., *The Columbian Exchange: Biological and Cultural Consequences of 1492* (Westport CT: Greenwood Press, 1972); Russell Thornton, *American Indian Holocaust and*

Survival: A Population History since 1492 (Norman: University of Oklahoma Press, 1987), and *The Cherokees: A Population History* (Lincoln: University of Nebraska Press, 1990); Peter H. Wood, "The Changing Population of the Colonial South: An Overview by Race and Region, 1685–1790," in *Powhatan's Mantle: Indians in the Colonial Southeast,* ed. Peter H. Wood, Gregory A. Waselkov, and M. Thomas Hatley (Lincoln: University of Nebraska Press, 1989), 35–103; and Henry F. Dobyns, *Their Numbers Become Thinned: Native American Population Dynamics in Eastern North America* (Knoxville: University of Tennessee Press, 1983).

30. Edward Gaylord Bourne, ed., *Narratives of the Career of Hernando de Soto,* 2 vols. (New York: Allerton Book Co., 1922), 1:65–72; John Lawson, *A New Voyage to Carolina,* ed. Hugh T. Lefler (Chapel Hill: University of North Carolina Press, 1967), 25; Alexander S. Salley Jr., ed., "A Relation of a Voyage on the Coast of the Province of Carolina, 1666, by Robert Sandford," *Narratives of Early Carolina, 1650–1708* (New York: Charles Scribner's Sons, 1911), 90. See also Martha W. McCartney, "Cockacoeske, Queen of Pamunkey: Diplomat and Suzeraine" in Wood, Waselkov, and Hatley, eds., *Powhatan's Mantle,* 173–95.

PART I: A WOMAN'S WORLD

1. See Bennie C. Keel, *Cherokee Archaeology: Study of the Appalachian Summit* (Knoxville: University of Tennessee Press, 1976), and Roy S. Dickens Jr., *Cherokee Prehistory: The Pisgah Phase in the Appalachian Summit Region* (Knoxville: University of Tennessee Press, 1976).

2. James Mooney, "Myths of the Cherokee," *Nineteenth Annual Report,* Bureau of American Ethnology (Washington DC: Government Printing Office, 1900), 239–40, 244–45.

3. Charles Hudson, "The Cherokee Concept of Natural Balance," *Indian Historian* 3 (1970): 51–54.

4. Mooney, "Myths," 142–49.

5. According to the myth, "the strange boy sprang from the blood of the game which Selu had washed off at the river's edge." In *The Southeastern Indians* (Knoxville: University of Tennessee Press, 1976), Charles Hudson suggests that "this may be an oblique way of saying that Selu put menstrual blood into the river" (p. 515 n. 49). Wild Boy referred to himself as "elder brother" to Kana'ti and as Selu's son.

1. CONSTRUCTING GENDER

1. Adair, *History,* 435.

2. John Howard Payne Papers, typescript, 14 vols., Newberry Library, Chicago, 4:27 (hereafter cited as Payne Papers). As late as the 1950s, the Eastern Cherokees in

North Carolina performed some labor communally. Formed into work companies called *gadugi,* individuals joined together to work in the fields and offer assistance to members in need. See John Gulick, *Cherokees at the Crossroads* (Chapel Hill: University of North Carolina Institute for Research in Social Science, 1960), 88–94.

3. Adair, *History,* 436–37.

4. The Cherokees grew corn, beans, sunflowers (and the species called Jerusalem artichokes), squash, pumpkins, and gourds before contact with Europeans. After contact, they quickly added watermelons, sweet potatoes, and peas. Gary C. Goodwin, *Cherokees in Transition: A Study of Changing Culture and Environment prior to 1775* (Chicago: University of Chicago Department of Geography, 1977), 51–55.

5. Goodwin, *Cherokees in Transition,* 51–55; Mooney, "Myths," 423–24. "Most of these customs have now fallen into disuse excepting among the old people," Mooney wrote when he recorded the rituals associated with corn cultivation in the late nineteenth century. Based on disparities between eighteenth-century accounts of the Green Corn Ceremony and Mooney's account, I suspect that women originally had a far more prominent role than the informants remembered or Mooney recorded. In any event, the genderless "owner of the field" who conducted or participated in these ceremonies almost certainly would have been a woman in the eighteenth century and either a man or women in Mooney's time. In the 1960s, Mollie Sequoyah confided to Ray Fogelson "that women did not want men in the fields, that the growing of maize was a sacred activity involving specialized magical and practical knowledge, that men were unclean—'bloody' was how she expressed it—and that the presence of 'bloody young men' in the cornfields could endanger the crops." See Raymond D. Fogelson, "On the 'Petticoat Government' of the Eighteenth-Century Cherokees," in *Personality and the Cultural Construction of Society: Papers in Honor of Melford E. Spiro,* ed. David K. Jordan and Marc J. Swartz (Tuscaloosa: University of Alabama Press, 1990), 174.

6. Cyrus Kingsbury Journal, 13 February 1817, Papers of the American Board of Commissioners for Foreign Missions, Houghton Library, Harvard University, Cambridge MA (hereafter cited as ABCFM); Diary of the Moravian Mission at Springplace, June 1801, trans. Carl C. Mauleshagen, typescript, Georgia Historical Commission, Department of Natural Resources, Atlanta (hereafter cited as Moravian Diary).

7. Hudson, *Southeastern Indians,* 293–94. Corn and beans are also nutritionally complementary. See Goodwin, *Cherokees in Transition,* 52.

8. Adair, *History,* 436.

9. Henry Timberlake, *Lieut. Henry Timberlake's Memoirs, 1756–1765,* ed. Samuel Cole Williams (1927; Marietta GA: Continental Book Company, 1948), 68.

10. Adair, *History,* 438.

11. Louis-Philippe, *Diary of My Travels in America,* trans. Stephen Becker (New York: Delacorte Press, 1977), 88.

12. William Bartram, "Observations on the Creek and Cherokee Indians, 1789," *Transactions of the American Ethnological Society* 3, pt. 1 (1853): 31; Samuel Cole Williams, ed., "Journey of the Moravians to the Cherokee and Cumberland Countries (1799)," *Early Travels in the Tennessee Country, 1540–1800* (John City TN: Watauga Press, 1928), 478; Payne Papers, 4:196; Butrick to Worcester, 2 July 1818, ABCFM; Benjamin Hawkins, Journal, 4 Dec. 1796, in *Letters of Benjamin Hawkins, 1796–1806,* vol. 9 of *Georgia Historical Society Collections* (Savannah: Georgia Historical Society, 1916), 24, (hereafter cited as Hawkins, *Letters*). Among the wild foods that Cherokees in the east still enjoy are *sochani* (*Rudbeckia laciniata*); creases (*Barbarea vulgaris,* in Cherokee, *oo-li-si*); poke (*Phytolacca americana,* in Cherokee, *tla-ye-de*); and ramps (*Allium tricoccum,* in Cherokee, *wa-s-di*). See Mary Ulmer and Samuel E. Beck, *Cherokee Cooklore* (Cherokee NC: Museum of the Cherokee Indian, 1951), 47, and Paul B. Hamel and Mary U. Chiltoskey, *Cherokee Plants and Their Uses: A Four Hundred Year History* (Sylva NC: Herald Publishing Co., 1975), 30, 31, 50, 52.

13. Adair, *History,* 94.

14. Adair, *History,* 436.

15. Williams, "Bro. Schneider's Journey to the Cherokee Country (1783–84)," *Early Travels,* 261.

16. Payne Papers, 4:74; Adair, *History,* 442.

17. Payne Papers, 4:28; Adair, *History,* 447; Louis-Philippe, *Travels,* 73.

18. Payne Papers, 4:27–28, 73, 199; Adair, *History,* 446.

19. Payne Papers, 4:27–28. Cherokees continue to eat a number of these dishes, particularly bean bread and *ga nu ge* (*kenuche; connutche*), or hickory nut soup. See Ulmer and Beck, *Cherokee Cooklore,* 44–45, 48; Ruth Bradley Holmes and Betty Sharp Smith, *Beginning Cherokee* (2d ed., Norman: University of Oklahoma Press, 1977), 47.

20. Williams, "Moravians," *Early Travels,* 479; Adair, *History,* 447.

21. Adair, *History,* 438, 46.

22. Bartram, "Observations," 82.

23. Adair, *History,* 456.

24. Williams, "Schneider's Journey," *Early Travels,* 257.

25. Sarah H. Hill, *Weaving New Worlds: An Ecological History of Southeastern Cherokee Women and their Basketry* (Chapel Hill: University of North Carolina Press, 1997).

26. Adair, *History,* 456.

27. Adair, *History,* 454.

28. Payne Papers, 4:28.

29. Williams, "Schneider's Journey," *Early Travels*, 257–58; Lawson, *Voyage to Carolina*, 36, 195; Hawkins, Directions for Tanning, in Hawkins, *Letters*, 426–27.

30. Bartram, "Observations," 31.

31. Payne Papers, 4: 28, 72.

32. Romans, *Concise History*, 41.

33. Louis-Philippe, *Travels*, 73. For the role of women in the horticulture of another Indian people, see Joan Jensen, "Native Women and Agriculture: A Seneca Case Study," *Sex Roles: A Journal of Research* 3 (1977): 423–42. Judith K. Brown suggests that "the degree to which women participate in subsistence activities depends on the compatibility of the latter with simultaneous child-care responsibilities" (1074) in "A Note on the Division of Labor by Sex," *American Anthropologist* 72 (1970): 1073–78.

34. Adair, *History*, 436.

35. John Norton, *The Journal of Major John Norton*, ed. Carl F. Klinck and James J. Talman (Toronto: Champlain Society, 1970), 125–26.

36. Payne Papers, 4:27.

37. Anon., "Reflections on the Institutions of the Cherokee Indians," *Analectic Magazine* 36 (1818): 43 (hereafter cited as "Reflections").

38. Bartram, "Observations," 66.

39. Cephas Washburn, *Reminiscences of the Indians* (Richmond: Presbyterian Committee on Publications, 1869), 206–7.

40. James Mooney, "Sacred Formulas of the Cherokees," *Seventh Annual Report*, Bureau of American Ethnology (Washington DC: Government Printing Office, 1886), 401.

41. Adair, *History*, 410; Payne Papers, 6:209; Frans M. Olbrechts, "Cherokee Belief and Practice with Regard to Childbirth," *Anthropos* 26 (1931): 23.

42. Norton, *Journal*, 130; John Philip Reid, *A Law of Blood: Primitive Law of the Cherokee Nation* (New York: New York University Press, 1970), 138; Payne Papers, 6:209; Olbrechts, "Cherokee . . . Childbirth," 17–33. In *Cherokee Prehistory*, Dickens points out that in the Pisgah Phase (c. 1250–1450 A.D.) "fur-bearing mammals . . . were hunted as much for their fur as for their meat." In the Qualla Phase (c. 1450–1650 A.D.), "evidence points to maize-bean-squash cultivation, supplemented by hunting, fishing, and gathering," pp. 14, 203.

43. Payne Papers, 1:43.

44. Adair, *History*, 105–15, 462.

45. Mooney, "Myths," 423.

46. Adair, *History*, 105–15, 462; Timberlake, *Memoirs*, 64, 88; Mooney, "Myths," 423.

47. Bartram, "Observations," 40.

48. Hudson, *Southeastern Indians,* 209–10, 223. Hudson discusses Natchez and Creek redistribution in particular.

49. Williams, "Schneider's Journey," *Early Travels,* 262.

50. Timberlake, *Memoirs,* 100. The herbs that the woman used to make medicine held special significance for the Cherokees. Laurel (probably both *Rhododendron maximum* and *Kalmia latifolia*), along with cedar, pine, spruce, and holly, held the distinction of remaining green all year, an attribute acquired when the earth was first made and these plants stayed awake for seven days while other plants dozed. As a result, the evergreens became the "greatest for medicine." Mooney, "Myths," 240.

51. Mary Douglas, *Purity and Danger: An Analysis of Pollution and Taboo* (London: Routledge and Keegan Paul, 1966), 94–95. I have narrowed Douglas's definition of "pollution" along lines suggested by Ray Fogelson in "On the 'Petticoat Government' of the Eighteenth-Century Cherokees," 172–73.

52. Mooney, "Sacred Formulas," 370, 375, 380–81.

53. Hudson, "Uktena: A Cherokee Anomalous Monster," *Journal of Cherokee Studies* 3 (1978): 62–75; Douglas, 96; Olbrechts, "Cherokee . . . Childbirth," 21.

54. Adair, *History,* 129–30.

55. Mooney, "Sacred Formulas," 330–31.

56. Adair, *History,* 129–30.

57. Payne Papers, 3:76, 4:63, 91; Mooney, "Sacred Formulas," 325.

58. Payne Papers, 1:38, 3:76–77, 4:218.

59. Adair, *History,* 130. The Choctaws used the term *Ishtohoolo Aba* to refer to the sun, the giver of life.

60. George Devereux long ago suggested that menstrual taboos actually indicate a superior status for women; see "The Psychology of Feminine Genital Bleeding," *International Journal of Psychoanalysis* 31 (1950): 237–57. Nevertheless, Frank Young and Albert A. Bacdayan attributed menstrual taboos to male dominance in "Menstrual Taboos and Social Rigidity," *Ethnology* 4 (1965): 225–40. Phillip M. Bock criticized Young and Bacdayan for ethnocentrism and maintained that menstrual taboos do not discriminate against women; see "Love, Magic, Menstrual Taboos, and the Facts of Geography," *American Anthropologist* 69 (1967): 213–17. Marla N. Powers demonstrated that the menstrual taboos of the Oglala emphasized and celebrated the female reproductive role; see "Menstruation and Reproduction: An Oglala Case," *Signs* 6 (1980): 54–65. Thomas Buckley found menstruation to be a source of spiritual power for women in "Menstruation and the Power of Yurok Women." More recently, Patricia Galloway challenged archaeologists to pursue an archaeology of women centered on menstrual huts and ceremonial objects; see "Where Have All the Menstrual Huts Gone? The Invisibility of Menstrual Seclu-

sion in the Late Prehistoric Southeast," Southeastern Anthropological Society meeting, 1990; revised version presented at the Appalachian State University Conference on Women in Anthropology, 1994.

61. Mooney, "Myths," 319–20.

62. Olbrechts, "Cherokee . . . Childbirth," 21–24; Mooney, "Myths," 422; Payne Papers, 4:282.

63. Olbrechts, "Cherokee . . . Childbirth," 21–24.

64. Olbrechts, "Cherokee . . . Childbirth"; Payne Papers, 3:77. Rayna Green has suggested to me that accounts of these restrictions may result from misunderstanding or misrepresentation by observers, which certainly is possible. It may also be the case that Cherokees did not seriously expect the outcomes predicted—just as many people avoid walking under a ladder but do not really believe that doing so brings bad luck.

65. Olbrechts, "Cherokee . . . Childbirth," 19–21.

66. Olbrechts, "Cherokee . . . Childbirth," 24–29; Payne Papers, 4:94.

67. Mooney, "Sacred Formulas," 363–64.

68. Olbrechts, "Cherokee . . . Childbirth," 24–29; Payne Papers, 4:94.

69. Timberlake, *Memoirs,* 90; Payne Papers, 1:21, 4:94.

70. Olbrechts, "Cherokee . . .Childbirth," 24–29.

71. Mooney, "Myths," 284, 306, 308–9, 424.

72. John Gerar William de Brahm, *De Brahm's Report of the General Survey in the Southern District of North America,* ed. Louis De Vorsey Jr. (Columbia: University of South Carolina Press, 1971), 108; Adair, *History,* 6.

73. Timberlake, *Memoirs,* 90.

74. Hudson, *Southeastern Indians,* 231. The enactment of a law prohibiting infanticide implies that the practice still existed in the early nineteenth century. *Laws of the Cherokee Nation: Adopted by the Council at Various Times, Reprinted for the Benefit of the Nation,* vol. 5 of *The Constitutions and Laws of the American Indian Tribes* (Wilmington DE: Scholarly Resources, 1973), 79. For an archaeological investigation of infanticide, see Louise M. Robbins, "The Story of Life Revealed by the Dead," in *Biocultural Adaptation in Prehistoric America,* ed. Robert L. Blakely (Athens: University of Georgia Press, 1977), 10–26. Although it was illegal, women in both England and New England committed infanticide for social and economic reasons. See Peter Hoffer and N. E. H. Hull, *Murdering Mothers: Infanticide in England and New England, 1588–1803* (New York: New York University Press, 1984).

75. Olbrechts, "Cherokee . . . Childbirth," 19.

76. Payne Papers, 3:77.

77. Timberlake, *Memoirs,* 90.

78. Payne Papers, 3:76–77.

79. These two realms should not be considered analogous to the Christian concept of heaven and hell.

80. Mooney, "Myths," 240. See also Hudson, *Southeastern Indians,* 127–28.

81. Payne Papers, 4:341; Adair, *History,* 167–78; Thomas Griffiths, "Journal of a Visit to the Cherokees, 1767," Treasurers and Comptroller's Papers: Indian Affairs and Land, North Carolina Archives, Raleigh, 7. Also see Fogelson, "On the 'Petticoat Government' of the Eighteenth-Century Cherokees," 174–75.

82. Payne Papers, 4:346.

83. Adair, *History,* 172.

84. Payne Papers, 3:43–45, 6:209.

85. Adair, *History,* 140–41.

86. Mooney, "Myths," 432.

87. Mooney, "Sacred Formulas," 319–22, 370–71.

88. Hudson, *Southeastern Indians,* 320–21.

89. Hudson, *Southeastern Indians,* 128.

90. In "Cherokee Notions of Power," Raymond D. Fogelson points out that power "was open to anyone who applied himself over the course of a lifetime to patient accumulation of knowledge, conscientious attention to ritual detail, and maintenance of a moral relationship to fellow Cherokees." Power could be dissipated and had to be renewed, and the attainment of old age confirmed the possession of power. In Fogelson and Richard N. Adams, *The Anthropology of Power* (New York: Academic Press, 1977), 185–94.

91. Adair, *History,* 109, 127, 169. For beloved women, see below.

92. Timberlake, *Memoirs,* 100; Norton, *Journal,* 124, 135. The Cherokees used the term *beloved* to apply to women and men who were repositories of spiritual knowledge and power. The title was individually acquired—the wives of beloved men were not necessarily beloved women and vice versa. Normally these people would have been quite elderly, and they commanded great respect.

93. Adair, *History,* 109.

94. Romans, *Concise History,* 82–83.

95. Quoted in Walter L. Williams, *The Spirit and the Flesh: Sexual Diversity in American Indian Culture* (Boston: Beacon Press, 1986), 4.

96. Adair, *History,* 163. Apparently, men trained as priests were exempt from war and the hunt in order to spare them the pollution of spilling blood. Griffiths, "Visit," 7.

97. Mooney, "Myths," 250, 297–98, 327–29; Hudson, *Southeastern Indians,* 147–48.

98. "List of Indian Towns and Head Men," in William L. McDowell, ed., *Documents Relating to Indian Affairs, May 21, 1750–August 7, 1754* (Columbia: South

Carolina Archives Department, 1958), 164–65; De Brahm, *General Survey,* 109; Payne Papers, 4:170, 3:124; Mooney, "Myths," 395, 419; Moravian Diary, 5 July 1807. Gambold was visiting in the polygamous household of James Vann, whose family is discussed in chapter 2.

99. Bartram, "Observations," 32.

100. Mooney, "Myths," 395; Payne Papers, 6:220; Alexander Longe, "A Small Postscript on the Ways and Manners of the Indians called Cherokees," ed. David H. Corkran, *Southern Indian Studies* 21 (1969): 14, 16, 20, 22, 24.

101. Mooney, "Myths," 250, 297–301.

102. Henry S. Sharp, "Asymmetric Equals: Women and Men among the Chipewyan," in Klein and Ackerman, eds., *Women and Power,* pp. 68–69. Durbin Feeling, *Cherokee-English Dictionary* (Tahlequah: Cherokee Nation of Oklahoma), xiii. The numbers in Feeling's spelling indicate pitch in pronunciation.

103. As we shall see, Cherokees organized their world in terms of kinship rather than gender.

104. Peggy R. Sanday, "Theory of the Status of Women," *American Anthropologist* 75 (1973): 1682–1700.

2. DEFINING COMMUNITY

1. J. P. Evans, "Sketches of Cherokee Characteristics," *Journal of Cherokee Studies* 4 (1979): 10.

2. Lawson, *Voyage to Carolina,* 57.

3. Evans, "Sketches," 10.

4. Payne Papers, 4:355, 6:202; William H. Gilbert, "Eastern Cherokee Social Organization" in *Social Anthropology of North American Tribes,* ed. Fred Eggan (Chicago: University of Chicago Press, 1955), 287; "Reflections," 45.

5. Williams, "Schneider's Journey," *Early Travels,* 255.

6. Norton, *Journal,* 69.

7. Norton, *Journal,* 49.

8. Moravian Diary, 14 January 1814.

9. Payne Papers, 4:266.

10. Adair, *History,* 449–50; De Brahm, *General Survey,* 110; Williams, "Schneider's Journey," *Early Travels,* 260–61; Romans, *Concise History,* 67.

11. Longe, "Ways and Manners," 32.

12. Mooney, "Myths," 337–41, 345–47.

13. Payne Papers, 4:94, 170.

14. Moravian Diary, 8–9 Feb. 1829.

15. Longe, "Ways and Manners," 32.

16. Mooney, "Sacred Formulas," 307, 376.

17. Payne Papers, 3:35, 4:276; Adair, *History,* 198.

18. Butrick to Worcester, 1 January 1819, ABCFM.

19. "Reflections," 48; Alice Schlegel, *Male Dominance and Female Autonomy: Domestic Authority in Matrilineal Societies* (New Haven: Yale University Press, 1972), 87–88. Ray Fogelson cites evidence for the marriage of mother and daughter to the same man and offers explanations for such a union in "On the 'Petticoat Government' of the Eighteenth-Century Cherokees," 161–81

20. Mooney, "Myths," 291–93.

21. Moravian Diary, 1 Sept. 1813.

22. Lawson, *Voyage to Carolina,* 192.

23. Moravian Diary, 9 Jan. 1824.

24. Longe, "Ways and Manners," 30, 32.

25. Norton, *Journal,* 56.

26. Mooney, "Myths," 456.

27. Mooney, "Myths," 440.

28. Adair, *History,* 18–19.

29. Longe, "Ways and Manners," 32; Payne Papers, 8:12.

30. Gilbert, "Eastern Cherokee Social Organization," 296–97.

31. Evans, "Sketches," 10.

32. Griffiths, "Visit," 6.

33. Mooney, "Myths," 239.

34. Jack Frederick Kilpatrick and Anna Gritts Kilpatrick, *Run toward the Nightland: Magic of the Oklahoma Cherokees* (Dallas: Southern Methodist University Press, 1967), 31–33.

35. Payne Papers, 3:10, 11:110.

36. For examples, see The Head Men and Warriors of the Lower Cherokees, 10 May 1751, and Talk of the Raven and Others, 9 Aug. 1751, McDowell, *Documents, 1750–1754,* 62–63, 118–19. Newton D. Mereness, ed., "Journal of Colonel George Chicken's Journey from Charleston, S.C., to the Cherokees, 1726," in *Travels in the American Colonies* (New York: Macmillan, 1916), 128.

37. Mooney, "Myths," 368–69.

38. Theda Perdue, *Nations Remembered: An Oral History of the Five Civilized Tribes, 1865–1907* (Westport CT: Greenwood Press, 1980), 93.

39. Mooney, "Sacred Formulas," 338–39.

40. Adair, *History,* 19, 188–89.

41. Theda Perdue, "People without a Place: Aboriginal Cherokee Bondage," *Indian Historian* 9 (1976): 31–37.

42. John Phillip Reid, "A Perilous Rule: The Law of International Homicide"

in *The Cherokee Indian Nation: A Troubled History,* ed. Duane H. King (Knoxville: University of Tennessee Press, 1979), 39–40.

43. Lud. Grant to Governor Glen, 20 Aug. 1755, William L. McDowell Jr. *Documents Relating to Indian Affairs, 1754–1765* (Columbia: University of South Carolina Press, 1970), 74–75.

44. Adair, *History,* 162–63.

45. "Reflections," 42; Payne Papers, 4:331; Adair, *History,* 157.

46. Payne Papers, 7:7; Adair, *History,* 157.

47. Payne Papers, 2:28, 4:49.

48. Moravian Diary, May 1806. Other interpretations exist. Norton attributed Vann's death to the fact the he "was not generally beloved," *Journal,* 68. The anonymous author of "Reflections," 42–43, claimed that a black slave was offered in Vann's stead and was killed. If this account is accurate, Vann's death was more likely a political assassination than an act of vengeance.

49. "Reflections," 43; Adair, *History,* 156; Moravian Diary, 3 Feb. 1802.

50. Adair, *History,* 155; Payne Papers, 2:31–39.

51. Adair, *History,* 19; "Reflections," 43.

52. Longe, "Ways and Manners," 32; Lawson, *Voyage to Carolina,* 208; Adair, *History,* 158, 161.

53. Payne Papers, 7:17; Longe, "Ways and Manners," 32.

54. Adair, *History,* 408, 410, 412–13; Timberlake, *Memoirs,* 93.

55. Payne Papers, 3:74, 4:335, 4:342; Mooney, "Myths," 376, 390–91.

56. Mooney, "Myths, " 360, 363; Timberlake, *Memoirs,* 82; De Brahm, *General Survey,* 108–9; Adair, *History,* 418–19.

57. Timberlake, *Memoirs,* 94; John Haywood, *The Natural and Aboriginal History of Tennessee Up to the First Settlements Therein by the White People in the Year 1768* (1823; Jackson TN: n.p., 1959), 278. Ward permitted the women to torture and kill a boy who had been captured along with Mrs. Bean.

58. Deposition of William Springstone, 11 Dec. 1781, William P. Palmer, ed., *Calendar of Virginia State Papers and Other Manuscripts, 1652–1781, Preserved in the Capitol at Richmond,* 11 vols. (Richmond: Superintendent of Public Printing, 1875–1893) 1:446–47.

59. Adair, *History,* 161.

60. Williams, "Journal of Antoine Bonnefoy (1741–42)," *Early Travels,* 152.

61. David Menzies, "A True Relation of the Unheard-of Sufferings of David Menzies, Surgeon, among the Cherokees, and of His Surprising Deliverance," *Royal Magazine,* July 1761, 27.

62. Menzies, "True Relation," 27.

63. Proceedings of Sir William Johnson with the Indians, 4–12 March 1768, E. B. O' Callaghan and B. Fernow, eds., *Documents Relative to the Colonial History of the State of New York,* 15 vols. (Albany: Weed, Parsons, and Company, 1853–87), 8:38–53.

64. South Carolina Journal, Minutes of 9 Feb. 1757, Quoted in Reid, *A Law of Blood,* 69.

65. Timberlake, *Memoirs,* 93.

66. "Reflections," 41–42; Timberlake, *Memoirs,* 93.

67. Adair, *History,* 459–60.

68. Oral traditions suggest that a priestly clan once ruled the Cherokees, but it had been overthrown by the people for violating incest taboos and otherwise abusing its authority. Daniel Butrick, from whom Payne received much of his information, thought it probable "that they did not adhere to the same form of government at all times." Payne Papers 7:7; Norton, *Journal,* 80; Mooney, "Myths," 392–93. Also see Raymond D. Fogelson, "Who Were the Ani-Kutani? An Excursion into Cherokee Historical Thought," *Ethnohistory* 31 (1984): 255–63.

69. Adair, *History,* 127; Louis-Philippe, *Travels,* 86; Norton, *Journal,* 80; Payne Papers, 4:44; Timberlake, *Memoirs,* 93.

70. Adair, *History,* 261; Norton, *Journal,* 39.

71. Adair, *History,* 460.

72. Anthropologist Robert K. Thomas, a participant in the University of North Carolina's Cross Cultural Laboratory, articulated this concept in the 1950s. See Gulick, *Cherokees at the Crossroads,* 121–53.

73. Adair, *History,* 152.

74. Mooney, "Sacred Formulas," 380, 382.

75. Payne Papers, 1:36–37.

76. Louis-Philippe, *Travels,* 72.

77. Norton, *Journal,* 70.

78. Adair, *History,* 153.

79. Longe, "Ways and Manners," 32.

80. Louis-Philippe, *Travels,* 71–72.

81. Longe, "Ways and Manners," 30; Timberlake, *Memoirs,* 89.

82. Adair, *History,* 153.

83. Longe, "Ways and Manners," 30.

84. Adair, *History,* 480.

85. Adair, *History,* 244.

86. Payne Papers, 4:346.

87. Payne Papers, 4:227.

PART 2: CONTACT

1. Nathaniel Green Papers, Library of Congress, Washington DC, quoted in Samuel Cole Williams, *Tennessee during the Revolutionary War* (1944; Knoxville: University of Tennessee Press, 1974), 201.

2. See Sara M. Evans, *Born for Liberty: A History of Women in America* (New York: Free Press, 1989), 21–23, 46–47; Linda K. Kerber, *Women of the Republic: Intellect and Ideology in Revolutionary America* (Chapel Hill: University of North Carolina Press, 1980), and "'History Can Do It No Injustice': Women and the Reinterpretation of the American Revolution," in *Women in the Age of the American Revolution,* ed. Ronald Hoffman and Peter J. Albert (Charlottesville: University Press of Virginia, 1989), 3–42; Mary Beth Norton, *Liberty's Daughters: The Revolutionary Experience of American Women, 1750–1800* (Boston: Little, Brown, 1980); Ruth H. Block, "The Gendered Meanings of Virtue in Revolutionary America," *Signs* 13 (1987): 37–58; and Marylynn Salmon, *Women and the Law of Property in Early America* (Chapel Hill: University of North Carolina Press, 1986). For a good discussion of the position of classical philosophy and Catholicism on women in general and Native women in particular, see Karen Anderson, *Chain Her by One Foot: The Subjugation of Women in Seventeenth-Century New France* (London and New York: Routledge, 1991).

3. Tom Hatley, *The Dividing Paths: Cherokees and South Carolinians through the Era of Revolution* (New York: Oxford University Press, 1993), 148–50.

3. TRADE

1. The best discussion of the early Cherokee trade is found in John Phillip Reid, *A Better Kind of Hatchet: Law, Trade and Diplomacy in the Cherokee Nation during the Early Years of Contact* (University Park and London: Pennsylvania State University Press, 1976), 23–38. Also see the Verner Crane's classic *The Southern Frontier, 1670–1732* (Durham NC: Duke University Press, 1928). For an insightful study of Cherokee political and economic relations with the colony of South Carolina, see Hatley, *Dividing Paths.* Also useful is Chapman J. Milling, *Red Carolinians* (Columbia: University of South Carolina Press, 1969).

2. Williams, "Colonel George Chicken's Journal (1725)," *Early Travels,* 100.

3. Reid, *A Better Kind of Hatchet,* 25–28; Theda Perdue, *Slavery and the Evolution of Cherokee Society, 1540–1866* (Knoxville: University of Tennessee Press, 1979), 19–35; J. Leitch Wright, *The Only Land They Knew: The Tragic Story of the American Indians in the Old South* (New York: Free Press, 1981), 126–50.

4. Crane, *Southern Frontier,* 112–13.

5. Wright, *Only Land They Knew,* 252–60.

6. Instructions for Theophilus Hastings, 10 July 1716, 23 Nov. 1716; Instructions to Capt. Charlesworth Glover, 29 Nov. 1716; Journals of 7, 11 June 1717, William L. McDowell, ed., *Journals of the Commissioners of the Indian Trade, Sept. 20, 1710–Aug. 29, 1718* (Columbia: South Carolina Archives Department, 1955), 85–87, 129, 134, 186.

7. Alexander S. Salley, ed. *Journals of the Commons House of Assembly of South Carolina for 1703* (Columbia: Historical Commission of South Carolina, 1934), 75; Perdue, *Slavery,* 26.

8. George Chicken, "A Journal from Carolina in 1715," ed. Langdon Cheeves, *Yearbook of the City of Charleston, 1894,* 331.

9. Griffiths, "Visit," 5.

10. Charles Hart to Mr. St. Julian, 19 Aug., 1713, McDowell, *Journals of the Commissioners,* 49; Wright, *Only Land They Knew,* 149.

11. Wright, *Only Land They Knew,* 148–50, 248–78.

12. Leland Ferguson, *Uncommon Ground: Archaeology and Early African America, 1650–1800* (Washington DC: Smithsonian Institution Press, 1992).

13. Alexander Hewatt, *An Historical Account of the Rise and Progress of the Colonies of South Carolina and Georgia,* 2 vols. (London: Alexander Donaldson, 1779), 1:241.

14. Journal, 11 June 1717, McDowell, *Journals of the Commissioners,* 186.

15. Journals, 4, 5, 6, 7, 20 May 1714; An Ordinance of the General Assembly, 15 Dec. 1716; Resolution, 10 May 1717, McDowell, *Journals of the Commissioners,* 53–57, 140, 179; Timberlake, *Memoirs,* 82.

16. Perdue, *Slavery,* 46–49.

17. Journal, 16 Nov. 1716; Instructions from the Assembly, 24 Nov. 1716; Journals, 30 Nov. 1716, 9 Dec. 1717, McDowell, *Journals of the Commissioners,* 127–28, 131, 135, 239; Perdue, *Slavery,* 37–39.

18. Journal, 16 Nov. 1716; Instructions from the Assembly, 24 Nov. 1716, McDowell, *Journals of the Commmissioners,* 127–28, 131.

19. De Brahm, *General Survey,* 109.

20. De Brahm, *General Survey,* 107.

21. Crane, *Southern Frontier,* 110–12; Hatley, *Dividing Paths,* 70.

22. Lud. Grant to Governor Glen, 27 March 1755; James Beamer to Governor Glen, 11 Feb. 1756, McDowell, *Documents, 1754–1765,* 44–45, 94–95.

23. Williams, "Schneider's Journey," "Francis Baily's Tour (1797)," "Moravians," *Early Travels,* 258, 402–3, 457; Journal, 3 Dec. 1796, Hawkins, *Letters,* 23; Payne Papers, 4:142, 43–47; Reid, *A Law of Blood,* 134; Reid, *A Better Kind of Hatchet,* 171.

24. Alan Klein described such a process among buffalo-hunting peoples of the

northern plains in "The Political Economy of Gender: A Nineteenth Century Plains Indian Case Study," in Albers and Medicine, eds., *The Hidden Half,* 143–74. On the other hand, Henry S. Sharp described Chipewyan men of the subarctic as being dependent on the women who processed raw materials, a circumstance that linked a man's status to the ability and willingness of the women attached to him to work (46–74).

25. Sattler, "Women's Status," 223–24.

26. Kathryn E. Holland Braund, *Deerskins and Duffels: Creek Indian Trade with Anglo-America, 1685–1815* (Lincoln: University of Nebraska Press, 1993), 67–69.

27. Braund, *Deerskins and Duffels,* 67. Also see Braund, "Guardians of Tradition and Handmaidens to Change: Women's Roles in Creek Economic and Social Life during the Eighteenth Century," *American Indian Quarterly* 14 (1990): 239–58.

28. Daniel H. Usner Jr., *Indians, Settlers, and Slaves in a Frontier Exchange Economy: The Lower Mississippi Valley before 1783* (Chapel Hill: University of North Carolina Press, 1992).

29. Anne Matthews, "Memoir," 2, typescript in the South Caroliniana Library, Columbia, quoted in Hatley, *Dividing Paths,* 89–90.

30. Richard White has examined the Choctaw attitudes toward gift giving and trade in *The Roots of Dependency: Subsistence, Environment, and Social Change among the Choctaws, Pawnees, and Navajos* (Lincoln: University of Nebraska Press, 1983), 73, 80–81.

31. "Mr. Carteret's Relation of their Planting at Ashley River '70," in Salley, *Narratives,* 117–18. The people described by Carteret were not Cherokee, of course, but Cherokees probably reacted similarly to early traders and explorers.

32. Adair, *History,* 462–63. Although his visit was to coastal tribes rather than the inland Cherokees, John Lawson chronicled many acts of hospitality by his Native hosts. Interestingly, it usually was the women who provided him with food; for examples, see *Voyage to Carolina,* 34–36. As late as 1796, Louis-Philippe was offered food immediately upon his entrance into a Cherokee home "according to the rules of Indian hospitality" (84).

33. Captain Rayd. Demere to Governor Lyttleton, 23 June 1756, 2 Jan. 1757, McDowell, *Documents, 1754–1765,* 126, 303; Journal, 28 March 1797, Hawkins, *Letters,* 110.

34. Goodwin, *Cherokees in Transition,* 125–46.

35. Thomas Hatley, "Cherokee Women Farmers Hold Their Ground," in *Appalachian Frontiers: Settlement, Society, and Development in the Preindustrial Era,* ed. Robert D. Mitchell (Lexington: University of Kentucky Press, 1991), 37–51.

36. Commission of Captain Charlesworth Glover, 29 Nov. 1716; Journals, 2 Dec. 1717, 9 May 1718, McDowell, *Journals of the Commissioners,* 135, 236–37, 273.

37. Captain Rayd. Demere to Governor Lyttelton, 23 June 1756, McDowell, *Documents, 1754–1765,* 125–26.

38. Governor Glen to The Little Carpenter, 17 Feb. 1756; Governor Lyttleton to Old Hop, 3 June 1756; Captain Rayd. Demere to Governor Lyttleton, 24 June 1756, 2 Jan. 1757, McDowell, *Documents, 1754–1765,* 99–100, 115–16, 126–27, 303.

39. De Brahm, *General Survey,* 102–4; Timberlake, *Memoirs,* 89–90.

40. Adair, *History,* 456.

41. See Hill, *Weaving New Worlds.* Journal, 1, 16 Nov. 1716; Commission to Capt. Charlesworth Glover, 5 Feb. 1716/17, McDowell, *Journals of the Commissioners,* 120, 128–29, 158.

42. Col. John Barnwell to Commission 23 Jan. 1716/17; Charite Hagey to Commission, 25 Jan. 1716/17; Journals, 26, 28 Jan. 1716/17, McDowell, *Journals of the Commissioners,* 149–50, 151–54.

43. Adair, *History,* 456. Ancient skills did not disappear completely, of course. In 1802, Moravian missionaries reported that they had "bought several earthen crocks from an Indian woman who made them." Pottery, however, came closer to extinction than did basketry, and Catawba potters who lived among the Cherokees in the nineteenth century are credited with reinvigorating its production. Contemporary Cherokees still make traditional crafts, largely for the tourist trade, but pottery and basketry are no longer gender-specific crafts. Moravian Diary, 21 April 1802; Rodney L. Leftwich, *Arts and Crafts of the Cherokee* (Cherokee NC: Cherokee Publications, 1970), 76–77

44. Adair, *History,* 9.

45. Information of George Johnston, 2 Oct. 1754, McDowell, *Documents, 1754–1765,* 11; Payne Papers, 7:2.

46. An Account of the Price of Goods, settled between Col. James Moore and the Conjuror, 30 April 1716; A Schedule of the Stated Prices of the Goods, 9 Aug. 1716; Commission to Capt. Charlesworth Glover, 3 June 1718, McDowell, *Journals of the Commissioners,* 89, 104, 281. Captain Raymond Demere to Governor Lyttelton, 21 July 1756, McDowell, *Documents, 1750–1754,* 146–47.

47. White, *Roots of Dependency,* 84–86. Also see Peter C. Mancall, *Deadly Medicine: Indians and Alcohol in Early America* (Ithaca: Cornell University Press, 1995).

48. Louis-Philippe suggested that Indians drank less than their white neighbors and gave the following evidence: "During the last war the bodies of Indians killed in battle were still fresh when the Americans' were already rotting. I believe the Americans' immoderate consumption of whiskey accelerates putrefaction." He went on to observe: "The southern Indians would also indulge to excess if they could procure whiskey, but they cannot distill it and outsiders sell them very little." Louis-Philippe, *Travels,* 70–71. Adair, *History,* 6, 122–23, 315, 326–28.

49. Peter C. Mancall, "Men, Women, and Alcohol in Indian Villages in the Great Lakes Region in the Early Republic," *Journal of the Early Republic* 15 (1995): 425–48.

50. Captain Rayd. Demere to Governor Lyttelton, 23 June 1756, 26 Oct. 1756, McDowell, *Documents, 1754–1765,* 125–26, 231. The chief complaint, however, was about "the White People getting drunk."

51. John Herbert, *Journal of John Herbert, Commissioner of Indian Affairs for the Province of South Carolina, October 17, 1727 to March 19, 1727/8,* ed. Alexander S. Salley (Columbia: Historical Commission of South Carolina, 1936), 18.

52. Lud. Grant to Governor Glen, 27 March 1755, McDowell, *Documents, 1754–1765,* 43.

53. Journals, 10 Sept. 1717, 19 July 1718, McDowell, *Journals,* 205, 306; Williams, "Moravians," 463.

54. Journals, 18 July 1716, 23, 24 Oct., 27 Nov. 1717, McDowell, *Journals,* 82, 219, 221, 232; Reid, *A Better Kind of Hatchet,* 82–83, 168–70.

55. Journals, 9 July 1717; 2, 8 May 1718; 12 June 1718; Commission to William Hatton, 11 June 1718, McDowell, *Journals of the Commissioners,* 194, 271, 272, 287, 290–91; Williams, "Journeys of Needham and Arthur (1673)," *Early Travels,* 28–29; Mereness, "Chicken's Journal," 154; Orders by Captain Rayd. Demere, 25 Aug. 1756, McDowell, *Documents, 1754–1765,* 172.

56. Carol I. Mason, "Eighteenth-Century Culture Change among the Lower Creeks," *Florida Anthropologist* 16 (1963): 65–81.

57. Captain Rayd. Demere to Governor Lyttelton, 23 June 1756, McDowell, *Documents, 1754–1765,* 125–26.

58. Timberlake, *Memoirs,* 92–93.

59. Williams, "Schneider's Journey," *Early Travels,* 262.

60. Mooney, "Myths," 323–24.

61. Williams, "Schneider's Journey," *Early Travels,* 255, 257, 262. Unlike some Native societies, Cherokees do not seem to have created fictive kin in order to conduct trade. For an example of fictive kin see Gary Clayton Anderson, *Kinsmen of Another Kind: Dakota-White Relations in the Upper Mississippi Valley, 1650–1862* (Lincoln: University of Nebraska Press, 1984).

62. Lawson, *Voyage to Carolina,* 35–36.

63. Louis-Philippe, *Travels,* 77.

64. Captain Rayd. Demere to Governor Lyttelton, 16 Oct. 1756, McDowell, *Documents, 1754–1756,* 225.

65. Moravian Diary, 2 July 1810.

66. Adair, *History,* 443.

67. James Beamer to Governor Glen, 22 Sept. 1754; Lud. Grant to Governor Glen, 27 March 1755; Captain Raymond Demere to Governor Lyttelton, 9 June

1756, 10 June 1756, 15 June 1756, 2 July 1756, McDowell, *Documents, 1754–1765,* 8–9, 44–45, 119, 120, 122, 130–31.

68. Mooney, "Myths," 250–51.

69. Norton, *Journal,* 130.

4. WAR

1. Lud. Grant to Governor Glen, 20 Aug. 1755, McDowell, *Documents, 1754–65,* 74; Adair, *History,* 158, 163, 261.

2. Norton, *Journal,* 47.

3. Adair, *History,* 438; Mooney, "Myths," 365–66, 369, 374; Mereness, "Chicken's Journal," 103.

4. Ludovic Grant to Governor Glen, 22 July 1754, 29 April 1755; Captain Rayd. Demere to Governor Lyttelton, 2 July 1756, McDowell, *Documents, 1754–1765,* 18, 19, 54, 131; John Gardiner's Journal or Narrative on Oath, 15 December 1736, J. H. Easterby et al., eds., *The Journals of the Commons House of Assembly,* 13 vols. to date (Columbia: Historical Commission of South Carolina, 1951–), *Journal . . . , November 10, 1736–June 7, 1739,* 134.

5. Williams, "Chicken's Journal," *Early Travels,* 100–101.

6. Joyce Rockwood vividly portrays this very crisis in her anthropological novel, *Long Man's Song* (New York: Holt Rinehart Winston, 1975).

7. Captain Rayd. Demere to Governor Lyttelton, 10 Aug. 1757, McDowell, *Documents, 1754–1765,* 400.

8. Adair, *History,* 261; Norton, *Journal,* 39.

9. Hudson, *Knights of Spain,* 238–43; Dobyns, *Their Numbers Become Thinned,* 174–89.

10. "An Account of the Province of Carolina, By Samuel Wilson, 1682," Salley, *Narratives,* 173.

11. Cherokee Head Men to Governor Glen, 21 Sept. 1754, McDowell, *Documents, 1754–1765,* 8.

12. Governor Glen to Malatchi, 2 Oct. 1754; Lud. Grant to Governor Glen, 27 March 1755, McDowell, *Documents, 1754–1765,* 9, 40; Abstract of Despatches from Canada, 7 June 1759, O'Callaghan and B. Fernow, eds., *Documents Relative to . . . New York,* 10:974.

13. Herbert, *Commissioner's Journal,* 25–26; Reid, *A Better Kind of Hatchet,* 30, 59.

14. Adair, *History,* 416; Timberlake, *Memoirs,* 150; Crane, *Southern Frontier,* 161; Wright, *Only Land They Knew,* 124–25.

15. Adair, *History,* 161–62, 416–17; Timberlake, *Memoirs,* 82.

16. Adair, *History,* 163; John Stuart to William Johnson, 1 June 1766, 30 March

1766, James Sullivan, Alexander C. Flick, Almon W. Lauber, Albert B. Corey, and Milton W. Hamilton, eds. *The Papers of Sir William Johnson,* 14 vols. (Albany: University of the State of New York, 1921–65), 5:234, 12:56–57. See also Perdue, "Cherokee Relations with the Iroquois in the Eighteenth Century," in *Beyond the Covenant Chain: The Iroquois and Their Neighbors in Indian North America,* ed. Daniel K. Richter and James H. Merrell (Syracuse: Syracuse University Press, 1987), 135–49.

17. Mereness, "Chicken's Journal," 120–21, 134–35.

18. Captain Raymond Demere to Governor Lyttelton, 12 Sept. 1756, 11 Dec. 1756, McDowell, *Documents, 1754–1765,* 201, 268.

19. Mereness, "Chicken's Journal," 131; Herbert, *Commissioner's Journal,* 13, 14; At a Council Held at Philadelphia, 1 June 1758, Samuel Hazard, ed., *Minutes of the Provincial Council of Pennsylvania,* 16 vols. (Harrisburg: Theo. Fernon, 1838–53), 8:124–25.

20. Journal of Sir William Johnson's Proceedings with the Indians, 31 July–20 Sept. 1757; Proceedings of Sir William Johnson with the Indians, 4–12 March 1768, O'Callaghan and Fernow, eds., *Documents Relative to . . . New York,* 7:324–28; 8: 38–53.

21. Adair, *History,* 460; De Brahm, *General Survey,* 113.

22. The classic study of eighteenth-century Cherokee political organization and change is Fred Gearing, *Priests and Warriors: Social Structures for Cherokee Politics in the Eighteenth Century* (Menasha WI: American Anthropological Association Memoir 93, 1962). While I agree with Gearing's central thesis that Cherokee government became increasingly centralized and coercive in the eighteenth century in order to control the raids of young warriors, I do not think the evidence supports the rigid moiety system he describes for Cherokee politics. Raymond D. Fogelson's suggestion that "red" and "white" designations were based in part on age makes more sense. Fogelson classifies women as "pink" because they mediated between "red" and "white." See his "Cherokee Notions of Power" in *The Anthropology of Power,* ed. Raymond D. Fogelson and Richard N. Adams (New York: Academic Press, 1977), 185–94.

23. Adair, *History,* 460.

24. Adair, *History,* 459; Herbert, *Commissioner's Journal,* 13, 14; Hewatt, *Rise of South Carolina and Georgia,* 2:4.

25. Reid, *A Better Kind of Hatchet,* 59; "Report of the Committee on Oglethorpe," *South Carolina Historical Society Proceedings* 4:141, 147, 155, 177; Mereness, "Chicken's Journal," 115–16.

26. Adair, *History,* 260–62.

27. Hatley, *Dividing Paths,* 100, 119–40.

28. Captain Christopher French, "Journal of an Expedition to South Carolina," *Journal of Cherokee Studies* 2 (1977): 284–85; Alexander Monypenny, "Diary of Alexander Monypenny," *Journal of Cherokee Studies* 2 (1977): 328.

29. Monypenny, "Diary," 324; French, "Journal of an Expedition," 287.

30. French, "Journal of an Expedition," 285; Jeffrey Amherst to William Johnson, 11 Aug. 1761, Sullivan et al., eds., *Johnson Papers* 3:517; "A Talk for the Cherokee Chiefs & Headmen of the Nation to their Father in Charles Town, 22 September 1766," Colonial Office, Class 5, Number 67: "Plantations General," 484–85, Public Record Office, London (microfilm, Western Carolina University); Adair, *History,* 239, 242.

31. Daniel L. Simpkins, "A Comparison of Pisgah Plant Food Remains from the Warren Wilson Site (31Bn29) with Related Archaeological Complexes and Records of the Historic Cherokee," in *The Conference on Cherokee Prehistory,* ed. David G. Moore (Swannanoa NC: Warren Wilson College, 1986), 20–41.

32. Contemporary estimates of Cherokee population before 1735 range from 10,000 to 22,000. Gary C. Goodwin includes a handy chart of various population estimates in the colonial period; see *Cherokees in Transition,* 111. Some demographers, such as Henry F. Dobyns, challenge these early censuses and the way in which total population figures have been extrapolated from available data. In *Their Numbers Become Thinned,* Dobyns multiplied the number of warriors by five in order to estimate the total Timucuan population, but he also pointed out that "projections from army size may underestimate true population" (174–89). For other views, see Thornton, *The Cherokees,* 5–46 and Peter Wood, "The Changing Population of the Colonial South" in Wood, Waselkov, and Hatley, eds., *Powhatan's Mantle,* 35–103.

33. Louis-Philippe, *Travels,* 74–75; Mooney, "Myths," 44; Adair, *History,* 239, 242.

34. Adair, *History,* 241.

35. De Brahm, *General Survey,* 102–4; Timberlake, *Memoirs,* 89–90.

36. Hatley, *Dividing Paths,* 90.

37. Arthur Campbell to Thomas Jefferson, 15 Jan. 1781, in Palmer, *Virginia State Papers,* 434–47.

38. Nathaniel Green Papers (Library of Congress), quoted in Samuel Cole Williams, *Tennessee during the Revolutionary War* (1944; Knoxville: University of Tennessee Press, 1974), 201.

39. War Woman of Chota to the Treaty Commissioners, 23 Nov. 1785, *American State Papers,* Class 2: *Indian Affairs,* 2 vols. (Washington DC: Gales and Seaton, 1832), 1:41.

40. Journals, 26 Jan. 1716/17, 2 Dec. 1717, 12 June 1718, McDowell, *Journals of the Commissioners,* 153, 236–37, 287.

41. Journals, 26 Jan. 1716/17, 29 Jan. 1716/17, 5 Feb. 1716/17, McDowell, *Journals of the Commissioners,* 153, 154, 158; Williams, "Cumming's Journal," *Early Travels,* 138–41.

42. Hazard, *Minutes of . . . Pennsylvania,* 7:553–56; Presents Given to the Cherokee Indians, 23 November 1751, McDowell, *Documents, 1750–1754,* 161–62; Adair, *History,* 463.

43. Journal, 30 Jan. 1716/17, McDowell, *Journals of the Commissioners,* 155; "Report of the Committee on Oglethorpe," 147; Estimate for Seige of St. Augustine, Easterby et al., eds., *Journals of the Commons House,* September 12, 1739–March 26, 1741, 271.

44. Presents Given to the Cherokee Indians, 23 November 1751, McDowell, *Documents, 1750–1754,* 161–62.

45. Adair, *History,* 186–87; 406.

46. Hewatt, *Rise of South Carolina and Georgia,* 1:67.

47. For Cherokee land cessions specifically, see Charles C. Royce, *The Cherokee Nation of Indians* (Chicago: Aldine, 1975). For all land cessions plus detailed maps, see Royce, "Indian Land Cessions in the United States," *Eighteenth Annual Report,* Bureau of American Ethnology (Washington DC: Government Printing Office, 1899).

48. For example, see the Treaty of Hopewell (1785) in Charles J. Kappler, ed. *Indian Affairs: Laws and Treaties,* vol 2: *Treaties* (Washington DC: Government Printing Office, 1904), 8.

49. Patrick Brown to Governor Glen, 25 April 1752; James Beamer and Richard Smith to Governor Glen, 2 May 1752; James Beamer to Governor Glen, 26 April 1752, McDowell, *Documents, 1750–1754,* 246–47, 249, 256–57. See David J. Hally, "The Cherokee Archaeology of Georgia," in *The Conference on Cherokee Prehistory,* 95–121.

50. Journal, 3 Dec. 1796, Hawkins, *Letters,* 23.

51. For shifts in Cherokee towns, see Betty Anderson Smith, "Distribution of Eighteenth-Century Cherokee Settlements," in King, *The Cherokee Indian Nation,* 46–60.

52. Journal, 28 Nov. 1796, Hawkins, *Letters,* 18.

53. Norton, *Journal,* 142.

54. Norton, *Journal,* 142; Journal, 27–28 Nov. 1796, 27 March 1797, Hawkins, *Letters,* 16–18, 108–9; Payne Papers, 4:95; Brainerd Journal, 29 Dec. 1818, ABCFM.

55. Norton, *Journal,* 141.

56. Journal, 30 March 1797, Hawkins, *Letters,* 112.

57. Payne Papers, 1:43.

58. Mooney, "Myths," 423–24.

59. Kilpatrick and Kilpatrick, *Run toward the Nightland,* 37.

PART 3: "CIVILIZATION"

1. Robert Beverley, *The History and Present State of Virginia,* ed. Louis B. Wright (1705; reprint, Chapel Hill: University of North Carolina Press, 1947), 159.

2. Thomas Jefferson, *Notes on the State of Virginia* (Boston: Lilly and Wait, 1832), 6, 63, 143, 145.

3. Roy Harvey Pearce, *Savagism and Civilization: A Study of the Indian and the American Mind* (1953; rev. ed., Berkeley: University of California Press, 1988), 66, 83–90; Berkhofer, *White Man's Indian,* 138.

4. George W. Corner, ed. *The Autobiography of Benjamin Rush: His "Travels through Life" Together with His Commonplace Book for 1789–1813,* Memoirs of the American Philosohical Society, vol. 25 (Princeton: Princeton University Press, 1948), 71; Benjamin Rush, "Medicine among the Indians," in *Essays Literary, Moral, and Philosophical* (Philadelphia: Thomas and Samuel F. Bradford, 1798), 290.

5. Henry Knox to George Washington, 7 July 1789, *American State Papers,* 1:53.

6. A Treaty of Peace and Friendship, 2 July 1791, *American State Papers,* 1:124–25.

7. G. Melvin Herndon, "Indian Agriculture in the Southern Colonies," *North Carolina Historical Review* 44 (1967): 283–97.

8. George Washington to the Cherokees, 1796, *Cherokee Phoenix,* 20 March 1828.

5. A CHANGING WAY OF LIFE

1. See Merritt B. Pound, *Benjamin Hawkins—Indian Agent* (Athens: University of Georgia Press, 1951); Frank L. Owsley Jr., "Benjamin Hawkins, the First Modern Indian Agent," *Alabama Historical Quarterly* 30 (1968); Florette Henri, *The Southern Indians and Benjamin Hawkins, 1796–1816* (Norman: University of Oklahoma Press, 1986).

2. Journal, 30 Nov.–3 Dec. 1796, Hawkins, *Letters,* 20–23. Hawkins also called on one family in which both father and mother were away hunting, and the daughters entertained him.

3. Journal, 28 Nov., 2 Dec. 1796, Hawkins, *Letters,* 18, 21–22.

4. Goodwin, *Cherokees in Transition,* 126–31.

5. Journal, 26 Nov., 2 Dec. 1796, Hawkins, *Letters,* 16, 21–22.

6. Jack Kilpatrick, ed., *The Wahnenauhi Manuscript: Historical Sketches of the*

Cherokees, Bureau of American Ethnology Bulletin 196 (Washington DC: Smithsonian Institution, 1966), 195.

7. Norton, *Journal,* 36, 51; Williams, "Moravians," *Early Travels,* 477.

8. Moravian Diary, 8 Oct. 1800.

9. Williams, "Moravians," *Early Travels,* 469–71, 485, 490.

10. Journal, 2 Dec. 1796, Hawkins, *Letters,* 21–22.

11. Charles Hicks to Return J. Meigs, 7 Sept. 1801, Records of the Cherokee Agency in Tennessee, 1801–35, U.S. Bureau of Indian Affairs, Record Group 75, National Archives, Washington DC, Microcopy M-208 (hereafter cited as M-208).

12. Meigs to Henry Dearborn, 30 Nov. 1801, M-208.

13. Charles Rogers to Meigs, 1 Feb. 1808, M-208.

14. Brainerd Journal, 2 June 1818, ABCFM.

15. Jefferson to Hawkins, 18 Feb. 1803, Paul Leicester Ford, ed., *The Writings of Thomas Jefferson,* 10 vols. (New York: G. P. Putnam's Sons, 1892–99), 8:213–14.

16. Meigs to Hawkins, 13 Feb. 1805, M-208.

17. Draft of Jefferson's Fifth Annual Message, Ford, *Writings of Jefferson,* 8:394.

18. Thomas Jefferson to John C. Breckinridge, 12 August 1803, Ford, *Writings of Jefferson,* 8:243–44.

19. Meigs to Dearborn, 31 May 1804, M-208.

20. Warriors in Council to Lieut. Col. Thomas Batten, 20 March 1801, M-208.

21. James Wilkinson, Benjamin Hawkins, and Andrew Pickens to Henry Dearborn, 6 Sept. 1801, Hawkins, *Letters,* 383–85.

22. Norton, *Journal,* 36, 59–60.

23. Some men valued the president's words even if, perhaps, they did not follow his advice. One of the headmen of Chota treasured a copy of Washington's letter, which agent Dinsmore had bound and given him. Williams, "Moravians," *Early Travels,* 469–71, 485, 490.

24. Goodwin suggests that the Cherokees did not keep livestock because they believed that by consuming beef and pork, they would acquire the slow, slovenly characteristics of the animals (*Cherokees in Transition,* 135).

25. Edward Morris to Colonel Mullryne, n.d., McDowell, *Documents, 1750–1754,* 82.

26. James Francis to Governor Glen, 24 July 1751, McDowell, *Documents, 1750–1754,* 29; Captain Raymond Demere to Governor Lyttelton, 24 June 1756, 19 July 1756; Isham Clayton to Captain Demere, 15 Aug. 1756, McDowell, *Documents, 1754–1765,* 127, 144, 168; Williams, "Cuming's Journal," *Early Travels,* 140 n. 50; Timberlake, *Memoirs,* 72.

27. Adair, *History,* 443.

28. Williams, "Moravians," *Early Travels,* 481–83.

29. "Reflections," 39.

30. Journal, 28 Nov., 4 Dec. 1796, Hawkins, *Letters,* 18, 24.

31. Receipts to Samuel Eckridge, 19 Oct. 1802, M-208.

32. Daniel Alexander to Meigs, 22 Feb. 1805, M-208.

33. "Reflections," 41.

34. Jedidiah Morse, *The American Universal Geography; or, A View of the Present State of All the Kingdoms, States and Colonies in the Known World* (Boston: Thomas and Andrews, 1812), 574.

35. Norton, *Journal,* 57.

36. Daniel S. Butrick to Samuel Austin Worcester, 2 July 1818; Ard Hoyt to Jeremiah Evarts, 8 Jan. 1819, ABCFM.

37. Doublehead to J. D. Chilsolm, 20 Nov. 1802, M-208.

38. Butrick to Worcester, 2 July 1818, ABCFM.

39. For example, see Abstract of Indemnification for Horses Stolen, 27 Oct. 1801; Meigs to Dearborn, 22 Feb. 1802; and List of Claims, 25 Oct. 1811, M-208. The Indians enjoyed sovereignty under the supervision of the federal government, but their lack of jurisdiction over whites and the absence of formal laws meant that the prosecution of whites was unlikely. The states, on the other hand, usually refused to admit Native testimony, and so the federal government attempted to intercede to prevent Indians' being tried in state courts.

40. Meigs to Dearborn, 19 Dec. 1807, M-208.

41. Norton, *Journal,* 54–55.

42. Meigs to Dearborn, 19 Dec. 1807, M-208.

43. Williams, "Moravians," *Early Travels,* 485.

44. William G. McLoughlin, "Cherokee Anomie, 1794–1810," in McLoughlin, *The Cherokee Ghost Dance: Essays on the Southeastern Indians, 1789–1861* (Macon GA: Mercer University Press, 1984), 3–37.

45. Hicks to Meigs, 31 March 1805; Meigs to the Chiefs, 2 April 1806, M-208.

46. Williams, "Moravians," *Early Travels,* 460; Journal, 30 April 1797, Hawkins, *Letters,* 133.

47. Meigs to Cherokee Nation, 14 Aug. 1807; J. D. Chilsolm to Meigs, 19 Aug. 1807; James Lusk to Gov. Sevier, 9 Dec. 1807; List of Claims, 25 Oct. 1811, M-208.

48. Black Fox & other chiefs to George Parris & Killachulla, 23 Aug. 1807, M-208.

49. Testimony of Return J. Meigs, 31 Dec. 1801, Statement of Elisha Winn and Elijah Pugh, 11 Oct. 1808, M-208.

50. James Vann to Meigs, 26 March 1803, M-208.

51. Thomas McKenney, *Memoirs Official and Personal; with Sketches of Travels*

among the Northern and Southern Indians, 2 vols. (New York: Paine and Burgess, 1846), 1:232–33.

52. A. O. Aldridge, "Franklin's Letter on Indians and Germans [1753]," *Proceedings of the American Philosophical Society* 94 (1950): 392.

53. McKenney, *Memoirs Official and Personal,* 1:232–33.

54. Ann Paine to Evarts, 8 Nov. 1821, ABCFM.

55. Moody Hall's Journal, 17 April 1822, 17 April 1823, ABCFM.

56. Norton, *Journal,* 36, 59–60.

57. Journal of Occurrences in the Cherokee Agency in 1802, M-208.

58. John Lowry to Meigs, 20 Oct. 1818; Names of Persons who are on land in Sequchee Valley, 22 April 1809; William Schrimsher and Richard Martins recommendation as croppers for Jn. Boggs, a Cherokee, 21 April 1808, M-208. All people mentioned as employers of share croppers were men except for Granny Maw and Nancy. Meigs to Chiefs, 27 March 1810, M-208.

59. Meigs to Chulisa and Sour Mush, 14 March 1808, M-208.

60. Meigs to William Eustis, 27 Feb. 1811, M-208.

61. See R. Halliburton Jr., *Red over Black: Black Slavery among the Cherokee Indians* (Westport CT: Greenwood Press, 1977), and Perdue, *Slavery.*

62. Joseph Phillips to Meigs, 12 Aug. 1807; Complaint of Griffin Minor, 5 May 1809, M-208.

63. Payne Papers, 7:58–59.

64. Morse, *Geography,* 574.

65. By 1835 nearly 1,600 residents of the Cherokee Nation were slaves, but less than 8 percent of the heads of household listed on this census owned slaves. Those who did were wealthy in every category listed on the census: they farmed more acres, raised more corn and wheat per acre, sold more of their produce, and owned a disproportionate number of mills and ferries. Cherokee Census of 1835 (Henderson Roll), U.S. Bureau of Indian Affairs, Record Group 75, National Archives, Washington DC, Microcopy T-496.

66. Journal, 3 Dec. 1796, Hawkins, *Letters,* 22–23.

67. Meigs to Dearborn, 7 Dec. 1801, M-208.

68. Muscle Shoals Chiefs to Meigs, 27 March 1804; Meigs to Black Fox and other Headmen, 29 August 1808; Memorandum of Corn Received of William Hicks, 6 March 1811, M-208.

69. Little Turkey to Meigs, 10 Dec. 1801; Upper Town Chiefs to the President, 25 April 1806; The Glass to Meigs, 8 Feb. 1808, M-208.

70. Bartlet was a white man "living in the Cherokee Nation with Nancy Falling," and Burns, who was married to Cherokee Aky Lowry, may well have been white because Lovely suggests that he would be "a good example to the Indians."

William L. Lovely to Meigs, 30 Jan. 1804; Statement of Bartlett Robbins, 25 Oct. 1808, M-208.

71. Little Turkey to Meigs, 10 Dec. 1801; Journal of Occurrences in the Cherokee Agency, 1802; List of Tools, etc., 28 May 1806; Dearborn to Meigs, 24 April 1807; Meigs to Eustis, 15 Dec. 1810, M-208.

72. Meigs to John Cocke, 7 April 1803; Meigs to Eustis, 15 Dec. 1810, M-208.

73. Meigs to Eustis, 10 May 1811, M-208. Plows were not evenly distributed throughout the Nation. Lower Towns in Georgia and Alabama received more than the Upper Towns in eastern Tennessee or the Valley Towns in western North Carolina. John Tinsley complained to Meigs that only one family in seven in his neighborhood had a plow. 10 June 1811, M-208.

74. The Church at Willstown, 10 Oct. 1828, ABCFM.

75. Butrick's Journal, 19 Feb. 1824; Butrick to Evarts, 9 May 1827, ABCFM.

76. Brainerd Journal, 22 April 1820, 5 Nov. 1821, ABCFM.

77. Journal of the Church at Willstown, 10 Oct. 1828, ABCFM.

78. Albert Gallatin, "Synopsis of the Indian Tribes within the United States East of the Rocky Mountains, and in the British and Russian Possessions," *Archaeologia Americana: Transactions and Collections of the American Antiquarian Society,* vol. 2 (Cambridge: Folsom, Wells, and Thurston), 108.

79. Gallatin, "Synopsis," 157.

80. Journal, 2 Dec. 1796, Hawkins, *Letters,* 21–22.

81. Journal, 28 Nov. 1796, Hawkins, *Letters,* 18.

82. Journal, 1–2 Dec. 1796, Hawkins, *Letters,* 21.

83. Meigs to Black Fox, 29 Aug. 1808, M-208.

84. Muscle Shoals Chiefs to Return J. Meigs, 27 March 1804, M-208.

85. Non-Indians living west of the continental divide had similar problems marketing their produce. Some resorted to making whiskey from their grain. The frustrations of Pennsylvanians with limited markets for grain and heavy taxes on spirits erupted in the "Whiskey Rebellion" in the 1790s. Distilling corn into whiskey simplified transport to market, but Cherokees had no tradition of fermenting and distilling grain.

86. Williams, "Moravians," *Early Travels,* 464; Norton, *Journal,* 125.

87. Thomas Johnson to Genl. Winchester, 20 April 1801, M-208.

88. Meigs to Israel Wheeler, 21 Nov. 1801, M-208. By the 1820s, those ostrich feathers at which the chiefs had sneered in 1801 had become so desirable that a case contesting ownership of them reached the Cherokee Supreme Court. *Betsey Walker vs. Chekayoue,* 24 Oct. 1827, Cherokee Supreme Court Docket, Tennessee State Archives, Nashville TN.

89. Morse, *Geography,* 574.

90. Meigs reported that in 1801 weavers produced 600 yards of cloth on one loom at Hiwassee. If weavers averaged that level of productivity, the total yards produced would be 280,200. Journal of Occurrences &c. relating to the Cherokee Nation [1801], M-208.

91. Ann Paine, Notebook 2, 20 Dec. 1820, ABCFM.

92. Brainerd Journal, 28 Oct. 1822, ABCFM.

93. Brainerd Journal, 14 Dec. 1822, ABCFM.

94. Little Turkey to Meigs, 10 Dec. 1807; Black Foxes Speech, 25 Feb. 1804; James Davis, Chief of Tusquitee, to Meigs 29 July 1804, M-208. One man, the Bold Hunter, learned to make looms. Journal of Occurrences &c. relating to the Cherokee Nation [1801], M-208.

95. Pathkiller and Toochalee to Meigs, 14 Sept. 1812, M-208.

96. Doublehead to Meigs, 8 June 1804, M-208.

97. Receipts to Samuel Eckridge, 19 Oct. 1802, M-208.

98. Receipt to Nancy Lin, 22 Aug. 1802; Receipt to Susannah Trembel, 23 July 1802; Receipt to Nancy Davis, 8 Sept. 1802, M-208.

99. Journal, 7 Aug. 1801, Hawkins, *Letters,* 360.

100. List of white men permitted to assist the Cherokees in 1811; An agreement between Doublehead & John Smith, Jr., 16 Nov. 1805. M-208.

101. Meigs to Hawkins, 28 Dec. 1802; Resolutions of the National Council, 10 April 1804, M-208.

102. Resolutions of the National Council, 10 April 1804; Lovely to Meigs, 4 Nov. 1803; Meigs to Col. Walter, 10 Jan. 1804; Charles Hicks to Meigs, 19 Aug. 1806; John Lowry to Meigs, 22 March 1807, M-208.

103. Meigs to Eustis, 1 Dec. 1809, M-208.

104. Meigs to Eustis, 1 Dec. 1809, M-208.

105. Nicholas Byers to Meigs, 28 Aug. 1805, M-208.

106. Meigs to Eustis, 1 Dec. 1809, M-208.

107. Meigs to Lovely [1801], M-208.

108. Dearborn to Meigs, 9 July 1801; Meigs to Dearborn, 8 June 1802; Meigs to Dearborn, 31 May 1804; Lovely to Chiefs, June 1805, M-208.

109. Meigs to Eustis, 1 Dec. 1809, M-208.

6. WOMEN IN THE EARLY CHEROKEE REPUBLIC

1. Meigs to the Chiefs, 2 April 1806, M-208.

2. For a discussion of property ownership, see Rennard Strickland, *Fire and the Spirits: Cherokee Law from Clan to Court* (Norman: University of Oklahoma Press, 1975), 93–98.

3. Warriors in Council to Lieut. Col. Thomas Batten, 20 March 1801, M-208. The

idea that Native people viewed the earth as their mother has been challenged by Sam D. Gill in *Mother Earth: An American Story* (Chicago: University of Chicago Press, 1987). I think that the council used the term as a metaphor in this case: they did not believe literally that the earth was their mother. Corn is more likely to be associated with motherhood.

4. Mooney, "Myths," 242–49.

5. The Chickamaugans, the last Cherokees to make peace with the United States, became the most aggressively capitalistic.

6. Meigs to the Chiefs, 2 April 1806, M-208.

7. Meigs to Henry Dearborn, 31 March 1802; Resolutions of the Cherokee Delegation to Washington, 4 Jan. 1806, M-208. On September 19, 1806, the council instructed Meigs that the annuity was not to be used to pay off individual debts.

8. Timberlake, *Memoirs,* 90–91; Dickens, *Cherokee Prehistory,* 102–32; Thomas M. N. Lewis and Madeline Kneberg, *Hiwasee Island: An Archaeological Account of Four Tennessee Indian Peoples* (Knoxville: University of Tennessee Press, 1946), 136–52.

9. Even the grave of a highly esteemed war chief who died about 1783 contained only his glasses, iron cup, buckle, and knife as well as beads, siltstone pipes, and vermillion. Duane H. King and Danny E. Olinger, "Oconostota," *American Antiquity* 37 (1972): 222–27.

10. Statement of William Bright, 14 July 1808, M-208.

11. John Finly to Meigs, 10 April 1811, M-208.

12. Strickland, *Fire and the Spirits,* 39. The Moravians, for example, recorded in their diary that "once they have a tool which they have broken and repaired they think it belongs to them." Apparently, for Cherokees labor conveyed title. Moravian Diary, 12 March 1802.

13. Saul K. Padover, *Thomas Jefferson on Democracy* (New York: New American Library, 1939), 106–7.

14. Benjamin Hawkins to James McHenry, 4 May 1797, Hawkins, *Letters,* 136.

15. *Laws of the Cherokee Nation,* 3–4 (quotation). On sporadic operation, see Lovely to Upper Town Chiefs, June 1804, M-208. The Lighthorse continued to operate, with expanded duties, until 1825 when the council repealed the 1808 law. Marshals, sheriffs, and constables already operated alongside the Lighthorse, and this law merely gave them exclusive authority for enforcing the law. *Laws,* 51.

16. See Theda Perdue, "The Conflict Within: The Cherokee Power Structure and Removal," *Georgia Historical Quarterly* 73 (1989): 467–91.

17. *Laws,* 53. A number of Cherokee wills survive. For example, see Young Wolf's Will, 12 March 1814, Payne Papers, 7:58; Rachel Ratcliff's Will, 15 May

1821, Richard Ratliff's Will, 25 Feb. 1833, Special Files, U.S. Bureau of Indian Affairs, Record Group 75, National Archives, Washington DC, M-574 (hereafter cited as M-574).

18. Meigs to the Chiefs, 2 April 1806, M-208.

19. Meigs to Dearborn, 4 Aug. 1805, M-208.

20. Meigs to William Eustis, 15 Oct. 1810, M-208.

21. Meigs to Black Fox in Council, 6 April 1808, M-208.

22. John Gambold to Meigs, 20 April 1809, M-208.

23. Among other violent acts, Vann killed his brother-in-law, John Falling, in a duel in 1806. William G. McLoughlin, "James Vann," in *The Cherokee Ghost Dance,* 56. The records of the Cherokee Supreme Court reveal that the family was particularly litigious. In 1826 (24 Oct.), for example, the widower of James Vann's earlier wife, Elizabeth, sued James and Elizabeth's daughter Deliliah McNair and her husband David for two slaves. Eddy Springston, Elizabeth's son by another husband, sued his brother-in-law for improvements (25 Oct. 1826). The next year, Springston's wife sued for a horse (24 Oct. 1827). And in 1828, Joseph Vann sued the McNairs "to recover certain property" (10 Nov. 1828). Cherokee Supreme Court Docket.

24. William Shorey's Will, April 1809, M-208.

25. John McDonald to Meigs, 20 April 1809; Elizabeth Lowry to Meigs, 26 April 1809; Pathkiller and Chureowee to Meigs, 27 May 1809; Elizabeth Lowry to Meigs, 2 October 1809, M-208.

26. Meigs to Col. Samuel Wear, 21 Sept. 1802, M-208.

27. Benjamin Hawkins to James McHenry, 4 May 1797, Hawkins, *Letters,* 136.

28. Meigs to Wear, 21 Sept. 1802, M-208.

29. Examination Respecting the death of an Indian, 22 Dec. 1802, M-208. The creation of the Lighthorse in 1808 raised the possibility that members of the company might suffer the penalty of clan vengeance even if they killed a person in their official capacity. Consequently, the council provided that "the blood of him or them shall not be required of any of the persons belonging to the regulators from the clan the person so killed belonged to." *Laws,* 3–4.

30. In council at Eustenaulee, 4 March 1804, M-208.

31. Meigs to Dearborn, 4 May 1806, M-208.

32. McLoughlin, "Cherokee Anomie," 25–29.

33. *Laws,* 4.

34. Meigs to Maj. Lovely, 10 June 1806, M-208.

35. V. Richard Persico Jr., "Early Nineteenth-Century Cherokee Political Organization," in King, *The Cherokee Indian Nation,* 92–109.

36. Pathkiller to Meigs, 27 Sept. 1809, M-208. For a detailed study of Cherokee political transformation, see William G. McLoughlin, *Cherokee Renascence in the New Republic* (Princeton: Princeton University Press, 1986).

37. *Laws,* 4–5.

38. Butrick's Journal, 21 Jan. 1824, ABCFM.

39. Moravian Diary, 20 April 1803.

40. Cephas Washburn and Alfred Finney, "Mission among the Cherokees of Arkansas," reprinted in Eugene L. Schwaab, ed., *Travels in the Old South Selected from Periodicals of the Time,* 2 vols. (Lexington: University of Kentucky Press, 1974), 1:156. Similarly, on occasions when their interests seemed to be at stake, women met in their own councils, and on at least three occasions, women's councils from particular locales petitioned the National Council. The petitions of these councils, discussed below, are reprinted in Theda Perdue and Michael D. Green, *The Cherokee Removal: A Brief History with Documents* (Boston: Bedford Books, 1995), 124–26.

41. Daniel S. Butrick, "A Brief Review of the History of the Cherokee Nation for a Few Years Past," Payne Papers, 9:53; *Laws,* 410–41.

42. Perdue, "The Conflict Within."

43. *Laws,* 4–5, 11–12. Districts were laid off in 1821, and the Supreme Court began sitting in 1822. *Laws,* 17–18, 22. Duane Champagne has suggested that the Cherokees were able to change their political system profoundly in relatively little time because, unlike the other large southern Indian tribes, they differentiated between kinship and political organization. See *Social Order and Political Change: Constitutional Governments among the Cherokee, the Choctaw, the Chickasaw, and the Creek* (Stanford: Stanford University Press, 1992).

44. *Laws,* 73–76, 120–21.

45. Norton, *Journal,* 135.

46. Census of 1835, T-496.

47. Ard Hoyt, Moody Hall, William Chamberlain, and Daniel Butrick to Samuel Worcester, 25 July 1818, ABCFM.

48. Ann Paine, Notebook 2, 20 Dec. 1820, ABCFM.

49. James Hall, *Sketches of History, Life, and Manners in the West,* 2 vols. (Philadelphia: H. Hall, 1835) 1:128.

50. *Laws,* 10.

51. *Laws,* 57.

52. John Ridge to Albert Gallatin, 27 Feb. 1826, Payne Papers, 8:111.

53. *Laws,* 57.

54. Meigs to Chulisa and Sour Mush, 14 March 1808, M-208. Silas Dinsmore had written to Meigs earlier that he had little confidence in the "civilizing" influence of the daughters of one white family who had lived in the Cherokee country:

"The girls are criminally lazy . . . and commit such excesses as make even savages ashamed!" 31 July 1802, M-208.

55. Captain Shoe Boots to the National Council, 20 Oct. 1824, Cherokee Nation Papers, Western History Collection, University of Oklahoma, Norman OK. Shoe Boots' previous wife was a white woman whom he had captured in late-eighteenth-century warfare. Many years after hostilities ceased, she decided to take their children and return to her family in Kentucky. See Adriane Strenk, "Tradition and Transformation: Shoe Boots and the Creation of a Cherokee Culture," M.A. thesis, University of Kentucky, 1993.

56. For details, see Thurman Wilkins, *Cherokee Tragedy: The Story of the Ridge Family and the Decimation of a People* (New York: Macmillan, 1970), 119–52.

57. Chamberlain's Journal, 24 Aug. 1825, ABCFM. When Milo Hoyt, son of American Board missionary Ard Hoyt, married Cherokee Lydia Lowry in 1820, however, there had been some disagreement among missionaries over the propriety of Milo's action. Ann Paine, Notebook 2, 20 Dec. 1820, ABCFM.

58. *Laws,* 79.

59. *Panoplist,* 22 July 1805, 408.

60. *Missionary Herald* 25 (1829): 60.

61. For example, see the *Latter Day Luminary* 2 (1820): 198–99. According to Josephine McDonagh, writers in this period used infanticide as a literary trope for two reasons: (1) "infanticide marks the epitome of savage behavior," and (2) infanticide provides "a humanitarian critique of rational society" by demonstrating the savagery to which industrialization had reduced the working class in England. See "Infanticide and the Boundaries of Culture from Hume to Arnold," in *Maternal Culture: Politics, Biology, and Literature, 1550–1865,* ed. Carol Barash and Susan Greenfield (Lexington: University of Kentucky Press, forthcoming).

62. Mooney, "Myths," 240. Also see Hudson, *Southeastern Indians,* 231.

63. *Cherokee Phoenix,* 18 Feb. 1829.

64. My own views on the effects of the "civilization" program have changed slightly since I published "Southern Indians and the Cult of True Womanhood," in *The Web of Southern Social Relations: Women, Family, and Education,* ed. Walter J. Fraser Jr., R. Frank Saunders Jr., and Jon L. Wakelyn (Athens: University of Georgia Press, 1985), 35–51. I now think that the "cult of true womanhood" was largely superficial. Because of the prominent position of the women who subscribed to it, however, it remains an important feature of life in the early Cherokee republic.

65. William Chamberlain's Journal, 24 Aug. 1825; Samuel A. Worcester to Jeremiah Evarts, 24 Oct. 1825, ABCFM.

66. Ann Paine, Notebook 2, 20 Dec. 1820, ABCFM.

67. Cherokee Supreme Court Docket, 18 Oct. 1833.

68. *Laws,* 38.

69. Daniel Butrick to Samuel Worcester, 2 July 1818, ABCFM.

70. *Laws,* 133.

71. Chamberlain's Journal, 13 Aug. 1827, ABCFM.

72. Payne Papers, 7:114.

73. *Laws,* 5.

74. *Laws,* 10.

75. *Laws,* 111.

76. *Laws,* 142–43.

77. Report of Stocks destroyed by the army marching through the Cherokee against the Hostile Creeks, 27 Sept. 1814; A duplicate Report on Battle Creek Claims by a Board at the Cherokee Agency, 13 July 1819, M-574.

78. John Ridge to Albert Gallatin, 27 Feb. 1826, Payne Papers, 8:109.

79. Condition of the Indian Tribes, Senate Report 165, 39th Cong. 2d sess. (Washington DC: Government Printing Office, 1867).

80. Hoyt to Evarts, 6 Sept. 1822, ABCFM.

81. The average slaveholding in the Cherokee Nation was 7.6 slaves while women slaveholders owned an average of 6.5 slaves. Unlike their male counterparts, women slaveholders concentrated their assets in farming: none owned a mill or ferry, and almost all had only one farm. Census of 1835, T-496; Halliburton, *Red over Black,* 190.

82. Will of Rachel Ratcliff, 15 May 1821, M-574. Rachel did not follow a matrilineal line of descent. Her half siblings were the children of her father by a woman other than her mother. Her half sister Nancy Ratcliff Griffin later contested ownership of the slaves. Jane Griffin to Maj. B. J. Curry, 4 Oct. 1835, M-574.

83. Meigs to James Barbour, 34 Dec. 1826, Letters Received, 1824–1881, U.S. Bureau of Indian Affairs, Record Group 75, National Archives, Washington DC, M-234. Register of Reservations in the Cherokee Agency under the Treaty of 1817, Cherokee Claims for Life Reservations (1819), Treasurers and Comptrollers Papers, Indian Affairs and Land, North Carolina Archives, Raleigh NC.

84. Census of 1835, T-496. Robert Bushyhead, a native speaker of Cherokee, helped me identify the gender of names on the census. Some names were used by both men and women, and many have not been used within Bushyhead's memory. Therefore, my sample was not a scientific one, but one based on English given names and Cherokee names used in the last one hundred years. I suspect that the proportion of women heads of household listed on the census may be higher than I was able to determine.

85. *Laws,* 7–8.

86. Cherokee Supreme Court Docket, 22 April 1820.

87. Approximately 60 of the 270 cases involved women. Gender is often difficult to determine. A woman lost only one of the cases in which farms or improvements were contested. Cherokee Supreme Court Docket, 9 Oct. 1823, 10 Oct. 1823, 25 Oct. 1824, 29 Oct. 1825, 22 Oct. 1833.

88. Women won four cases involving slaves and lost three. They won eight livestock cases and lost five. Cherokee Supreme Court Docket, 1823–25.

89. Cherokee Supreme Court Docket, 24, 26 Oct. 1827. The woman who sued for damage to glassware lost. The gender of the winner in the ostrich feather case is unclear, but the loser was a woman. The ostrich feathers have an interesting, if somewhat irrelevant, history. They had been part of an annuity that the chiefs protested because the Cherokees had little use for the items, such as morocco leather shoes and ostrich feathers. In less than thirty years, the feathers had become so desirable that people went to court over them.

90. Prince apparently purchased his own freedom. Supreme Court Docket, 20 Jan. 1834, 10 Aug. 1829.

91. Valuation 28, 7 Dec. 1833, M-574. Meigs ultimately found for Cow because "Cow made the improvements."

92. Ann Paine, Notebook 2, 20 Dec. 1820, ABCFM.

93. Louis Wyeth to R. Chapman and C. C. Clay, 16 May 1838; Writ of the Morgan County [AL] Court, 9 June 1838, M-234; Joel R. Poinsett to Brigadier General Matthew Arbuckle, 17 Dec. 1838, John Ross to Poinsett, 18 July 1839, John Ross Papers, Thomas Gilcrease Institute, Tulsa OK.

94. Valuation 72, 21 Dec. 1833, M-574.

95. Meigs to Dearborn, 12 July 1801, M-208.

96. *Laws,* 4–5.

97. *Laws,* 23–24.

98. *Laws,* 44–45.

99. *Laws,* 118–19.

100. *Laws,* 136.

101. *Laws,* 9–10, 19, 56, 80, 139–41.

102. Presidential Papers Microfilm: Andrew Jackson (Washington DC, 1961), series 1, reel 22; Cyrus Kingsbury Journal, 13 Feb. 1817, ABCFM.

103. Brainerd Journal, 30 June 1818, ABCFM.

104. Not only had John Ridge and Elias Boudinot married women from New England, but several other members of the Treaty Party also apparently had white wives. Royce, "Indian Land Cessions in the United States," 684–85, 696–97; Census of 1835, T-496.

105. *Cherokee Phoenix,* 12 Nov. 1831. The petition is dated 17 Oct. 1821, but the year is almost certainly a typographical error.

7. SELU MEETS EVE

1. Barbara Welter, "The Cult of True Womanhood, 1820–1860," *American Quarterly* 18 (1966): 151–74. Although Welter begins her study in 1820, the "cult" had been emerging since the mid–eighteenth century.

2. McKenney, *Memoirs Official and Personal,* 1:236.

3. For early-nineteenth-century evangelicalism and missions, see John A. Andrew III, *Rebuilding the Christian Commonwealth: New England Congregationalists and Foreign Missions, 1800–1830* (Lexington: University of Kentucky Press, 1976). For the impact on the Cherokees, see Andrew, *From Revivals to Removal: Jeremiah Evarts, the Cherokee Nation, and the Search for the Soul of America* (Athens: University of Georgia Press, 1992), and William G. McLoughlin, *Cherokees and Missionaries, 1789–1839* (New Haven: Yale University Press, 1984).

4. Robert F. Berkhofer Jr., *Salvation and the Savage: An Analysis of Protestant Missions and the American Indian Response, 1787–1862* (Lexington: University of Kentucky Press, 1965), 6–9.

5. Sarah Tuttle, *Letters and Conversations on the Cherokee Mission* (Boston: T. R. Marvin for the Massachusetts Sabbath School Union, 1830), 24, 26.

6. Elizabeth Taylor to Miss D. Gould, 20 May 1828, Payne Papers, 8:9.

7. Brainerd Journal, 1 Nov. 1820, ABCFM.

8. The notable exceptions are the Baptist missionaries John and Evan Jones, who fostered a syncretic Christianity among the conservative Cherokees living in what is today western North Carolina. See William G. McLoughlin, *Champions of the Cherokees: Evan and John B. Jones* (Princeton: Princeton University Press, 1990).

9. Butrick's Journal, 6 Sept. 1826; Cyrus Kingsbury, Daniel S. Butrick, Moody Hall, and Loring S. Williams to Samuel Worcester, 18 March 1818; Report on the Station at Candy's Creek, Jan. 1828, ABCFM; Butrick to Corresponding Secretary, 12 May 1831, Payne Papers, 9:17; Berkhofer, *Salvation and the Savage,* 79.

10. Tuttle, *Letters and Conversations,* 58.

11. Jedidiah Morse, *A Report to the Secretary of War of the United States on Indian Affairs* (1822; New York: A. M. Kelley, 1970), 74. For one example of the application of this policy, see Mary E. Young, "Women, Civilization, and the Indian Question," in *Clio Was a Woman: Studies in the History of American Women,* eds. Mabel E. Deutrich and Elizabeth C. Purdy (Washington DC: Howard University Press, 1980).

12. *Latter Day Luminary* 2 (1821): 331.

13. *Latter Day Luminary* 5 (1824): 242–43.

14. *Latter Day Luminary* 6 (1825): 34–35.

15. *Latter Day Luminary* 2 (1821): 336.

16. Cyrus Kingsbury to Samuel Worcester, 28 Nov. 1816; Brainerd Journal, 27 May, 29 Oct. 1819, ABCFM. Boarding schools often proved necessary because the Cherokee population, particularly the more highly acculturated part, was so widely dispersed. Cyrus Kingsbury to Samuel A. Worcester, 8 May 1816, ABCFM. By the mid-1820s, most mission societies had begun to turn to day schools because they cost less to operate and more children could be reached. Letter from Evan Jones and T. Dawson, 28 March 1825, *Latter Day Luminary* 6 (1825): 147–48.

17. Payne Papers, 8:10–12, 35; William Potter to Jeremiah Evarts, 16 Aug. 1826, ABCFM.

18. Thomas Roberts to Rev. O. B. Brown, 22 Jan. 1822, *Latter Day Luminary* 3 (1822): 91. In American Board missions, the number of children with only Cherokee ancestry steadily declined. However, it is difficult to distinguish racism from ethnocentrism. William G. McLoughlin points out that Baptists were far more interested in "full-bloods" and tolerant of traditional culture than other missionaries, but McLoughlin uses *full-blood,* a racial categorization, to describe a cultural preference. Therefore, I find his discussions of "full-bloods," unlike virtually everything else he wrote, to be confusing and troubling. I no longer use the racial designations (mixed-blood, full-blood) to describe Cherokees because I find these terms offensive and, in the ways in which they commonly are used, inaccurate. The terms may be a convenient shorthand (and many Native people themselves use them), but I see no sense in perpetuating nineteenth-century linkages between race and culture that have caused so much suffering and have so little basis in fact. See McLoughlin, "Two Bostonian Missionaries" in *The Cherokees and Christianity, 1794–1870: Essays on Acculturation and Cultural Persistence,* ed. Walter H. Conser Jr. (Athens: University of Georgia Press, 1994), 66–69.

19. Brainerd Journal, 24 June 1818, ABCFM; Nancy Reece to Mrs. Conner, n.d., Payne Papers 8:10.

20. Sophia Sawyer to Jeremiah Evarts, 21 Aug. 1824; Appendix to Memoranda of the Cherokee Mission, 16 May 1822; Brainerd Journal 14 Dec. 1822, 11 June 1823, ABCFM; Payne Papers 8:6, 9, 11, 18, 39.

21. Isaac Proctor to Jeremiah Evarts, 21 April 1828, ABCFM.

22. Adam Hodgson, *Letters from North America, Written during a Tour of the United States and Canada,* 2 vols. (London: Hurst, Robinson, 1824), 1:277–78. Another father had heard rumors that the missionaries kept the boys for the purpose of fieldwork. The missionaries convinced him that the rumor was unfounded, and he decided "that it was very good for them to work part of the day, for he wanted his boys to work for a living when they left school." Brainerd Journal, 20 July 1819, ABCFM.

23. Brainerd Journal, 19 June 1818, 2 Aug. 1821; Memoranda of the Cherokee Mission, No. 2, May 1822; Ann Paine to Jeremiah Evarts, 8 Nov. 1821, ABCFM; Payne Papers 8:51.

24. Cyrus Kingsbury to Samuel A. Worcester, 30 June 1817, ABCFM.

25. *Latter Day Luminary* 5 (1824): 167–68.

26. Letter of Evan Jones and T. Dawson, 28 March 1825, *Latter Day Luminary* 6 (1825) 147–48.

27. Brainerd Journal, 21 Dec. 1824, ABCFM.

28. William G. McLoughlin, "Native American Reactions to Christian Missions" and "Two Bostonian Missionaries" in *Cherokees and Christianity*, 28–29, 55–56. Baptists were least likely to do this.

29. For example, see Butrick's Journal, Feb., March 1822, 15 Aug. 1832, ABCFM.

70. Members of the Church at Brainerd exclusive of the missionaries, Also of the Church at Creek Path, May 1822; Report on the Station at Haweis, Jan. 1828, ABCFM.

31. Ann Paine, Notebook 2, 20 Dec. 1820, ABCFM.

32. Brainerd Journal, 26 Jan. 1819, ABCFM. The American Board did send itinerating ministers to this region ocasionally, but frequently the itinerants could not be spared from the stations.

33. Brainerd Journal, 29 July 1819, ABCFM.

34. Daniel Butrick to Jeremiah Evarts, 24 Nov. 1824, ABCFM.

35. Appendix to Memoranda of the Cherokee Mission, 16 May 1822, ABCFM.

36. Letter of Evan Jones, 17 Aug. 1822, *Latter Day Luminary* 3 (1822): 310.

37. Nancy Reece to Mrs. Elizabeth Preston, 27 July 1828, Payne Papers, 8:12.

38. Report on the Station at Haweis, Jan. 1828, ABCFM.

39. Memoranda Relative to the Cherokee Mission, No. 1, April and May 1822, ABCFM.

40. Sophia Sawyer to Jeremiah Evarts, 21 Aug. 1824; Elizur Butler to Jeremiah Evarts, 3 Aug. 1829, ABCFM; Payne Papers 8:34, 49.

41. Lucy A. Butler to Daniel Green, 29 Sept. 1832, ABCFM.

42. Brainerd Journal, 18 Sept. 1823, ABCFM.

43. Memoranda Relative to the Cherokee Mission, No. 1, April and May 1822; Daniel Butrick to Jeremiah Evarts, 17 Oct. 1824; Sophia Sawyer to Evarts, 11 Aug. 1825, 19 Oct. 1827, ABCFM; Moravian Diary, 1 June 1828.

44. Moravian Diary, 11 April 1813; Frederick Ellsworth to Jeremiah Evarts, 25 May, 12 Aug. 1825, ABCFM. Despite the missionaries' misgivings, both girls became respectable married women. Nancy Watie married John Wheeler, a printer who later became an editor in Fort Smith, Arkansas. Sally Ridge married a Georgia lawyer, George Washington Paschal.

45. Sophia Sawyer to Jeremiah Evarts, 21 Aug. 1824, ABCFM.

46. John Ridge to Albert Gallatin, 27 Feb. 1826, Payne Papers, 8:112.

47. Ann Paine, Notebook 2, 20 Dec. 1820; Sophia Sawyer to Jeremiah Evart, 25 June 1824, ABCFM; Payne Papers 8:39.

48. Brainerd Journal, 9 Aug. 1818, ABCFM; Payne Papers, 8:1, 20, 41. A Cherokee "Hymn" included in the American Board papers should have made impressionable children worry about their souls: "Remember sinful youth . . . To a dreadful Judgement day you are bound."

49. William Chamberlain to Jeremiah Evarts, 11 June 1823, ABCFM.

50. Berkhofer, *Salvation and the Savage,* 51–55.

51. Letter from Evan Jones, 17 Aug. 1822, *Latter Day Luminary* 3 (1822): 311.

52. Brainerd Journal, 19 Jan. 1817, 26 Jan. 1818, ABCFM.

53. Brainerd Journal, 9 April 1818, ABCFM.

54. Brainerd Journal, 2 March 1817, 2–14 Dec. 1817, ABCFM.

55. Brainerd Journal, 28 Jan. 1818, ABCFM.

56. Daniel S. Butrick to Samuel A. Worcester, 2 July 1818, ABCFM.

57. Brainerd Journal, 28 Jan. 1818, ABCFM; Tuttle, *Letters and Conversations,* 48.

58. *Latter Day Luminary* 6 (1825): 334–38.

59. *Latter Day Luminary* 6 (1825): 36–37.

60. Chamberlain's Journal, 5 July 1822, 19 April 1826, ABCFM. Kenneth G. Hamilton, ed. and trans., "Minutes of the Mission Conference Held in Springplace," *Atlanta Historical Bulletin* 16 (1971): 44.

61. Asa Hitchcock to the *Christian Gazette,* 8 June 1824, reprinted in *Latter Day Luminary* 5 (1824): 246.

62. Daniel Butrick to Samuel A. Worcester, 7 Sept. 1820; Butrick to Jeremiah Evarts, 11 June 1823; Brainerd Journal, 1 Feb. 1818, ABCFM. McLoughlin deals with the similarity of baptism to "going to water" in "Accepting Christianity, 1839–1860" in *Cherokees and Christianity,* 200–201. For mothers and children, see his *Champions of the Cherokees,* 69.

63. *Latter Day Luminary,* 6 (1825): 336. St. Paul issued the injunction on women: "Let women learn in silence with all subjection." 1 Timothy 2:11.

64. Payne Papers, 8:9, 16; William Chamberlain to Jeremiah Evarts, 8 Jan. 1829, ABCFM.

65. *Missionary Herald,* 4 July 1830.

66. Brainerd Journal, 28 June, 22 July 1822, ABCFM.

67. Frederick Ellsworth to Jeremiah Evarts, 1 March 1825, ABCFM. Missionaries also provided opportunities for mature women to acquire other accouterments of "civilization," particularly through Sabbath schools where they could learn to read and write English. Brainerd Journal, 28 June 1818; Hall's Journal, 13 July 1823,

ABCFM. Adult women also occasionally attended mission school. See Moravian Diary, 14 April 1802.

68. Rufus Anderson, *Memoir of Catharine Brown, a Christian Indian of the Cherokee Nation* (Boston: S. T. Armstrong and Crocker and Brewster; New York: J. P. Haven, 1825).

69. McLoughlin, "Native American Reactions to Christian Missions" in *Cherokees and Christianity,* 9–33; Charles Hudson, "The Cherokee Concept of Natural Balance," *Indian Historian* 3 (1970): 51–54.

70. Articles of Faith and Covenant adopted by the Church of Christ at Chickamauga, 28 Sept. 1817, ABCFM.

71. The point of this article, however, was not the origin of sin but the presence of sin, which the author thought should receive more attention. *Latter Day Luminary* 3 (1822): 267.

72. Sophia Sawyer to Jeremiah Evarts, 19 Oct. 1827, ABCFM.

73. McLoughlin, "Fractured Myths: The Cherokees' Use of Christianity" in *Cherokees and Christianity,* 173.

74. *Cherokee Phoenix,* 18 March 1829.

75. *Cherokee Phoenix,* 8 May 1830. Although there are no consistent membership lists, the records that are available do not suggest a disparity between male and female converts such as the one Carol Devens discovered in seventeenth- and eighteenth-century Canada. See her *Countering Colonization.* However, McLoughlin says that after removal, two-thirds of the converts were "full-blood" women and attributes this high rate of conversion to the mortality rate on the Trail of Tears. "Accepting Christianity," in *Cherokees and Christianity,* 109.

76. David Greene to Jeremiah Evarts, 28 Jan. 1828, ABCFM.

77. Samuel Worcester to Jeremiah Evarts, 28 July 1826, ABCFM.

78. For example, Brainerd enrollments for boys in 1823 ranged between 39 and 47 while girls' enrollment ranged between 11 and 33. The low point for both came in November after the harvest when corn would have been plentiful at home (Brainerd Journal, 31 Jan., 28 Feb., 11 June, 30 June, 30 Nov. 1823, ABCFM). Moravians reported 13 boys and 2 girls on 11 Sept. 1825, and 8 boys at the end of 1826 and 1827, but only 3 and 5 girls respectively (Moravian Diary). In 1822, Evan Jones reported that the school serving Valley Towns had 48 boys and 22 girls. *Latter Day Luminary* 3 (1822): 310.

79. John C. Ellsworth to Evarts, 16 Dec. 1824, ABCFM.

80. Ellsworth admitted another reason for declining enrollments: "Miss Sawyer and myself differ a little in regard to the management & studies of the girls school." Ellsworth to Evarts, 24 Feb. 1825, ABCFM.

81. Sally Reece to Mrs. Eleanor Fields, 7 June n.y., Payne Papers 8:35–36.

82. Brainerd Journal, 24 May 1822, 12 April 1823, ABCFM.

83. Sophia Sawyer to Jeremiah Evarts, 21 Aug. 1824, ABCFM.

84. Agent Meigs promoted education among the Cherokees as necessary for conducting "the ordinary business required in civilized life." Return J. Meigs to Benjamin Hawkins, 28 Dec. 1802, M-208. Cherokee leaders implied a connection between education and politics when they planned to locate a male academy, which never materialized, in the capital New Echota, while leaving the female academy at the American Board mission at Taloney (Carmel). Moody Hall to Jeremiah Evarts, 13 Sept. 1824, ABCFM.

85. Ard Hoyt, Daniel Butrick, and William Chamberlain to Samuel Worcester, 21 Dec. 1818, ABCFM. Just as some children refused to go to school, others decided independently to attend. Two small girls all alone traveled the forty miles to Brainerd because they could get no one to bring them. Brainerd Journal, 13 June 1821, ABCFM. A few parents adopted Anglo-American disciplinary techniques. When one young man ran away, his uncle brought him back and threatened to whip him if he ran away again. The missionaries considered this threat to be progress: "A few months ago this boy would have been pitied and excused." Hall's Journal, 21 Nov. 1822, ABCFM.

86. Polly Wilson to Jeremiah Evarts, 11 Feb. n.y., Payne Papers 8:51.

87. Moravian Diary, 30 Oct. 1803, 1:32.

88. Polly Wilson to Jeremiah Evarts, 11 Feb. n.y., Payne Papers 8:51.

89. Appendix to Memoranda of the Cherokee Mission, 16 May 1822, ABCFM. Missionaries explained their expenditure for labor to the board: "When we can profitably employ the Cherokees, we esteem it our duty and privilege as it may be of great benefit to them in a spiritual as well as a temporal point of view." Brainerd Journal, 28 Oct. 1822, ABCFM.

90. Mrs. Chamberlain clearly was in the process of having a breakdown: she did laundry herself outdoors at night in the rain. Memoranda of the Cherokee Mission, No. 2, May 1822, ABCFM.

91. For example, see Brainerd Journal, 2 Aug. 1821, ABCFM. Also see Wade Alston Horton, "Protestant Missionary Women as Agents of Cultural Transition among Cherokee Women, 1801–1839," Ph.D. diss., Southern Baptist Theological Seminary, 1991.

92. Ann Paine, Notebook 2, 20 Dec. 1820, ABCFM.

93. In this case, the children did not want to leave, and so the mother permitted her daughter to remain and took her son only for a short visit. In an unusual pattern, the father soon removed the children from the school to prevent their mothers from taking them away, but a settlement ultimately was reached whereby the children remained in school. Brainerd Journal, 5, 23 Sept., 20 Oct. 1818, ABCFM.

94. For example, see Brainerd Journal, 15 July, 14 Nov. 1818, 20 Sept. 1820, 7 May 1821, ABCFM.

95. Brainerd Journal, 21 July 1822, ABCFM.

96. Brainerd Journal, 5 Sept. 1818, 21 Nov. 1822; Daniel Butrick to Samuel Worcester, 6 Oct. 1818; Ard Hoyt, William Chamberlain, and Daniel Butrick to Worcester, 28 Oct. 1818; Hoyt to Jeremiah Evarts, 4 Aug. 1824, ABCFM.

97. Isaac Proctor to Jeremiah Evarts, 28 Aug. 1826, ABCFM.

98. Brainerd Journal, 25 Jan. 1818, ABCFM.

99. Butrick's Journal, 6 Oct. 1818, ABCFM.

100. Louis-Philippe, *Travels,* 72.

101. Moravian Diary, 9 Oct. 1800.

102. Butrick's Journal, 6 Oct. 1818, ABCFM; Moravian Diary, 22 June 1826.

103. Samuel Worcester to Ard Hoyt, 11 Nov. 1818; Hall's Journal, 21 April 1824; Daniel Butrick to Worcester, 1 Jan. 1819, ABCFM; McLoughlin, *Cherokees and Missionariew,* 204–5.

104. Brainerd Journal, 25 Jan. 1817, ABCFM.

105. Butrick's Journal, 13 Oct. 1838, ABCFM.

106. Butrick's Journal, 10 Aug., 10, 14 Dec. 1823, 21 Feb. 1824; Butrick to Samuel Worcester, 2 July 1818; Butrick's Journal, 23 Jan. 1824, 24 Sept. 1824, 22 Feb. 1823, ABCFM.

107. Daniel Butrick to Jeremiah Evarts, 8 May 1823, ABCFM.

108. "Extract from the Journal of the Mission at Spring Place," 30 July 1822, *Latter Day Luminary* 5 (1824): 340.

109. Brainerd Journal, 9 Feb. 1820, ABCFM.

110. McLoughlin, *Champions of the Cherokees,* 69.

111. Ann Paine, Notebook 2, 20 Dec. 1820, ABCFM.

112. The woman soon removed her daughter, however, "because she had heard that the child cried at night." Brainerd Journal, 14 Nov., 22 Nov. 1818, ABCFM.

113. Brainerd Journal, 7 May 1821, ABCFM.

114. Brainerd Journal, 7 May 1821, ABCFM.

115. Ann Paine, Notebook 2, 20 Dec. 1820, ABCFM.

116. McLoughlin suggests ways in which Christianity helped the Cherokees reorganize themselves socially as well as politically. See "Accepting Christianity, 1830–1860," in his *Cherokees and Christianity,* 109–12.

117. For example, Brainerd Journal, 27 Sept. 1819, Isaac Proctor to Jeremiah Evarts, 23 April 1827, ABCFM.

118. Rev. Roberts to Corresponding Secretary, 18 Sept. 1823, *Latter Day Luminary* 4 (1823): 369.

119. William Potter to Jeremiah Evarts, 1828, ABCFM.

120. Frances Paul Prucha, *American Indian Policy in the Formative Years: The Indian Trade and Intercourse Acts, 1790–1834* (Cambridge: Harvard University Press, 1962), chap. 6; Izumi Ishii, "The Cherokee Temperance Movement: An Internal Struggle for a Sober Nation before the 'Trail of Tears,'" M.A. thesis, University of Kentucky, 1996; *Laws,* 6–7, 24–25, 39–40.

121. *Laws,* 26–27, 36.

122. Moravian Diary, March 1813. In *Chain Her by One Foot,* Karen Anderson examined the increase in violence against women in Jesuit Christianized Huron and Montagnais societies. Whereas men traditionally vented socially disruptive feelings on war captives, they now turned on women who became "legitimate objects of aggression" because Christianity demanded their subjugation (223).

123. Zillah Haynie Brandon Diary, 1823–71, Alabama State Archives, Montgomery AL, 82–83, 85–86.

124. Daniel S. Butrick, "A Brief Review of the History of the Cherokee Nation for a Few Years Past," entry for 29 June 1838, Payne Papers, 9:81–82. This Butrick journal in the Payne Papers is a more personal commentary, unlike the Butrick journal in the American Board Papers (the one frequently cited in the current volume), which is a narrative of events.

125. Isaac Proctor to J. Evarts, 28 July 1827, ABCFM.

126. Butrick, "A Brief Review," 29 June 1838, Payne Papers, 9:83.

127. Samuel Worcester to Jeremiah Evarts, 28 July 1826, 29 March 1827, 19 Aug. 1829, ABCFM; McLoughlin, *Champions of the Cherokees,* 65.

128. McLoughlin, *Cherokees and Missionaries,* 35–53.

129. Brainerd Journal, 29 Oct. 1819, ABCFM.

130. William G. McLoughlin, "Cherokee Antimission Sentiment, 1823–24" in *Cherokee Ghost Dance,* 385–96; Perdue, "The Conflict Within," 467–91.

131. Elias Boudinot, "An Address to the Whites" in *Cherokee Editor: The Writings of Elias Boudinot,* ed. Theda Perdue (Knoxville: University of Tennessee Press, 1983), 77–78.

132. Chamberlain's Journal, 4 July 1822; Brainerd Journal, 5, 6 July, 1822, ABCFM.

133. Hudson, *Southeastern Indians,* 408–21.

134. Frank G. Speck and Leonard Broom, *Cherokee Dance and Drama* (Berkeley: University of California Press, 1951).

135. Brainerd Journal, 9 Aug. 1819, ABCFM.

136. Brainerd Journal, 3 July 1822, ABCFM.

137. Hudson, *Southeastern Indians,* 174–83.

138. Brainerd Journal, 28 May 1822, ABCFM.

139. Hall's Journal, 4 Oct. 1823, ABCFM.

140. John Ridge to Albert Gallatin, 17 Feb. 1826, Payne Papers, 8:110–11.

141. Raymond D. Fogelson, "The Conjuror in Eastern Cherokee Society," *Journal of Cherokee Studies* 5 (1980): 60–87.

142. Hall's Journal, 17 May 1822, ABCFM.

143. William Holland to Jeremiah Evarts, 14 Oct. 1826, ABCFM. As a postscript, Holland noted, "She returned last week mostly recovered."

144. Hall's Journal, 31 July 1823, ABCFM. One child died.

145. Rowena McClinton, "The Moravian Mission among the Cherokees at Springplace, Georgia," Ph.D. diss., University of Kentucky, 1996, 285–86, 397–99.

146. Elizur Butler to Jeremiah Evarts, 3 Aug. 1829, ABCFM. Unlike most other missionaries, Evan Jones tolerated traditional medical practices and other activities of conjurors when they did not come into direct conflict with Baptist theology. The result was a syncretic Christianity that proved far more popular among traditional Cherokees than the more intolerant Presbyterianism. See McLoughlin's *Champions of the Cherokees.*

147. Worcester to Evarts, 8 Dec. 1825, ABCFM.

CONCLUSION

1. Ard Hoyt, Moody Hall, William Chamberlain, and D. S. Butrick to Samuel Worcester, 25 July 1818, ABCFM.

2. Carroll Smith-Rosenberg, "Dis-Covering the Subject of the 'Great Constitutional Discussion,' 1786–1789," *Journal of American History* 79 (1992): 841–73.

3. Edmund S. Morgan, *American Slavery, American Freedom: The Ordeal of Colonial Virginia* (New York: W. W. Norton, 1975); Kenneth S. Greenberg, *Masters and Statesmen: The Political Culture of American Slavery* (Baltimore: Johns Hopkins University Press, 1985); William J. Cooper, *Liberty and Slavery: Southern Politics to 1860* (New York: Alfred A. Knopf, 1983).

4. Gallatin, "Synopsis," 151.

5. Reuben G. Thwaites, ed., *Original Journals of the Lewis and Clark Expedition, 1804–1806,* 8 vols. (New York: Dodd, Mead, 1904–5), 1:89; 6:80–94.

6. Native peoples who had been farmers for centuries must have been somewhat perplexed over treaty provisions promising assistance in their transition to "herdsmen and cultivators, instead of remaining in the hunter state." A Treaty of Peace and Friendship, 2 July 1791, *American State Papers,* 1:124–25.

7. Timberlake, *Memoirs,* 99.

8. Jefferson, *Notes on the State of Virginia,* 302.

9. Beverley, *History . . . of Virginia,* 156.

10. A. Whitney Griswold, "The Agrarian Democracy of Thomas Jefferson," *American Political Science Review* 40 (1946): 657–81; also see Joyce O. Appleby,

"Commercial Farming and the 'Agrarian Myth' in the Early Republic," *Journal of American History* 68 (1982): 833–49, and Stephanie McCurry, "The Two Faces of Republicanism: Gender and Proslavery Politics in Antebellum South Carolina," *Journal of American History* 78 (1992): 1245–64.

11. Corner, *Autobiography of Benjamin Rush,* 71; Rush, "Medicine among the Indians," in *Essays,* 290.

12. In his *Handbook of Federal Indian Law* (Charlottesville VA: Michie Company, 1982), 50, Felix Cohen supports the contention of Francisco de Victoria that "the aborigines in question were true owners, before the Spaniards came among them, both from the public and private point of view." He maintains that this recognition of Native title forms the basis of modern Indian law. While this may be true, late-eighteenth- and early-nineteenth-century writers subscribed to Vattel's opposing view that Natives had only limited rights, and failure to cultivate the soil was a major cultural feature restricting their absolute ownership. For example, Lewis Cass referred to Vattel by name in his formal justification of Indian removal; see "Removal of the Indians," *North American Review* 30 (1830): 95. Also see Berkhofer, *Salvation and the Savage,* 120–26, 129–32; Pearce, *Savagism and Civilization,* 70–71.

13. Wilson Lumpkin, *The Removal of the Cherokee Indians from Georgia,* 2 vols. (New York: Dodd, Mead, 1907), 2:150.

14. Andrew Jackson's Second Annual Message, in James D. Richardson, ed., *Messages and Papers of the Presidents* (New York: Bureau of National Literature, 1897–1911), 1083; Lewis Cass, "Removal of the Indians," 72–73.

15. Glenna Matthews, *Just a Housewife: The Rise and Fall of Domesticity in America* (New York: Oxford University Press, 1987). In this period, "manliness" involved self-discipline and restraint. Policy makers saw hunting as impulsive and, therefore, both "uncivilized" and unmanly. See David D. Gilmore, *Manhood in the Making: Cultural Concepts of Masculinity* (New Haven: Yale University Press, 1972). Although her book focuses on the end of the century, Gail Bederman examines the ideological process in which ideas about civilization and manhood intersected in *Manliness and Civilization: A Cultural History of Gender and Race in the United States, 1880–1917* (Chicago: University of Chicago Press, 1995).

16. Julian P. Boyd, ed., *The Papers of Thomas Jefferson,* 24 vols. to date (Princeton: Princeton University Press, 1950–), 11:415.

17. Gallatin, "Synopsis," 158.

18. Jefferson to the Senate and House of Representatives, 18 January 1803, Richardson, ed., *Messages,* 340; Draft of Jefferson's Fifth Annual Message, Ford, *Writings of Jefferson,* 8:394.

19. Albert Gallatin was one of the few people who explicitly stated that Native men must farm. Most others simply assumed that the plows sent under the aus-

pices of the civilization program would be taken up by men while women used their new spinning wheels and looms. Gallatin, "Synopsis," 152–53.

20. Gallatin, "Synopsis," 108.

21. Gallatin, "Synopsis," 157. Cass concurred ("Removal of the Indians," 71).

22. Cass, "Removal of the Indians," 67.

23. Jefferson wrote to John C. Breckinridge on 12 August 1803, concerning the Louisiana Purchase: "The best use we can make of the country for some time, will be to give establishments in it to the Indians on the East side of the Mississippi, in exchange for their present country." Jefferson also mentioned this use in a draft of a constitutional amendment providing for territorial acquisition. Ford, *Writings of Jefferson,* 8:243–45.

24. Hall, *Sketches of . . . the West,* 1:118.

25. Cass, "Removal of the Indians," 91–92, 121.

26. In *From Colonies to Commonwealth: Familial Ideology and the Beginnings of the American Republic* (Baltimore: Johns Hopkins University Press, 1985), Melvin Yazawa charts the demise of familial ideology in the early republic. Although citizens of the United States may no longer have viewed themselves as members of a patriarchal national family, they certainly understood other societies in terms of this familial ideology.

27. Isaac Proctor to Jeremiah Evarts, 9 Feb. 1825, ABCFM.

28. Cyrus Kingsbury to Samuel Worcester, 28 Nov. 1816, ABCFM.

29. Gallatin, "Synopsis," 108.

30. Cass, "Removal of the Indians," 73–74, 91.

31. Kerber, *Women of the Republic,* 287.

32. Adair, *History,* 153.

33. Cadwallader Colden, *History of the Five Indian Nations of Canada Which Are Dependent on the Provinces of New York,* 2 vols. (1747; reprint, New York, 1922), 1:xxxiii.

34. "Reflections," 51.

35. Hall, *Sketches of . . . the West,* 1:128.

36. Samuel Stanhope Smith, *Essay on the Causes of the Variety of Complexion and Figure in the Human Species,* ed. Winthrop D. Jordan (1810; reprint, Cambridge MA, 1965), 235–41.

37. Hall, *Sketches of . . . the West,* 1:128.

38. Cass, "Removal of the Indians," 117.

39. Cass, "Removal of the Indians," 71.

40. Benjamin Currey to Cass, 1 Oct. 1831, Senate Document 512, 23 Cong., 1st sess.; 2:612–15.

41. This proposal was aimed, in particular, at John Martin and Joseph Vann. Sworn Statement of Thos. Shirley Jr., 31 March 1834, Payne Papers, 7:158–59.

42. "Communication of 'A Traveler' on the Condition of the Cherokees," reprinted in Schwaab, ed., *Travels in the Old South,* 1:224–5.

43. In December 1831, Curry reported that seventy-one families had enrolled to go west voluntarily. These included twenty-one families headed by white men, thirty-four "mixed-bloods," and one white woman with Cherokee children. While the visitor from Connecticut may have exaggerated, he inflated the figures only slightly. Senate Document 512, 2:707–8.

44. Mankiller and Wallis, *Mankiller.*

45. *Cherokee One Feather,* 4 Oct. 1995.

INDEX

In the Indians of the Southeast series

William Bartram on the Southeastern Indians
Edited and annotated by Gregory A. Waselkov and Kathryn E. Holland Braund

Deerskins and Duffels
The Creek Indian Trade with Anglo-America, 1685–1815
By Kathryn E. Holland Braund

Searching for the Bright Path
The Mississippi Choctaws from Prehistory to Removal
By James Taylor Carson

Cherokee Americans
The Eastern Band of Cherokees in the Twentieth Century
By John R. Finger

Choctaw Genesis 1500–1700
By Patricia Galloway

The Southeastern Ceremonial Complex
Artifacts and Analysis
The Cottonlandia Conference
Edited by Patricia Galloway
Exhibition Catalog by David H. Dye and Camille Wharey

An Assumption of Sovereignty
Social and Political Transformation among the Florida Seminoles, 1953–1979
By Harry A. Kersey Jr.

The Caddo Chiefdoms
Caddo Economics and Politics, 700–1835
By David La Vere

Cherokee Women
Gender and Culture Change, 1700–1835
By Theda Perdue

The Brainerd Journal
A Mission to the Cherokees, 1817–1823
Edited and introduced by Joyce B. Phillips and Paul Gary Phillips

The Cherokees
A Population History
By Russell Thornton

American Indians in the Lower Mississippi Valley
Social and Economic Histories
By Daniel H. Usner Jr.

Powhatan's Mantle
Indians in the Colonial Southeast
Edited by Peter H. Wood, Gregory A. Waselkov, and M. Thomas Hatley

Creeks and Seminoles
The Destruction and Regeneration of the Muscogulge People
By J. Leitch Wright Jr.